THE
EVERYTHING®
GUIDE TO SELLING
ARTS & CRAFTS ONLINE

I've been active on the Internet as a website owner and web designer since 1995, when the term "online" first arrived in my rural corner of northern California. I have been an artist and an art educator for even longer. I had to learn how to write HTML code the hard way (by looking at the source code for other web pages and then changing little bits until I turned it into a unique code) when I designed my first website for my watercolor paintings. Every year since then, the Internet has gotten easier—and richer—and I've never looked back!

The Internet has changed my world, and the lives of almost everyone in our culture. It has opened vast stores of human knowledge and made communication easier than ever. It has even revolutionized industries, including the process of selling arts and crafts. No longer do artists and artisans need to depend on agents and galleries to become successful. The era of successful online entrepreneurs has arrived.

The Internet is bursting with venues where artists and crafters can sell their own work, attract supporters and customers, and communicate with their fans easily and enjoyably. Each year the online tools get easier to use and the opportunities expand. My goal with this book is to introduce you to the abundant resources available for selling arts and crafts on the Internet. I hope it enriches your life as much as it has mine.

Kim Solga

www.solga.com
www.SellingArtsandCraftsOnline.com

Welcome to the EVERYTHING® Series!

These handy, accessible books give you all you need to tackle a difficult project, gain a new hobby, comprehend a fascinating topic, prepare for an exam, or even brush up on something you learned back in school but have since forgotten.

You can choose to read an Everything® book from cover to cover or just pick out the information you want from our four useful boxes: e-questions, e-facts, e-alerts, and e-ssentials.

We give you everything you need to know on the subject, but throw in a lot of fun stuff along the way, too.

We now have more than 400 Everything® books in print, spanning such wide-ranging categories as weddings, pregnancy, cooking, music instruction, foreign language, crafts, pets, New Age, and so much more. When you're done reading them all, you can finally say you know Everything®!

QUESTION

Answers to
common questions

FACT

Important snippets
of information

ALERT

Urgent
warnings

ESSENTIAL

Quick
handy tips

PUBLISHER Karen Cooper

MANAGING EDITOR, EVERYTHING® SERIES Lisa Laing

COPY CHIEF Casey Ebert

ASSISTANT PRODUCTION EDITOR Alex Guarco

ACQUISITIONS EDITOR Pamela Wissman

DEVELOPMENT EDITOR Eileen Mullan

EVERYTHING® SERIES COVER DESIGNER Erin Alexander

Visit the entire Everything® series at *www.everything.com*

THE EVERYTHING®

GUIDE TO SELLING ARTS & CRAFTS ONLINE

How to sell on Etsy, eBay, your storefront,
and everywhere else online

Kim Solga

Avon, Massachusetts

To Steve for his support, ideas, and dining room table space.

An Everything® Series Book.
Everything® and everything.com® are registered trademarks of F+W Media, Inc.

Published by
Adams Media, a division of F+W Media, Inc.
57 Littlefield Street, Avon, MA 02322. U.S.A.
www.adamsmedia.com

ISBN 10: 1-4405-5919-8
ISBN 13: 978-1-4405-5919-8
eISBN 10: 1-4405-5920-1
eISBN 13: 978-1-4405-5920-4

Printed in the United States of America.

10 9 8 7 6 5 4 3 2 1

Library of Congress Cataloging-in-Publication Data
Solga, Kim.
  The everything guide to selling arts and crafts online : how to sell on Etsy, eBay, your StoreFront, and everywhere else online / Kim Solga.
    pages cm -- (An everything series book)
  Includes bibliographical references and index.
  ISBN-13: 978-1-4405-5919-8 (pbk. : alk. paper)
  ISBN-10: 1-4405-5919-8 (pbk. : alk. paper)
  ISBN-13: 978-1-4405-5920-4 (alk. paper)
  ISBN-10: 1-4405-5920-1 (alk. paper)
  1. Selling--Handicraft. 2. Handicraft--Marketing. 3. Electronic commerce. I. Title.
HF5439.H27S65 2013
745.5068'8--dc23

2013015430

Cover images © 123RF.com, Veer.com, and iStockphoto.com/MilesSherrill.

This book is available at quantity discounts for bulk purchases.
For information, please call 1-800-289-0963.

Contents

Screenshots and photographs provided by:

Denise Ackerman, The Knotty Needle

Deborah Babcock, Blue Sky Pottery

Brandon Bird, Artwork by Brandon Bird

Sarah Crawford, Renewed Upon a Dream (*www.Etsy.com/shop/ RenewedUponaDream*)

Jeanne Fry, Conscious Art Studios

Alyssa Gillooley, Clay de Lys

Elizabeth Hildreth, Mad Scientist Designs

Jenny Hoople, Jenny Hoople Authentic Arts

Julie Lyderson-Jackson, Spool + Sparrow

Carol Jenkins, Carol Jenkins Art

Heather Jessica, Papertique

David Joaquin, Twohawk Studio

Niccy Jordan, Scrapunzel, Photography by Nick Lawrence

Kevin McCorkle, Palletso

Ashley Pasquan, Adam Rabbit

Kathleen Selvaggio, In Vintage Heaven

Amilia Smith, Holdman Studios

Lauri Sturdivant, Lauri Sturdivant, Artist

Tana Taylor, Prairie Primitives Folk Art

Christina Winstanley, Jackdaw

The Top 10 Habits of Successful Online Entrepreneurs

1. Enjoy being online, and they are comfortable with the Internet and their computers.

2. Love to create, and they are masters at what they do.

3. Reduce big tasks into simple steps.

4. Document what they do, so things that work can be repeated. Good record keeping is the key.

5. Understand that the more places they appear on the Internet, the more easily their work can be discovered.

6. Know exactly who is most likely to buy their work.

7. Know how to take great photos with a digital camera. When all a customer can see is a photo, each photo must be excellent.

8. Can write about their work, and know that the story of the product communicates its value.

9. Price their work fairly.

10. Go out of their way to take great care of people.

Introduction

HANDMADE GOODS HAVE NEVER been so popular. More and more people are seeking one-of-a-kind treasures instead of mass-produced consumer products. They are choosing hand thrown pottery rather than dishes from some overseas ceramics factory. They are wearing tailor-made jackets, painted silk scarves, handstitched moccasins, and custom-designed jewelry. They are framing and hanging artwork created by an artist with a personal story, an artist they have come to know and love. From holiday ornaments to new furniture, people are buying handmade items that are uniquely designed, clever, well made, and filled with meaning.

The Internet is the key to this growing trend. With the help of this immense worldwide electronic system, buyers and sellers are connecting in deeply personal ways. A woman needing a new handbag will find ideas and possibilities on websites such as Etsy and ArtFire. She will check out the fashions that her friends share on Pinterest. She will narrow down her search for her perfect handbag by learning about the designers themselves, reading their stories on profile pages, their blogs, and reviews written by other customers. She will e-mail questions and get personal answers. And she will eventually buy a one-of-a-kind handbag that is perfect for her needs, from an artisan who will most likely become an online friend.

How do you become a part of this amazing online explosion of handmade sales? How do artists and crafters realize their dreams of turning artwork into cash online? It's easy when you take it step by step. It's not prohibitively expensive and it can be a great deal of fun. Successful online artists and crafters come from many different backgrounds. Some have advanced art and design degrees from prestigious universities, while others are self-taught. Some businesses start with abundant funding and support, while others operate on a shoestring budget and grow over time. There are multitudes of venues for selling artwork, from craft fairs to high-end art galleries in great cities. No matter where you begin or where you eventually find your greatest sales, marketing yourself and your artwork on the Internet will help your art career!

Selling your artwork online is serious business. It can be your road to success at whatever level you imagine, from turning your hobby into a satisfying small part-time business, to creating a substantial full-time job and income for yourself. The secret to your success will be a combination of talent, quality, and intuition. But the main ingredient will be your ability to get down to work, because selling your artwork online is a job. It is a serious commitment to thinking like, acting like, and becoming a professional.

This guide will provide you with detailed information on how to start and build an online presence, how to promote yourself and your unique artist's personality, and how get your creations to buyers. From setting up your own website and establishing good business systems to navigating popular online craft venues and using the best marketing techniques, your online arts business can be up and running in no time. Just remember, you have the power to make your business a success!

CHAPTER 1

The Possibilities

What does a successful online arts and crafts business look like? Almost anything! From small shops selling a few beautiful items, to companies with thousands of orders each month, every successful online business is unique. How do they measure success? Quite simply, an online business is successful when it fulfills the goals of its owner.

Seller Success Stories

There are many reasons to start selling art and handcrafts online. Some artists want to start a new career, develop recognition for their artwork, and generate an income that will support them as they rise to success in their field. Other artists and crafters are already well established, but wish to expand their markets. And still other new online sellers simply want to share the artwork they love, and perhaps make enough pocket money to buy new materials. Here are just a few success stories that are possible for online arts entrepreneurs.

Successful online artists and crafters come from many different backgrounds. Some have advanced art and design degrees from prestigious universities, while others are self-taught. Some businesses start with abundant funding and support; others begin on a shoestring and grow in the spare time between other jobs and responsibilities. But there are a few things that successful online sellers have in common, no matter what their situation.

Part-Time Hobby Seller

Ashley is a busy special education teacher. She loves her career and has no desire to leave her job, but she also loves creating jewelry. Crafting exquisite jewelry with raw crystal, stone, and wood provides the relaxation she needs to balance her high-stress profession. Ashley opened *Adam Rabbit* on Etsy to share her artwork and find new homes for the many wonderful earrings and necklaces she has made. She enjoys the friendship of other Etsy sellers and customers she has met online. "It has helped with my self-confidence and I have joined a great community on Etsy," says Ashley. Ashley's online business, small and part-time, is a complete success. (*www.etsy.com/shop/AdamRabbit*)

FACT

Online selling venues such as Etsy, eBay, CafePress, and ArtFire receive millions of online visitors per month. In November 2012, Etsy reported having 20 million members in nearly 200 countries, and had passed the $700 million mark for sales (compared to $525 million for all of 2011). And the 2012 holiday season was still to come!

Stay-at-Home Parent Supplementing Family Income

Denise opened *The Knotty Needle* in 2012. "Before I had my first child, I was webmaster for an international law firm in Washington, D.C. For the next four years I was fortunate to be able to continue that work from home, but after the birth of our third child, there just wasn't enough time in the day to care for the children and keep up with the workload. Returning to a conventional nine-to-five job wasn't in the cards for me. While I still do some freelance work, my main passion in life has always been seeking a creative outlet," says Denise.

Denise spends most of her free time either knitting or crocheting. *The Knotty Needle* carries her handmade accessories in unique and luxurious fibers, as well as knit and crochet beaded jewelry. "Not only is my online shop fulfilling a life-long dream of using my creativity to earn extra money, but it also allows me the freedom to drive my children to school every day, help them with their homework, cheer them on from the sidelines at their activities, and keep my dog company during the day!" she says. Denise also writes a blog. She explains, "Writing about my experiences selling online, as well as hoping to inspire others to follow their creative paths in life, has been great fun. With so many online opportunities to promote your own business these days, it is increasingly easy to make, or help supplement, your income from home while doing something you really enjoy!" (*www.etsy.com/shop/ TheKnottyNeedle* and *created.pookalooka.com*)

Inspired by Life's Changes

Sam of Perth, Western Australia, runs Humperdincks on Etsy, with a charming line of quirky, handmade, nursery rhyme–themed art prints for kids' rooms. Sam is a graphic designer by trade. When a bouncy bundle of joy came her way, she found herself at a loss for what to hang on the walls in the newly furnished nursery, and decided to create something herself. Her designs began with "Pop Goes the Weasel" and "Twinkle, Twinkle" . . . and then Sam just couldn't stop. Now her world is full of nursery rhymes, stories, songs, and games, and Sam says she had no choice but to open an Etsy shop. (*www.etsy.com/shop/Humperdincks*)

Career Change by Choice

Selene lived a busy life, commuting to a high-stress city job with a high-cost urban lifestyle, until she decided to bail out and move to a rural community. She started *Designs in Tile*, her own ceramic tile business specializing in reproductions of classic styles from Victorian to Craftsman. The business has changed through the years. She now sells tile murals online, but her website is primarily a catalog featuring amazing tile installations. Photos showcase Selene's work, from private kitchens and bathrooms to public spaces in hotels and offices. Her website allows her to successfully reach new customers and collaborate with architects and designers around the world. (*www.designsintile.com*)

Career Change by Necessity

Kevin created *Palletso* to sell rustic furniture and home décor made with wood reclaimed from shipping palettes. Following service in the U.S. Navy, Kevin explored various businesses, until he discovered himself without a job or car, and essentially stranded at his sister's house in southern California. "But I saw the positive side of things and decided that it was a good chance to work on this pallet idea. I put it into play and opened an Etsy account. I was definitely motivated by unemployment!" he explains.

Kevin creates palette wood products ranging from large chests and tables to small magnets and candleholders. "I've always been eco-conscious. I love the recycling part, and most of all I started to fall in love with the creative side of myself. It's fun inventing new ideas for furniture and home décor, creating whatever inspires me and makes me smile," says Kevin. His new Etsy shop is already gaining sales and success. "I do plan on making this something bigger, but for now Etsy is a great start." (*www.etsy.com/shop/Palletso*)

Seller Passionate about Raising Awareness

Lin creates vintage-style collage art, quirky greeting cards, magnets, and more for her *Rhody Art* shop, and is a passionate advocate for artists with disabilities. "For me, art is therapy. I deal daily with a severe mental illness that has caused several hospitalizations. Having a creative outlet helps me maintain an equilibrium that keeps me functional," she explains. Lin speaks about her journey in her blog, on her Etsy shop profile, and wherever her art is shown. "I'm passionate about representing those with mental illness. I want to show in my life and work that a person with severe mental illness is functional and a contributor to society," she writes. Along with her vibrant online presence, Lin volunteers at PeaceLove Studios where those with mental illness and those from the wider community come together to make art. (*www.etsy.com/shop/rhodyart*)

Life-Long Crafter Selling Retail and Wholesale

Tana, the creative spirit behind *Prairie Primitives*, remembers sewing doll clothes by hand when she was six years old. "Selling what I made came naturally. One of my favorite venues in the early years was a weekly 'Saturday Market' in my midwestern hometown. When I was still in high school, I'd take a big bag of stuffed animals and pillows that I'd made and a blanket to set them on and walk downtown to the market. If I had a really good day, I'd splurge, and take the bus home," she says. Working from her northern California studio, Tana sells retail on eBay; Etsy; at antique and craft fairs; and wholesale to several dozen gift shops across the country (and one shop in Japan!). (*www.etsy.com/shop/PrairiePrimitives* and *myworld.ebay.com/prairieprimitives*)

Artisan Studio Expanding Their Customer Base

Holdman Studios in Utah began blowing glass in 2005 and offering glass vases and platters for sale on the eBay auction website. Their success on eBay has expanded their clientele, both for hot glass collectibles as well as for the large architectural installations for which they are best known. (*stores.ebay.com/Holdman-Studios* and *www.holdmanstudios.com*)

Bricks-and-Mortar Store Seeking New Online Markets

Jayne uses recycled materials to create eye-catching glass jewelry, sculptures, collages, fine watercolors, mosaics, and unique gifts. "Everything I make is from found or donated recycled materials, with the exception of the ear wires. I have a line of wire-wrapped glass jewelry from recycled bottles and leftover fused glass. Copper earrings are made from old copper roofing shingles. I believe in the adage 'waste not, want not,'" she says. Jayne opened *Ruddle Cottage*, her gift-shop gallery, in a small northern California town twenty years ago. For many years the tourist trade and holiday sales were the backbone of her income, but the recent economic downturn inspired her to search for new markets. Moving her work online was the key to her current success. Today her online sales, both retail and wholesale, far exceed sales at her gallery. (*www.ruddlecottage.net* and *www.etsy.com/shop/ruddlecottage*)

A Husband and Wife Partnership

Conscious Art Studios is a business run by Jeanne and John, a husband-and-wife team from the Appalachian mountains of North Carolina. Their distinctive line of artwork includes native tradition flutes and music, drums and rattles, gourd art, and folk art in many different media. Their shop on ArtFire is the hub for an online presence that also includes their own website, blog, Facebook, and Twitter profiles. (*www.artfire.com/ext/shop/studio/ConsciousArtStudios*)

Shop Developed into a Major Family-Run Business

Dennis's family-centered *Anderson Soap Company* is consistently one of the Etsy top ten sellers, with more than 47,000 items sold by early 2013. Yet less than a decade ago Dennis was a temporary day laborer, at times living out of his car. In 2007, he quit his day job to become a full-time crafts seller. When he first heard about Etsy, Dennis invested about $40 into a product he could sell online—handmade soap. "After about a year or so on Etsy, it got too busy for me to be able to hold on to my low-paying job. Three years ago we moved the family to Portland, Oregon. I'm not well off, not by far, as all the money I make either goes toward the company or bills, but making soap has sustained me for nearly five years," he explains. Dennis continues to reinvest profits back into his handmade business, creating new and popular products like Spiced Mahogany Soap, Peppermint Oatmeal Scrub, and Chocolate Drizzle Soap in a Jar. His rise to success is one of the classic Etsy success stories. (*www.andersonsoapcompany.com/products* and *www.etsy.com/shop/AndersonSoapCompany*)

An Artist's Career Takes Off

David Joaquin is an incredibly gifted painter who ventured online several years ago with his own website for *Two Hawk Studio*. But the most remarkable expansion of his work happened when he and his wife began selling on

Etsy. His work was "discovered," not only by hundreds of enthusiastic customers and collectors, but by publishing companies, galleries, and writers requesting to use David's work to illustrate books. His new work is rich with the images and relationships he has developed through his online success. (*www.twohawkstudio.com* and *www.etsy.com/shop/PaintedMoonGallery*)

Selling Online: Is It Right for You?

Whatever your definition of "success," there are amazing opportunities for you online. The Internet is rich with different selling platforms, systems you can use to create your own website, and opportunities to blog and connect with other artists and customers worldwide.

Starting an online business is an attractive idea. Most people like the thought of being their own boss, working from home, and making money doing what they love to do. But is it right for everyone? Is it right for you?

Before you jump into this fabulous adventure, take a look again at The Top 10 Habits of Successful Online Entrepreneurs. As you read this list, do you nod your head and think, "Yup, that's me"? When you recognize these traits in yourself, you may be ready to consider a serious online business. If you think you have what it takes to start an online arts and crafts business, ask yourself a few questions first, and do yourself a favor with utterly honest answers.

ESSENTIAL

Entrepreneurs think creatively! Artists and crafters often have a head start in this quality. Successful new business owners are able to think of new ideas. They can imagine new ways to solve problems. If your creative spark gives you insights on how to take advantage of new opportunities, starting your own online business may be a good fit.

- Will I enjoy doing my artwork as a job?
- Will the work I create be popular with customers?
- Can I research my competition, and the artwork they sell?
- Am I willing to adjust the type of work I make in order to create better products?

- Am I prepared to spend the time and money needed to get my business started?
- Do I have the energy and health it takes to start an online business?
- Do I have a good source of income or savings to keep me going during the startup months, until I'm finally able to take money out of my new online business?
- Do I have, or can I get, the tools and equipment I'll need to get this started?
- Will I be able to run this business out of my home, or do I need to rent business space?
- How will I price my work compared to my competition?
- Am I ready to go public; get the licenses and permits I need; prepare for the taxes I will need to pay; and find the business insurance I'll want?
- Am I ready, willing, and able to learn all the skills I'll need to run a business?

Using Your Skills

Most online businesses, at the beginning, are a one-person show. Unless you have abundant funding for startup, you will need to do all the jobs required in setting up your small business. You will be the manufacturer, the marketing director, the customer service manager, and the Internet technology department. You will do the bookkeeping, the inventory control, and the shipping. When you need help during busy holiday sales, you will hire and manage employees. You will do your own product development research, seek your own legal advice, handle your own taxes and business licensing, and manage your own money. Here are just a few of the things you will need to teach yourself as your new online business grows:

- How to get organized
- How to brainstorm and test new products, marketing ideas, and solutions to problems that arise
- How to motivate yourself, day after day, to stay focused and productive
- How to get better at making your artwork and products

- How to copyright and license your original designs
- How to budget the money that is earned and spent by your business
- How to use the Internet to gather information, communicate with people, and set up your own web pages on different venues
- How to write clearly, correctly, and quickly, whether you're creating e-mails, product descriptions, or newsletter articles
- How to balance your personal life with the demands of your business

It is not necessary to start out in control of all these things. What *is* necessary is a willingness to be open to change, work hard, have patience, and learn.

ALERT

Doing business on the Internet comes with its own set of legal and financial considerations, particularly in the areas of privacy, security, copyright, and taxation. You must know and follow the rules and regulations for selling online and collecting customer data.

How Do You Define Success?

In the end, success comes down to a personal definition. You decide how you will measure success. Success is what feeds your soul. Sometimes the bottom line is not about money—it is about the way we walk through the world, the message we seek to convey through arts and crafts, the creation of beauty. Our artwork would be our passion whether or not we make money with it. For many artists and crafters, true success is simply being free to do our artwork and share it with the world.

Selling your artwork online is serious business. It can be your road to success at whatever level you imagine, from turning your hobby into a satisfying small part-time business, to creating a substantial full-time job and income for yourself. The secret to your success will be a combination of talent, quality, and intuition. But the main ingredient will be your ability to get down to work, because selling your artwork online is a job. It is a serious commitment to thinking and acting like a professional, and ultimately will lead your business to success.

CHAPTER 2

Developing Your Product Line

Artists and artisans enter the world of Internet sales in many different ways. Some are already successful sellers, experienced in art walks and gallery sales, craft fairs, and shops. Others may be just starting their professional art life online, with little or no experience actually selling the things that they love to make. No matter how they arrive, they all face the same initial question: Will my work sell online?

Successful Online Arts and Crafts

The wide variety of arts and crafts available exemplifies the diversity of the Internet's worldwide market. There truly is room for every seller and every artistic tradition online, from traditional to contemporary, Victorian to primitive, elegant to shabby chic. There are also tried and true sales models that will help guarantee success.

Quality Work at a Reasonable Price

The best way to guarantee success is to sell quality products at reasonable prices. The best and most successful handmade sellers fall into this delightful category. Offering quality products is essential from the beginning. Online customers are an amazingly sophisticated crowd, and the Internet is filled with fabulous arts and crafts choices. Examine your work with a critical and impartial eye. Be your own best critic. If your work is not already professional quality, then spend some time improving your skills before you venture online. Take classes and workshops to learn professional techniques. Invest in high-quality materials. Offer your items for sale at craft fairs and local events, and seek feedback from your customers.

QUESTION

How close are you to mastering your art?
In his bestselling book, *Outliers: The Story of Success*, Malcolm Gladwell suggests that it takes about 10,000 hours of dedicated practice to truly master a skill, be it playing the piano, surfing, or creating professional artwork. If you work 20 hours per week at your art, this will take nearly 10 years.

Work with a Special Meaning for People

Online customers have so many options that it takes something extraordinary to attract them to your product. Successful artwork stands out from a crowd of competitors. It appeals beyond its basic quality and beauty. When you look at the most successful online artists and artisans, you will often discover that their artwork carries some sort of deeper meaning for the customer. This might be of a spiritual nature, inspirational, motivational, etc. The art might appeal to customers' romantic or nostalgic roots. It may incorporate symbols of popular culture, heroes, a sport or lifestyle, a team, or a unique place in the world. It might connect with a deeply held value such as ecology, diversity, or peace. Successful artwork tells a story, and the customer is buying the story as much as the handcrafted item.

There is a special place on the Internet for clever artwork that makes you smile. There's even a new word for this attribute. "Etsy-esque" has come to mean the sweet, handmade quality of successful artwork sold on the giant Etsy.com. If your work falls into this genre, you have a step up on success.

An Idea That Catches On, and Goes Viral

If you happen upon this stroke of good luck, your online success is guaranteed. The "Keep Calm" phenomenon is a great example here. We've all seen variations of the classic "Keep Calm and Carry On" slogan. This vintage phrase was originally a little-used public-safety slogan from World War II era Great Britain. Now, various iterations of the saying have flooded the Internet on handcrafted products from posters to cups, iPhone covers, bookmarks, bags, and T-shirts. The *Keep Calm Shop* on Etsy (*www.etsy.com/shop/Keep CalmShop*) has sold more than 11,000 "Keep Calm" products. You too may come up with an idea that is utterly original, a first-of-its-kind design that takes off on various social networks and Internet sites.

Your Primary Product

Take a look at your online competition and at your own artwork. Choose one top-quality item you create to become the model for your primary product. This should be your favorite kind of artwork, the work you love to make with a style that truthfully reflects your personal values, because this primary product will become the core of your online business. This isn't etched in stone— you can always change things along the way. You will go on to develop related product lines. You will experiment with new styles and products. You may discover that customers actually prefer some new item you didn't even imagine would be popular. But you still need to begin somewhere, and you want your beginning to look as unified and professional as possible.

Get ready for online sales by creating a decent inventory of items that fit into the definition of your primary product. If you can assemble fifty or more excellent pieces, both small and large, you will gain the practice you need to begin production on a commercial level. You will know how long each piece takes to create, and what the materials will cost when purchased in quantity. Most importantly, you will be able to open your website or marketplace shop with sufficient items to become professional, and provide a variety of choices for your early customers.

The More (Products) the Merrier

To be successful, you need to have consistent sales. And to have sales, you need lots of products. Sarah, owner of *DodelineDesign* on Etsy, took note of this as she celebrated her 500th sale after two years on Etsy. "I tried one of those Etsy myths, that you need 120 items listed to get consistent sales. I will tell you, in my experience that is true! As soon as I increased my shop listings to around that number, I did much better," she writes on her blog, (*http://blog.dodelinedesign.com*). It took Sarah a year to get 100 products sold on Etsy, two years to get to 500, and her shop boasted more than 1,200 in sales in early 2013.

Having a multitude of items attracts customers. You simply have that many more products to search for, tags to use, and options to provide. Most of the time, you will make 80 percent of your profit on customers buying the same basic items, but the other products will attract new shoppers. Keep to your niche though. Random varieties confuse your buyers. If you are a jewelry maker, it might not be a good idea to sell doll clothes on the same website or shop space. You are seeking to brand yourself as you also add diversity.

Expand Your Product Line

Once you have opened an online space offering your highest quality primary product, you should immediately begin thinking about expanding your product line. Begin with your basic product or process, and brainstorm what else might work. A successful online artist will have a variety of great products and different price ranges, all of them fitting into your signature look and feel.

Here is a list of things to consider when growing your product line:

- **Expanding your product line often means creating both lower-priced and higher-priced items.** If you are selling original watercolor paintings priced in the $200–$400 range, you might offer limited-edition prints in the $100 range, and greeting cards for $4. Many online customers will test your business by purchasing an inexpensive item to see if its quality and your customer service are adequate before they take the plunge to buy an expensive original.
- **Duplicate your design successes.** If a particular style or image proves to be popular, use it to create other works. Put that block print on smocks, tea towels, and pillows. Create different sizes. Make small wooden trays and bowls with the hardwoods that customers love in your jewelry boxes. Make the same popular item in different trending colors, or that popular color combination in different items.
- **Pay attention to your customers.** Ask for feedback. If people tend to ask more questions about how you achieve a certain effect in your glass pendants, consider selling the information and materials as a kit as well as the finished pieces you make yourself.
- **Pay attention to trends.** The Etsy Blog (the site's online support system) is particularly good about sharing upcoming trends in color, style, and gifting. The current trends page (*www.etsy.com/trending*)

notes the popularity of dots and geometric patterns, oversized flowers, emerald green, and reclaimed materials. ArtFire's "Nosh" blog (*www.artfire.com/nosh*) features inspiration for upcoming seasons and styles. Searching for terms such as "selling art crafts trends" or "spring fashion trends" will reveal links for design blogs and articles highlighting the latest colors, styles, and "must have" accessories, all of which can inform your own new product creation.

- **Look at the part of the creative process that you enjoy the most.** If you particularly like stamping sweet little messages into antique spoons you sell as plant markers, consider making other stamped products, such as polymer clay pendants, silver bracelets and rings, or leather medallion key chains. Perhaps it's the unexpected "haiku" poetry of the message that becomes your signature style, not the silverware.

- **Here's something to go with that: Think of your products in terms of sets or collections.** Develop coordinated items that match one another. Your customers will return to purchase more of your wonderful products, to buy the salad bowls that match the serving platter, to get the clutch purse that goes so well the shawl. Simply offering a group of items at a discount, such as "Three $8.95 earrings for only $19.95," is an expansion of your product line.

- **Look at what makes you the best profit.** Maybe some of your items are easier to ship, or the materials are easier to find, or could be ordered in discounted quantities from a number of different suppliers. Perhaps a product is easier to make in quantity, lending itself to batch production.

- **Remember special occasions.** People are often online seeking a special gift for a wedding, graduation, Christmas, Halloween, or a birthday. Make a product tailored to those gifting and special occasions. Try to have something unique for different times of the year.

Market Research: What Do the People Want?

Developing a great product line is about quality, intuition, and good listening skills. Base your product line on work you love to create. This love is the foundation of your success. But be sure to add a huge dose of common sense, and take a look at what customers really want. Just because you love making a particular type of artwork does not necessarily mean that other people love it or will buy it. You never know until you test things. Craft fairs and art walks are great for giving your ideas a trial run because you can engage interested customers in conversation, ask questions, and get immediate feedback. Social media sites like Facebook and Pinterest can be a platform for posting a new product and posing a question such as, "New garden pots for spring planting . . . what do you think? Pastel colors best or neutral tans and sages?" Followers will freely share their opinions and help you determine the most popular path for your work.

Successful sellers are inspired by feedback from their customers. They will change and adapt, and in the end make much better products. However, the very nature of handmade products implies that the artwork and handcrafts come primarily from the heart and soul of the artist. All the market research in the world should never take the place of your creative intuition.

Words of Wisdom

Julie Lyderson-Jackson, owner of the Spool + Sparrow studio in Seattle, Washington, is a great example of someone who has developed a product line that she loves. Julie specializes in natural fiber, with many items handprinted using her own carved block designs. Her products include clothing, home décor, and handbags, three related categories that blend together beautifully in her online shop and her life.

"I have always been a maker," Julie shares, "but it wasn't until becoming a parent that I saw the opportunity to pursue my creative spark in a more formalized way. My love for handmade products and the whole do-it-yourself ethos led me to Etsy, first as a shopper in 2006, then to opening the Spool + Sparrow shop in 2009. Etsy provided the ideal venue for me to easily and quickly set up shop, connect directly with customers, and focus my work hours between 9 P.M. and 3 A.M. . . . so I could spend my days with my kids until they reached school age."

Julie's first products were block-printed dresses for children, aprons, and throw pillows. It has expanded to include delightfully textural handbags, skirts, tea towels, and a changeable lineup that arises from Julie's own intuition.

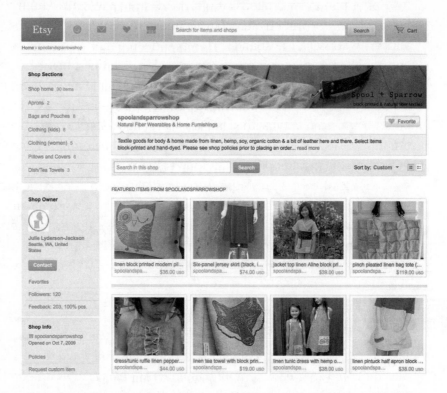

Spool + Sparrow Natural Fiber Wearables and Home Furnishings on Etsy.com.

Her signature handprinted designs, pintuck detailing, and natural-fiber cloth define her style. "I like to work with fabrics derived from sustainable crop fibers, most commonly linen, hemp, organic cotton, and soy. Each piece of fabric I purchase is always a bit different from the last, especially with linen. I find the natural imperfections of my medium to be part of its appeal. All of my products—wearable and nonwearable—are about quality construction, enduring design, and environmental sensitivity. I love rustic, raw edges and signs of the maker's hand in every piece," she says.

"Product life cycle is an important consideration when it comes to anything I make. I want my products to be durable and provide years of use. When possible, I design children's garments to accommodate rapidly growing bodies; a dress, for instance, that may later be worn as a tunic. At the end of an item's usable life, biodegradability is paramount."

Spool + Sparrow printed designs derive from a woodcarving course with a master carver, a keen interest in Japanese woodblock techniques, and life with a woodworker husband. "The imperfections of block printing suit my aesthetic better than the precise quality of screen printing. I delight in the fact that every time I press block to fabric the result is somewhat different."

Julie expands her product line through a very personal process. "It pretty much begins and ends with, 'Do I love it?' I consider myself to be among my target audience. I greatly value input from my customers and want them to be completely happy with any purchase. When it comes to final design decisions, however, I go with what works for me. Selling your handmade creations is such a personal endeavor. I need to be completely invested in each piece." You can find Julie's work at *www.spoolandsparrow.com* and *www.etsy.com/shop/spoolandsparrowshop.*

The Bottom Line

What's the bottom line? Be passionate about what you create. Begin with the work you love most. Display your products widely, in a variety of public venues, from exhibitions and juried shows to fairs and art walks. Ask for criticism. One of the most important parts of an arts education is the "critique," where colleagues and instructors let you know not only what is good about your work, but also what needs improvement, and how you can get better. Accept suggestions enthusiastically.

Expand your product line slowly and carefully. When you add a new design or variation, listen to the feedback and watch for sales before you invest time and resources into making hundreds of your new product. On marketplace websites like Etsy and ArtFire, you can keep track of the page views, product likes, and treasuries for your newest designs. If the reception is lukewarm, be ready to move on and try something else.

Keep true to your own artistic vision. Believe in your products and in yourself.

CHAPTER 3

Setting Up Your Workspace

The very first step in building a successful online arts business is to create your workspace. It does not need to be elaborate, and it certainly doesn't need to be perfect, but it is incredibly symbolic. It is where you first say to yourself, and to your family, friends, and the world at large, "I am serious! This is no longer a hobby. I am in business."

Studio Space and More

Successful businesses have been started in the most humble of home offices. In fact, one of the richest companies in the world, Apple Inc., was started in a garage! Home offices can be created in a spare bedroom, in a corner of the living room, in a nook of the upstairs hallway, a kitchen niche, even in a big closet. People renovate old garden sheds, attic space, and travel trailers to create home offices. It's quite the urban trend to buy a used cargo container and turn that into an office. One entrepreneur bought a metal storage shed and set it up inside her two-car garage. There are no limitations here!

You will need five different spaces to carry out the tasks that your business requires:

1. A place to do your artwork and crafting
2. An office space for your computer and files
3. A shipping space where you can process and pack orders
4. A photography space for consistently good photos
5. Organized storage for finished items

These five spaces can be separate areas if you have the room, or they can all fit into a single area. If your space is limited and needs to be multiuse, you'll find it a great advantage to be well organized. We'll show you how to accomplish this!

Begin with a Good Housecleaning

There are some people who thrive in chaos. Go to Google Images, and search for "Alexander Calder studio" to see a classic example from this famous American sculptor. If you are one of these rare creative geniuses, feel free to ignore the following advice. But if you aren't, pay attention to organizing your workspace, and regularly decluttering it. If you already have art studio and office space:

- Clear out papers, files, books, and computer manuals . . . any and all stuff that is not regularly used.
- Get rid of excess and duplicate files on your computer, and while you are at it, organize existing files into folders.

- Get rid of anything you do not like, even if it is useful or expensive. Replace it (you can buy a better office chair at a thrift store) or change it (a couple cans of spray paint will do wonders for that dingy filing cabinet).
- Read just a little bit about the ancient philosophy of *feng shui*. In *feng shui*, clutter complicates your life, disturbs your space, and steals your vital energy.
- Let go of the idea that you do not have enough space for your business. Open yourself to the possibility that you can do everything you need to do in the space that you have.

Build Your Workspace

If you have always imagined a beautiful home office with great colors, clever furnishings, and creative energy, go for it! This is your opportunity to shine. Your workspace does not need to be expensive or expansive. You can do wonders with simple recycled furniture and cans of paint. The Internet is filled with inspirational examples. Just search Pinterest for "home office ideas." The creativity of small workspaces is seemingly endless. Allow yourself the time and commitment to set up a space where you will love to go to work!

A Place to Do Your Artwork

Each art or craft practice has unique requirements for studio space, tools, materials, and safety. A glassblower needs an industrial area. A clothing designer will have a wide layout table next to the sewing machine and plenty of storage for bolts of fabric. A watercolor artist needs an adjustable drafting table to create different effects.

You are probably very accomplished at your art or handcraft. You may have even already created your own studio space. Though your studio space can most likely be updated, it is important to note that this area will not be your office space. It may be adjoining, perhaps, but not used for both, since most artists and crafters fill their studio with lots of messy art stuff. This is not the place for an office. You don't want to get clay and sawdust in your computer, and you shouldn't need to put away ongoing projects every time you ship an order.

Keep the space you already use to create your artwork, but think about how to make it more functional for your new business. To advance from hobby to professional level, here are some studio features to evaluate and improve your space:

- **Tools.** Do you really have the tools you need to create top-quality products? Invest in the best available if you can. Set up a budget for investing in new and better tools.
- **Materials.** Are there higher-quality materials you should be incorporating into your professional products? Use the best you can afford, price your products accordingly, and always strive to upgrade. Set up a system to store and keep track of your raw materials.
- **Lighting.** Amazingly, good lighting is one of the often-overlooked aspects of studio space. Invest now in full-spectrum lighting that welcomes you to work!
- **Organizers.** Use containers to organize tools and materials. Clear plastic bins are great. Sturdy cardboard boxes are free from your local grocery store. Cardboard bankers boxes with lids can be found for less than a dollar each when ordered a dozen at a time. You can paint cardboard and write labels identifying contents. Use chalkboard paint and a fat stick of white chalk for a great utilitarian effect. Other creative storage containers include vintage suitcases, high school lockers, and crates that once held milk bottles.

However you choose to set up your workspace, make sure that you feel comfortable and inspired when you are there.

An Office Space for Your Computer and Files

When it comes to setting up your new business office, a small desk (with a comfortable chair) is the core requirement. If you'll need to do shipping and photography in this space, trade that small desk for a larger table. Whether your home office has a room of its own depends on the space available in your house or apartment. A separate office is great. However, many successful businesses have been launched from the corner of a kitchen. As your business grows, your need for space will increase, and so will the part of your budget that is dedicated to paying for studio space. You may discover yourself building your dream office on your own property. Never let the lack of the ideal space stop you. Begin now and forge ahead with the best you have.

Office Equipment

First things first, you are going to need a good computer. This may be the main financial investment of your new online arts business. It does not matter if your computer is a laptop or desktop, PC or Mac, brand new or refurbished (but it should only be a couple years old). Some older machines can be upgraded with the latest operating systems and software like browsers and video applications. You do not want your new business to be handicapped by an old computer.

Your computer system also needs a regular backup system, either on an external hard drive, in the Cloud, or both. You don't want to find yourself in the unfortunate situation of your computer crashing and losing all of your files.

You will need a good Internet connection. If your connection to the Internet is too slow, the things you need to do online will simply take too long and you'll get frustrated. Get a broadband connection—DSL or cable. If you live in a rural setting and cannot get an Internet connection with decent speed—if the best you can get still makes you wait for web pages to slowly load as you move from site to site—then seriously consider finding an office space in town.

You'll want a printer for your computer. Most of your documents will be done online, but you will need hard copies every now and then. Most likely, you will have to print copies of each online order and include them in a packing slip when you ship a product. You may also find that ordering and printing postage and shipping labels online is a great time saver. Since printers are not expensive, treat yourself to a laser printer so you don't have to keep buying those pesky ink cartridges. Look for a printer that's also a scanner and a copier—three handy functions in one! What about a fax? You may be able to set your computer or your printer up to receive faxes. Check with a store employee before purchasing a new printer regarding this function.

Assuming you already have a phone (cell or land line), be sure your phone plan allows you sufficient time and the ability to call nationwide without excessive charges, so you can provide excellent customer service. Be aware that some United States telephone providers charge more for business phone lines.

Paperwork

Once you have paperwork, you need a place to file it. A vintage filing cabinet or even a stack of cardboard bankers boxes will do. Assemble your files into systems that will be easy for you to maintain. Remember, your goal is to be able to put your fingers on any document you might need at a moment's notice.

Here are a few tips to help you tame the slush pile:

- Set up one place to keep all your financial, legal, insurance, and other business records. Here's where you will file your business license, your resale permit, domain name records, website passwords, PayPal account information, and much more.
- Save all your purchase receipts—everything that has to do with your business. Pay for all business items with a check or credit card so there is a record of each transaction. At the beginning of each year, make a set of file folders labeled with the business deduction categories you use when filing your taxes. As you gather receipts through the year, stick them into the appropriate folder. When tax time comes at the end of the year, just pull the folders and pop them into a box . . . no sorting receipts or scurrying to remember everything.
- Keep good inventory records. Fortunately, there are many online inventory management systems available, even systems that connect with your Etsy shop or other common online e-commerce systems. Once you get everything set up, inventory management will track your raw materials, your finished items, and your sales. Some systems further integrate with accounting software such as QuickBooks. Inventory management systems may cost a fee per month based on your sales. Stitch Labs (*www.stitchlabs.com*), Bizelo (*www.eretail .bizelo.com*), and CraftyBase (*www.craftybase.com*) are great possibil-

ities. You might also be able to get software for free, like Run|Inventory (*www.runinv.com*).

- Keep track of all your sales. You can set up simple spreadsheets online and print as needed to back up your information. Most online systems will automatically track sales for you, but remember to include all of your sales—craft fairs, art walks, consignment sales at your local gallery, or folks who simply drop by your studio and buy something.
- Explore the various computer programs that make bookkeeping easy. Along with standard accounting software like QuickBooks and the simpler Quicken, there are computer programs and online services to manage your accounts, do your taxes, keep your records, organize e-mail, and save passwords.
- Get into good habits from the beginning. Establish listing, selling, and shipping processes that keep your space clean, organized, and productive.

Ideas for an Amazing Office Space

Boundaries are important in a home office, primarily as a signal that you are leaving your living space and "going to work." To accomplish this, you might, for example, use a different floor covering in your office space, such as an area rug in a different color. You might set things up so you have a threshold to cross—that is, a way into the office, especially if it's not in a separate room of its own. A pretty folding screen or a curtain hung in a doorway can create a partition.

Boundaries also help you define the square footage of your office space for insurance or tax reasons. In the United States, for example, you are able to take a deduction for a home office on your income tax form. In that case, you'd measure and document the exact area of your home that is used exclusively and regularly for business.

Office design gurus recommend that you arrange your desk so you sit at an angle to the room, facing the door rather than facing a wall. This is a psychological power position, allowing you to have greater awareness of what's happening around you. You see what is coming, and don't feel isolated. You may find yourself settling down to work more easily, and staying productive longer when your desk is in this position. It will certainly be easier to keep an eye on the kids if you are a multitasking parent!

On the other hand, you may be one of those people who need quiet and complete focus to do your best work. In that case, tuck your office into the coziest, out-of-the-way nook you can find, invest in some good sound-blocking earphones, and learn how to get to work early, before other family members are around.

Surround Yourself with Inspiration

Include lots of bulletin boards in your home office. Minimize clutter, but maximize inspiration. Embellish your office with things that enrich your life: photos, sketches, motivational bits, humor, and beautiful items. Rotate your visual collection often so you continually cast your eyes on fresh treasures. Hang your ideas on a wall covered with soft fiberboard. Just cut the fibrous board to size, mount it, and paint it the same color as your walls to create giant bulletin boards that last forever. Want a decorative statement? Cover big sheets of inexpensive insulation foam with brightly patterned fabric secured by packing tape. You can buy cork boards, or make your own with cork tiles glued onto a backing. Or, simply string a line against an open wall and use wooden clothespins to hang paper and small objects.

Most importantly, hang a whiteboard front and center in your office. Write the following numbers on it, and update weekly!

- Number of views you had in your marketplace shop the past week
- Number of visitors to your website in the past week
- Number of people subscribing to your newsletter
- Number of people who follow you on Twitter, Facebook, Pinterest, etc.

Remember the part about good lighting in your art studio? The same applies to your office. Make the best use of natural light, situating your office next to a window if possible. Install gentle, full-spectrum lighting overhead. Use smaller lights for specific tasks, gooseneck lamps, spots, and clip-ons. Finally, add ambient lights, those out-of-sight light sources that illuminate dark corners and provide a soothing glow.

Shipping Space

Packing all those online orders is a pleasant task to contemplate, and it will become one of your top business priorities. Using attractive, secure packaging and a speedy shipping service is one of the best opportunities you have to impress your customers.

To set up a shipping center in your office, you will need:

- Table space
- Places to store boxes
- Envelopes
- Packing tape
- Bubble wrap and foam
- A place to store all the items awaiting processing
- A place for the packages already wrapped and ready to go out

You can pack on a tabletop or at a counter. You may find it easier to stand for wrapping and packing chores, especially if your products are larger and call for boxes and bubble wrap. If so, make sure your workspace is high enough for comfort. A good digital scale is essential, and easy access to your computer and printer will be handy for purchasing and printing paid shipping labels.

ESSENTIAL

United States Postal Service Priority Mail Flat Rate packaging is usually the best way to send heavier items. The boxes are free from the post office, it does not matter what the package weighs as long as the contents fit, and the shipments are now trackable online. Priority Mail within the United States is usually delivered in 2–3 days.

Your Photography Studio

Consistent, high-quality product photos are essential to your online selling success. It would be nice to have a professional photographer on your payroll, but this is simply not affordable for most artists and artisans. As a new business owner and online seller, you are going to need to develop a process for taking your own product photos. The area you need for this will depend on the size of the artwork you create. Ideally, your photo space will be:

- Indoors at your workspace so you don't have to transport new items somewhere else, pray for good weather, or otherwise wait until the moment is right
- So easy to set up that you can quickly photograph new work and get it online fast
- Equipped with the right lights to capture natural color without shadows
- Incorporating carefully chosen backgrounds and props so your photos have a consistent look and feel throughout your website or market-place shop

Most artists and crafters with products small enough to sit on a table-top will be able to accomplish all of the above right in their home offices. It will take some experimentation, perhaps some do-it-yourself construction of simple light boxes and reflecting sheets, but it can be done, even in small spaces. Imagine carefully organized boxes of photography supplies transforming your office worktable into a photo studio at the drop of a hat. Picture yourself setting up new products with tried and true lighting and backgrounds, and snapping dozens of digital photos. Make it simple and you will be successful.

Artisans creating larger items—such as furniture, large canvas paintings, quilts, and clothing—have more challenging requirements for photography space and setup. You may need an entire corner of a room rather than a tabletop. There may be models involved. Stick to the basic principles of easy setup, great indoor lighting, and consistent settings. Spend the time it takes to invent a system that works for you.

Safe, Secure Storage

The final space to plan when setting up your home office is a storage system for all the fabulous products you're making. As with your studio space, the system you'll need depends on the kind of art or craftwork that you create.

From furniture to photographs, pottery to prints, you need to come up with storage that will keep items safe, keep them clean, and keep them well organized.

Each product is a precious investment of time and materials. It is not just the hours it took you to make that item, but also its share of all the hours you've spent building your online business. The only way to cash in is to sell the product. If the item gets damaged before it can reach the customer, all your investment is wasted. Customers expect and deserve excellence. Your handcrafted artwork must be in perfect condition, and the way you store your finished products assures this.

Here are some guidelines on how to pack your products:

- Prints, drawings, paintings on paper, and photographs should be encased in plastic or cellophane sleeves, and protected with acid-free board backing. Store flat art standing upright, not in flat stacks, and be especially careful to protect it from direct sunlight and damp areas.
- Paintings on canvas should be utterly dry before storing. Wrap canvases in bubble wrap, or acid-free paper, and stand them upright.
- Fabric items should be clean and folded, tucked into plastic zip-top bags, and stored in a place that is free from sunlight or odors.
- Ceramics and glass items should be wrapped and ideally boxed. If you must stack things, use plenty of protective separating layers.
- Woodwork with oil or painted finishes should be thoroughly dry before being placed into storage. Woodshops are especially dusty, so take good care to wrap items with protective plastic, paper, or cloth.
- Anything fluffy or three-dimensional (wreaths, clay sculptures, fabric flowers, paper constructions, etc.) should be boxed before storage.
- Jewelry is easy. Individual plastic zip-top bags do the trick nicely.

An information sheet should be included with each item you place into storage so it is ready to be shipped when the item sells. This information sheet tells the story of the piece: what it is made from, and how it is best used and cared for. Anything special about the product should be noted at the time it is made and stored.

Along with being clean and safe, products need to be well organized. When something sells online, you should be able to find and ship that item with ease. Likewise, the materials you use to create your artwork should be kept track of, so it is easy to reorder before you run out of supplies. Decide on the inventory management system you want to use, whether online or on your computer, or even on paper with your own system. Stick to your management system carefully.

Build a Good Relationship with Your Workspace

The time you spend planning and creating your home office and studio is similar to your investment in other meaningful relationships in your life. The more attention you give, the better it will be. Since this is where you will be spending a significant amount of time once you become a successful online seller, it makes sense to have a welcoming and supportive home office right from the start.

CHAPTER 4

Taking Your Work Seriously

Starting a business requires not only careful planning of space, time, and money, but also a commitment to taking care of legal issues. The specific licenses, permits, and tax authorizations you'll need depend on where you live. Figuring out what is required for your specific location can be challenging, but it's very important—if you ignore key permits and paperwork, it could lead to costly fines and penalties down the road. Doing things right from the beginning makes great business sense.

What to Do First

When it comes to legal matters, keep in mind that Australia has different rules than the United States. California has different rules than Ohio. Rural locations have different rules than towns or cities.

So what do you need to do? First, find out what is required for starting a business at your location. If you have access to a small business development organization, check out this valuable resource. Services are often free or available at a reasonable cost for small business startups. Their experts can guide you through the maze of requirements that are specific to you and your business. Just search Google for "small business development in (your town), (your state or province)" and explore the resulting links. Some small business development services are public agencies, provided by your government. Other organizations are independent nonprofits, and still others are businesses themselves selling consulting services.

ALERT

Internet businesses have unique needs. Before you seek advice from a business development specialist, be sure he has experience helping online sellers. Ask clear questions about his company's services and what he will charge.

Ask other small business owners what they've had to do to set up their business, especially people running online businesses in your region. Did they get good advice anywhere? Did they run into particularly helpful or unhelpful officials at local government offices? Do your best to get the actual names of bureaucrats who are easy to work with, and likewise those difficult officials you hope to avoid. Your banker and your tax preparer may have resources to help you move into small business mode. Ask plenty of questions wherever you go. Be respectful and patient with office staff. They will almost always appreciate your consideration, and help you toward your goal.

Legal Matters

Eventually, you will discover what official paperwork is required for your particular situation, and what is recommended, but optional. These licenses might include:

- Documents to define your business structure—in the United States, for example, you will typically choose from sole proprietorship, partnership, or corporation
- Registering your business to get an official identity number and all the needed tax forms required by your country
- Filing a fictitious name statement or "doing business as . . ." for your new business name
- Getting copyright or trademark protection for your business name and/or unique ideas
- Purchasing a business license
- Approval for a home-use permit
- Purchasing zoning and building permits if you intend to remodel your structure for your office or studio
- Going through various inspection requirements such as fire safety, health, and law enforcement
- Setting up a merchant tax account for collecting and turning in sales tax
- Registering for a reseller's license so you can purchase raw materials without paying sales tax
- Discovering the multitudes of rules and permits you may need if you plan to have employees
- Buying insurance for your business

Sole Proprietorship

There are many different ways to define a business. Most small arts and crafts sellers will do business by themselves, as a sole proprietorship. This is the simplest structure. Essentially, you are your business and you personally assume all the responsibility and risks involved. If the risk part makes you nervous, you can look into buying a personal liability umbrella insurance policy and still keep the simple sole proprietorship structure that is the easiest entity to manage.

Partnership

If you are starting your new online business with someone else, for example, as a mother-and-daughter team, you will want to set up a partnership. First, between the two of you, there should be a precise understanding of who does what; how each of you will share the financial risks and profit, and how you will make future decisions. Talk these things over. Communicate. Write things down. You may want to have a lawyer draw up a partnership agreement, or you can search online for information on defining your own partnership. Different countries have different regulations about partnerships as well as all the other legal complexities of doing business together. Take the time to be clear with each other from the beginning, and set the stage for long-term success.

Business structures get progressively more complex when there are several people involved. Partnerships may apply to more than two people. Look also into your country's legal definition for a cooperative. There may be advantages to this business definition.

Corporation

You may want your business to become a corporation, with its own unique identity separate from your personal status. Even if you begin your business as a sole proprietorship, you may want to incorporate later. It is imperative to understand the advantages and disadvantages of incorporating, and the process involved. There are many types and levels of corporations, and different fees and tax structures for different countries, states, and provinces. If you do feel that incorporating is in your best interest, research your options carefully. Here are some of the reasons you might want to incorporate:

- Personal asset protection—You can separate and protect your personal assets from those of the company, limiting your liability for business debts and obligations.

- Additional credibility—Adding "Inc." after your business name can add instant authority with customers and others who may prefer to do business with an incorporated company.
- Name protection—In most states, other businesses may not file your exact corporate name in the same states.
- Perpetual existence—Corporations continue to exist even if ownership or management changes. For example, if you die or leave the business, someone else can take over.
- Tax benefits—There are tax benefits to incorporation, such as being able to deduct normal business expenses, including salaries.

Registering Your Business

Each country will require a business identification number, primarily for tax and regulation purposes. This will differ from nation to nation. It is your responsibility to find out what is required of you. Talk to other small business owners, and business development agencies in your area. Keep the following information in mind:

- In the United States, a sole proprietorship simply requires the owner's own identification (your Social Security number). However, as soon as employees may be involved, or if your business is a partnership or incorporation, an Employer Identification Number is required. You can read more at the U.S. Small Business Administration website, *www.sba.gov.*
- In Australia, you may need an Australian Business Number (ABN) for your small arts and crafts business. Find forms and information at the Australian Business License and Information Service site, *https://ablis.business.gov.au.*
- In European Union countries, you may need a VAT, or Value Added Tax identification number, along with the business registration number required by your nation.
- Canadian arts and crafts sellers may need a business number. Find out more at the Canada Revenue Agency, *www.cra-arc.gc.ca.*
- You can find a lot of information about what it takes to start a business in different countries at *www.doingbusiness.org*, a project of The World Bank, which tracks business regulations around the world.

There are often fees involved with getting a business identification number, though many countries have no charge for filing this paperwork. The appropriate form may be available online for you to download and print, or it may be simply filled out and submitted online. Always print the form or make a copy of anything you submit, and save these in your office. Make notes of renewal dates if there are any, and plug these dates into your calendar to give yourself plenty of time to take care of renewals.

ESSENTIAL

When filling out forms, do not exaggerate the amount of money you plan to make from your new business. This is no place to broadcast lofty intentions. Be honest, but practical, because there are often simpler requirements, and less-expensive fees, for small, part-time, low-income businesses.

Doing Business As

If you name your business anything other than your own personal name, you'll most likely need to register it with the appropriate authorities. In the United States, this is known as filing a DBA, or "doing business as." In Canada, it's called "operating as," or O/A. In Great Britain, it's referred to as "trading as," or T/A. Each country, and indeed each state or province within a country, will have different rules for registering and using a business name.

Protecting Your Intellectual Property

Intellectual property is a term used for things you have created that may be commercially valuable. This can include names, artwork, designs, symbols, written material, and inventions. Once you have a great business name, a logo, and unique product designs, you may want to take extra steps to protect these. This is optional, but certainly smart. Here's where patents, trademarks, and copyrights come in. Copyrights will protect a painting, a jewelry design, or a book or article you have written. It does not protect the idea, only your particular expression of an idea. A trademark protects a business name, symbol, or logo. Patents protect inventions or innovative processes.

You can learn more about intellectual property rights on the U.S. Small Business Administration website, *www.sba.gov/content/intellectual-property-law.*

Copyright

In the United States, copyright protection automatically exists the moment a work is created. You don't "officially" have to do anything. You can use the copyright symbol (®) whenever you post or publish your items. This lets viewers know the item is uniquely yours and they cannot use it without your permission. You can also, for a fee, register your work with the United States Copyright Office, *www.copyright.gov.* There are similar systems in most countries.

ALERT

The process known as "poor man's copyright"—essentially mailing yourself a photo of your work and saving the unopened, postmarked envelope in your files—does not give you any copyright protection beyond the automatic copyright that exists the moment your work is created.

So what's the bottom line? If you discover that someone is using your work without your permission, you can demand that they stop, or ask for an appropriate fee for use of your work. You might decide to take legal action and sue for damages. The registration process with the United States Copyright Office gives you an official, dated document proving your copyright, a document you can use in court. Copyright is recognized internationally, though it is increasingly difficult to enforce in foreign nations.

Creative Commons (CC) (*www.creativecommons.org*) is an online system that lets you approve limited use of your images. Within the CC license, you specify how your image or design concept can be used, and how it must be attributed. Licensing work this way is becoming popular with many artists as a way to encourage others to share and reuse design ideas while promoting the original artist.

Trademark

Trademarking your business name or logo in the United States costs several hundred dollars, and can be done online at the U.S. Patent and

Trademark Office, *www.uspto.gov*. Trademarking your business name or logo means that no one else in your business category can use that specific name. If you intend to develop a major product line that will become a national or international brand, it is definitely a good idea to start with a business name you can trademark. You should search to see if the business name you are considering is available, because you may not use a business name so similar to a competitor's name that customers could be confused. Carefully select and trademark a unique business name. Make sure you can license your business name as an online domain name, too.

Patents

Patents apply to new techniques that you invent. If you come up with an entirely new design for an item, or a new way to do some sort of art or craft process, you might wish to apply for a design patent. Do lots of online research into the patent process and work with a trusted attorney. The U.S. Patent and Trademark Office offers information that may provide a good starting point. (*www.uspto.gov/patents/int_protect*)

Do You Need a Business License?

Business licenses are permits issued by government agencies, allowing you to do business within a particular jurisdiction. Almost every business, including Internet sales of art or craft products, requires some form of license to operate legally. Regulations will be different in each town, city, state, province, and country. It is your responsibility to find out what license or licenses you need. Operating a business without a business license is illegal in the United States. If you need a certain business license and don't have it, you could face penalties or be forced to close.

FACT

A business license is essentially an annual tax for doing business within that area. The most basic business license you'll need will be from the town or city where your office is located, so begin at your city offices. If you live outside of city limits, you will need a county business license.

A business license costs money each year, and the fee usually depends on the size of your business. Make sure you let authorities know that yours is an online business and that you will not be a location where customers come to shop. Most officials are accustomed to online businesses these days, but there may be offices where authorities will try to categorize you with the stores downtown and regulate you accordingly. Do your best to educate them. Honestly report your sales amount. When you are just starting out and have very low sales figures, you may qualify for an exemption from business license fees, but be assured that the officials will want to see your tax returns before they waive fees. Remember to renew your business license annually.

ESSENTIAL

In the United States, you can easily find a list of possible business license requirements for your location by following the links at the U.S. Small Business Administration's State Licenses and Permits page (*www.sba.gov*) and clicking on "what state license and permits does your business need?"

Working Out of Your Home

You may need to have an official home-use permit to run a business out of your home. All sorts of zoning regulations come into play here. These regulations essentially exist to protect your neighbors from any adverse effects that your home business might cause. Fortunately, a home-based Internet business has very little impact on others, and arts and crafts businesses are usually recognized as appropriate businesses for a home occupation.

Keep in mind that you may need to answer questions regarding the amount of noise or dust that comes from your art studio, the need for providing customer or employee parking, any higher-than-normal traffic from delivery vehicles, and the visibility and contents of your storage areas. Just imagine the questions you might have if your neighbor opened a business next door to your house or apartment.

Inspections by and permits from other agencies may be needed if your home business involves:

- Food production
- Lotions and cosmetics
- Installing a burglar alarm system
- Doing any construction to accommodate your office or studio
- Hiring employees
- Fire or safety concerns because of your art studio
- Any number of additional regulations specific to your location

ALERT

If you live in a planned neighborhood or condominium complex, check with your homeowners association to see if home business is regulated in your CC&R rules (covenants, conditions, and restrictions). These governing documents dictate how the homeowners association operates, and what rules the owners must obey.

Insurance

You can buy insurance for every conceivable risk your new business might face. It is up to you to decide what you need, and to look for the insurance company with the best rates. Since you will most likely be running your new business out of your home, the first place to seek advice is with your homeowner's insurance agent, though you should certainly shop around. Be sure to emphasize the online nature of your business and the fact that customers are not going to be coming to your office.

Additional policies, such as general and professional liability for yourself as business owner, could provide reassurance as you enter into business as a sole proprietor. You might want to have product liability, a policy that will cover you and your business if one of your products accidentally harms anyone. The need for this sort of insurance depends on what kind of artwork you create. It would not be very important for paintings or prints, but could prove necessary if you make products that are used in active sports, or are intended for children. If you begin to hire employees, there are all sorts of needs for health, injury, and unemployment insurance.

Taxes

Many different taxes can and will be applied to your new business. Depending on where you live, your new business will affect your income tax and possibly your property taxes. You may be required to submit inventory tax, business taxes, and collected sales tax. If you have developed a relationship with a small business development counselor, she will be able to guide you through the maze of tax requirements specific to your situation. You may discover that hiring a tax professional is well worth the cost.

One of the most important systems to set up as soon as you begin to sell any of your handcrafted artwork—whether online, in person at craft fairs, or to friends who drop by—is registering your new business with your tax officials. Most places in the world charge some sort of sales tax. You must collect this tax and send it to the government. It is important that you understand all of the rules and regulations you need to follow.

Here is a list of questions to consider about sales tax:

- Does your area have sales tax, and what is the rate?
- What sort of products and services are taxed, and what are not?
- Which online orders need to have sales tax added?
- How often and in what way is this collected tax sent to the government?

QUESTION

Do I need to collect sales tax online?
In the United States, if your business has a physical location in a particular state, you must collect sales tax from customers in that state. You do not need to collect sales tax from customers in states where you do not have a physical presence. Value-added tax (VAT) rules are similar for European Union countries. Canadian provinces use the harmonized sales tax system.

Most online shopping systems have processes built in for adding sales tax to an order. You simply specify which customers need to pay tax and what the tax rate should be. Say, for example, you live in Saint Petersburg, Florida, with an online business selling art prints on Etsy.com. You would need to collect a sales tax of 7 percent of the product cost from customers who live in Florida, or have orders shipped to Florida. So, you would set up your Etsy system to recognize Florida addresses, and compute 7 percent of the order subtotal for those customers. The Florida Department of Revenue regulates this process. You must register with them and submit your income figures on a regular basis, noting what part of your sales are exempt from Florida tax, what part had tax applied, and how much tax you collected. Then you send them a check for that amount.

Register with the tax officials for your location as soon as you begin selling your artwork. If you are caught selling without taking proper care of taxes, at the very least you may personally owe your state all the taxes for past sales. There could be hefty penalties imposed as well.

FACT

In the United States, you can find links for your state revenue agency at the Small Business Administration site, *www.taxadmin.org/fta/link*.

One positive outcome of registering with the proper tax authorities is that in many areas, merchants who make products are often eligible to avoid paying sales tax when they buy the raw materials and parts that go into their finished products. Depending on what you use to make your particular art or craft, this exemption could amount to significant savings over the year. Note that your suppliers will require documentation of your reseller's permit in order to sell to you without charging sales tax. They may also require this in order to give you wholesale pricing, another great savings tool as you move forward with your business.

Accounting Lets You Follow the Money

This brings us to accounting systems. You need to honestly, carefully record all of your business expenses and income. This is not optional. You are a real business, with responsibilities to tax officials, to your partners and colleagues (if you have any), and to yourself as business owner. Accurate accounting allows you to:

- See if you are making money with your business
- Easily balance your bank account
- Integrate all your income sources
- Set up budgets, and stick to them
- Report to tax officials when taxes are due
- Determine when, and how, to expand your business

Approaching Accounting

There are three basic ways to approach accounting. First, you can hire an accountant to do the bookkeeping for your business. Second, you can learn how to do it yourself. Or, third, you can hire an accountant to help you set up a system and teach you the basics, then take over and do it yourself.

Doing your own accounting has many advantages. Mainly, you will get to know the daily ins and outs of your business if you do the bookkeeping yourself. If you are bootstrapping your business (starting with very little funding), then you may not have the money to hire an accountant. If you do have some money in the beginning, there are fantastic accounting systems available: You can buy software for your computer, or use a myriad of online systems. Whichever one you select will require you make a serious commitment to learning how to use it before you are comfortable and competent. Do not underestimate the time and energy involved. Think of it as enrolling in a college class, but a class where you will be taught by online support videos and help files, with a class schedule you set yourself.

FACT

Your accounting system must integrate all the different ways you sell your artwork—online, mail order, face to face, retail, wholesale, and consignment.

If you are starting with a single online location, such as an Etsy shop, and do no other selling, you can simply look at the accounting modules that work with that particular system. Etsy sellers, for example, have a number of independent apps available at the Etsy Apps page, *www.etsy.com/apps/shop_tools*. Some of the accounting apps found on the Etsy Apps site include Outright (*www.outright.com/etsy*) and Wave (*www.waveapps.com/etsy-accounting-software*), in addition to others. These are online accounting programs created by independent companies. These systems are available for free, but they usually do have a way to make money for their developers. For example, Wave incorporates advertising to support their free system. Outright offers an expanded version available for a monthly fee, which they hope free users will purchase in order to get the additional features. These online systems will automatically connect with an Etsy shop, as well as your Etsy or PayPal payment gateway, to pull in your sales information such as product sales, shipping, and tax. You will need to manually enter your expenses. You can tour each system on their websites and search the Etsy discussion forums to read what other people have to say. Then you can decide if one of these systems is right for your needs.

If you are using other online stores to sell your goods in addition to Etsy, you will need to integrate all of your income sources. For example, you must enter your sales figures from the craft fair last month, the sales you made at your CafePress.com space, the piece you auctioned at eBay.com, that guy who bought a bunch of items wholesale for his gift shop, etc. If your business has already reached this level of complexity, or you have plans to, you may find that a more traditional and full-featured accounting system is a better choice than an online tool. The standard for small business is Intuit Quick-Books, available as a traditional desktop program that you purchase for your computer. You can get either the Pro program if your computer is a PC, or the Mac program for Apple computers. The QuickBooks system is also available in the cloud for a monthly fee. (See *http://quickbooksonline.intuit.com*.)

FACT

The availability of support and training is a key consideration if you choose an accounting system and plan to manage your business finances by yourself.

Because of its popularity, there are a lot of ways to learn QuickBooks. You can use support at Intuit's website; QuickBooks' online training videos at *www.youtube.com/quickbooksonline*; or online training sites like *www.lynda .com*. You can also find help in workshops and classes at community colleges, at small business development centers, and from professional accountants.

While QuickBooks might be the most widely used small business accounting system, there are alternatives. Other desktop programs for your computer include Sage 50 software and GnuCash. There are other online systems too, though most sport a hefty monthly fee. One great way to decide what system to use is to talk to an accountant. You may already use someone to prepare your taxes, even if you are not yet in business. Ask for his advice, and perhaps he can be hired to help you set up a system that you will eventually take over yourself. Whichever accounting system you use, here are a few basic tips and tricks that will help you start and stay organized:

- Tracking business finances is easiest if you keep business and personal accounts separate. Open a different bank account for your business. Get a separate credit card. Pay for every business expense with that card or a check so there is an easy record for keeping the books. Avoid paying cash for business items because those transactions take more of your effort to track.

- Schedule regular time to catch up on bookkeeping. Even a simple, regular, 20-minute session will help you stay on top of things. Post expenses weekly, balance your bank account monthly, and avoid that stressful panic at tax time when things really do have to be completed.

- Keep track of your time. As you start up your business, you are likely to be doing all the tasks yourself. And of course, since you are the owner and probably investing every cent you make back into your new business, you are not initially paying yourself for this labor. It is still essential that you keep track, because some day you may be hiring an employee to do certain tasks. You need to know how many hours various jobs take and what to budget in the future. Getting used to tracking time now will help you make better decisions down the road.

- If your new business is set up as a sole proprietorship and you end up having enough money to pay yourself for all this hard work (yes you will, eventually), you should take that money out as a draw. Do not plan on taking a lot of money out during the first year of business. Invest it back into building your business to ensure long-term success. In other words, keep your "day job" to pay your living expenses.

- When first setting up your bookkeeping system, work with a tax accountant to establish business-expense categories that exactly match what you will eventually use when you file your taxes. Learn which expenses go in each category so you can efficiently post everything you spend on your business. Set up manila folders to match each category so you have an easy place to stick receipts. When tax time comes, it will be a breeze.

Inventory

It is important to have an inventory system to allow you to keep track of your products. You will be very happy to have set this up at the beginning of your professional selling career. This is the essence of taking your work seriously!

There are various computer programs and online services designed to help artists and crafters, and many more systems designed by artists themselves. Essentially, you want an inventory management system that will keep track of everything that applies to your own artwork, including:

- The name of each piece you create
- The date it was finished
- A picture of the item, along with information on its digital files and where the files are kept
- The series or set it belongs to, and records of any related items
- Specs, such as size, media, or materials used; any specific glazes, dyes, etc.
- The current price and any price history
- Any awards this piece has received
- If the item is an art print, you need information on the limited edition, print numbers, and size options
- Its display history (where and when this item has been shown)
- If on consignment, where, when, and what terms
- The item's current location (at an outlet or in storage)
- If sold, to whom, when, from which outlet, for what price, etc.

Keeping Track by Hand or with a Spreadsheet

You can manage your inventory on paper if you don't have a lot of items and you have plenty of time. Create a separate sheet for each item, and pencil in its history as it happens. It is, at the very least, a place to begin.

If you'd rather keep digital files, you can use a spreadsheet application like Microsoft Excel to set this up on your computer. Create a spreadsheet with columns of data that are specific to your particular artwork, and simply keep updating the file with new information. Google Drive is a good online spreadsheet program that is free to use.

Add Power with a Database

You can have a computer expert set up a database on your computer using software such as Microsoft Access, FileMaker Pro, or even the open source MySQL. The advantage of having a database instead of the simpler spreadsheet is that you'll be able to sort by particular fields. Want to see the current items you have on consignment at the Western Star Gallery? Need to find all the items that are part of the "Openings" series of prints and paintings? Just specify your query and you'll find the list you seek.

Software for Your Computer

There are multitudes of computer programs for tracking inventory, from POS (point of sale) systems for stores, to inventory management systems for manufacturers. These software systems are elaborate databases already set up for a wide variety of functions, and each comes with a different cost. Artists and crafters can use (and afford) software targeted to small businesses, like inFlow (*www.inflowinventory.com*), which offers a downloadable version you can try for free for up to 100 products.

There are programs specific to certain industries. If you ask fellow artisans or search the Internet for these programs, you will find systems such as Jewelry Designer Manager (*www.jewelry.com*), Bead Manager Pro (*www.beading-software.com*), SoapMaker (*www.soapmaker.ca*), or My Art Collection (*www.my-artcollection.com*).

Management Systems in the Cloud

The latest tool in inventory management is an online system available for a monthly fee called a "cloud." There are several clouds that specifically target the arts and crafts market. These systems do amazing things, such as keep track of your finished items and selling history, and allow you to track your raw materials, the items and projects you have in progress, and even the time it takes to make each piece. You can obtain many reports from the information you enter such as interactive graphs that tell you which venues bring you the most sales, which of your products are selling the best, even which colors and sizes are the most popular. You will even find calculators to help determine a price for a finished item, selling modules to generate invoices, and packing slips for orders. These systems let you keep track of stores and selling locations, both consignment and wholesale, and individual customers themselves, complete with integrated e-mail lists. They can also connect online to a wide variety of shops to automatically import listings and sales data each month.

Stitch Labs inventory and order management system (*www.stitchlabs .com*) is very popular among serious Etsy sellers because it integrates seamlessly with the Etsy shop. Stitch Labs was developed as an API (application programming interface) for Etsy shops, but it goes far beyond. You can also connect to many other online selling platforms, from eBay to Shopify.com. There are modules to connect to PayPal's payment gateway and to Quick-Books for accounting. Stitch Labs is a management system with a huge potential for artists and crafters.

Craftybase (*www.craftybase.com*) is another online system made for professional crafters that allows you to track products, sales, and much more. It does an especially good job of tracking the creative process—the raw materials and the time that goes into making your items. Check out Bizelo (*www .eretail.bizelo.com/inventory*), a system designed for general online sellers, but with a new focus on Etsy and the arts marketplace. The Run|Inventory system (*www.runinv.com*), while simpler, is free.

Take Yourself Seriously!

Taking your work seriously is an important step for artists and crafters, but it can be a difficult transition for some. Creative minds often feel at odds with the number crunching, list making, and regulation that it takes to open a serious business. The many suggestions in this chapter are important for starting a business, but taking yourself seriously as an artist goes deeper. Taking your work seriously can be as fundamental as:

- Clearly signing each piece you make
- Finishing pieces rather than setting them aside incomplete
- Finding a mentor in your artistic field, and offering to assist them in exchange for advice and experience
- Taking classes and workshops
- Teaching classes and workshops (you could start by offering free classes at a school or a senior center)
- Entering your work in contests and exhibitions
- Donating your work to raffles and fundraisers for good causes
- Scheduling time to do your art or craft, and keeping this commitment to yourself

Simply start doing something—anything—each day toward your professional goal. Remember, one of the habits of a successful online entrepreneur is: "Reduce big tasks into simple steps." Taking your work seriously means integrating that habit into your whole life, not just your art.

CHAPTER 5

Writing a Great Business Plan

Most likely, you either have a plan for your new online selling business in place or are in the early stages of putting one together. Reading this book and exploring online selling platforms and resources should be the first steps in your plan. However, creating a checklist of things to do is only the beginning of your business plan. A formal business plan is a carefully prepared document describing the nature of your business, your sales and marketing strategy, and your financial background. Traditionally, it contains materials like a market analysis, a projected profit-and-loss statement, and details about the ownership of the company. Gathering this data, plugging in your own ideas, and writing everything down in a clear and concise plan are essential parts of growing a successful online business.

Do You Need to Write a Business Plan?

Creating a formal business plan is a daunting task, and many startup businesses delay this process for years. The most common reason why a new business needs a formal business plan is to seek loans or investors. The first thing a bank loan manager, angel investor, or venture capitalist will request is a copy of your business plan. If you are starting your online art or craft business with your own money, and bootstrapping and re-investing profits as you grow, you may not need to raise any money. If this is the case, then why bother with writing that business plan?

The answer is: because it works. Research on the business startup process has shown that in general, writing a business plan has a positive effect on a new business. It helps the owner find the information she needs to be successful, helps avoid common business mistakes as she learns what has worked for other businesses, and helps her organize her thoughts and actions. Simply committing your plans to paper helps to make them happen.

Writing down your business plan will:

1. Motivate you to make your goals happen
2. Clarify your strategic plans
3. Help you stick to the path you need to follow
4. Allow you to revisit, evaluate, and see your progress

ESSENTIAL

The U.S. Small Business Administration states, "A business plan is an essential roadmap for business success. This living document generally projects 3–5 years ahead and outlines the route a company intends to take to grow revenues."

Parts of a Business Plan

There are many different business plan formats, but all contain the following basic sections:

- Executive Summary: an introductory synopsis of the entire plan
- Company Description: clearly defining your business and the products and services you provide
- Market Analysis: who will purchase these services and products, and what is currently offered?
- Organization and Management: what is your business structure, and who are the principal people involved?
- Product Line: specifically, what do you sell, and what makes it stand out from your competition?
- Marketing Plan: what is your sales strategy?
- Financial Projections: how much money is being invested, and how much will be made over the next several years?
- Funding Request: if this is part of your plan, then what is needed now, what additional funding will be needed in the future, and how do you plan to pay it back?
- What are the twelve monthly landmarks for your business? (This is optional, but very helpful.)

Keep a Journal

As you continue to research the best-selling platform for your artwork, and what licenses and legal documents you need to open a home office, you are also completing your business plan. Record the things you discover. Start a notebook if you like to write by hand, or create a set of computer documents if you prefer to write electronically. Create a page for each of the elements of a traditional business plan. Jot down your ideas as you go. Don't try to write any polished, final copy, but write often and consistently.

Give yourself time to put your own thoughts together and to do research about some of these sections. Be sure to set a limit. A few weeks might be sufficient. At the end of that time, schedule an appointment with yourself to compile your notes and ideas into readable form, and write your business plan. Give yourself a whole day to do this. It may be the best day you will ever spend on your business. Follow the traditional format, described in detail in the following sections.

The Executive Summary

While this is the first section of a formal business plan, it will actually be the last section you write. The Executive Summary is a snapshot of all the other parts of your business plan. It should include your business contact information, your mission statement, a concise description of your business and your products, and your plan for growth. If someone reads only your Executive Summary, he should still come away with a clear understanding of your business and how you plan to develop over the next several years. He should know your strongest selling points and what makes your business unique. When you finally write this section, keep it to one page in length. Yes, one page. Two at the most, but one is better. Every word counts.

Company Description

This section of your plan you will specifically define your business, the products or services you will offer, and who will buy them and why. Is your business an existing company that is expanding, or is it brand new? Who are your customers? What is unique about your products? What will make you stand out in your market niche? Why will you be successful?

Being able to define these things demonstrates a lot about your capacity to run a business. This is where the very act of writing your business plan helps you succeed. "Heck, I just want to sell earrings to people," you may think at the start. If that is as far as you get with your plan, your chance of success is pretty small. But if you are forced to think about the customers you are selling to, what their needs are, and how you plan to fill those needs with features and services that make your earrings unique, then you are much closer to developing a business that will prosper.

ESSENTIAL

Talk to your customers and fans. Ask them what made them want to buy your products. Often you will hear about details that you never even imagined were important. Understanding what already differentiates you from your competitors can help you become even more memorable in the future.

Market Analysis

In this section of your business plan you'll get down to the details of the research you've completed. By checking out the websites mentioned in this book and looking at the shops and products of artists or crafters who are selling work similar to yours, you will have a better understanding of your industry. More information can be found through Internet searches, at various government agencies, and even from conversations with other business owners.

In this section of your plan, you will want to:

- Describe your industry. Dig deeper into the history of online selling. What is the current size of the market? How many visitors are there each month at Etsy, eBay, and Zazzle? How much money is made in total sales? What is the industry's recent growth and projected potential? What did these figures look like a year ago, and two years ago? Statistics are published online. Use Google searches to find the data.
- Describe your target market. Who shops online and buys the things you will sell? Be very specific. Your small business will be more successful if you target a realistic, narrow market rather than trying to please everyone. Again, spend some time looking for online data about how much money people spend for products like yours, what seasonal cycles are important, and any projections for the coming year.
- Explain how your products fit into industry trends. Search Google and follow the suggested links to read predictions in your market. Let's return to the earring maker as an example. A search reveals that earrings made out of vintage buttons, pearls, and geometric tribal designs have been seen on models at recent fashion shows, and that tangerine is predicted to be a popular color this coming year. Not only is this valid data to put into the Market Analysis section of your business plan, it is also (and primarily) great information to have when ordering supplies to make the next batch of earrings. Once again, the very act of writing a business plan can help you succeed.
- Define your pricing structure. How do your products fit in the range of competitors? What is your cost of goods (your wholesale and your retail price)? Very often your online research will reveal the prices that other successful online sellers offer.

- Write about any actual market testing you have done. For artists and crafters, local fairs and art walks are valid real-life testing possibilities, even before you sell online. What products have you presented? What has been the reaction? Have customers passed them by, or have they loved them? Have they purchased your product when it is priced really low, or are they just as likely to buy things at double the price?

QUESTION

Organization and Management

This section of your business plan describes the structure you have chosen for your business and the key people you will employ. This may be the easiest of all sections to complete, since most art and craft sellers will be describing a sole proprietorship and describing their own experience. Be sure to think deeply about the skills and strengths you bring to your business, and how these attributes can help you succeed. Write about your history, your training, your talent, the awards or recognition you have received, and the experiences in your life that will enable you to be a good business owner.

Product Line

You introduced your products in the Company Description section; now you are going to speak about them in detail. What are your product lines? What makes them unique? How do they meet the needs of your customers? As you write this section, you are actually involved in a personal exercise that is integral to your success as an online arts and crafts seller.

You will become used to thinking of your creative work as a product. Art itself is certainly not a product. It is a process that artists and crafters passionately practice, and will continue to do whether or not there's any money involved.

You will continually walk along the edge of this distinction as you go to your studio to create in the purest and most rewarding form, and then return to your office to analyze which of your creations actually help pay the bills. However, it is undeniable that successful online selling requires creating products that people want to buy.

Marketing Plan

Successful online sellers really love the marketing part of their businesses. Marketing online is fun. This section of your business plan gives you the opportunity to describe where and how you plan to market your product. Don't describe all the possibilities here; there are way too many. Instead, describe the promotions you plan to do during the next year.

Be sure to include:

- Where you will begin selling online and how you will expand. Will you open an Etsy shop, spend three months populating it with 100 items, and then start your own domain website showcasing those same items? Will you begin to incorporate eBay auctions for selected products? What's the plan?
- How will you reach your potential customers? Will you set up a blog, and begin regularly writing about your work? Perhaps you'll want to become a guest writer for other popular blogs and websites.
- Are you going to advertise online? Will you buy banner ads at targeted blog sites? Purchase feature spots on Etsy?
- What is your pricing strategy? How do your prices fit with the rest of the industry? Will you offer sales and discounts?
- How will you retain customers for repeated sales? Will you start a newsletter, create works in a series to encourage collectors, or start a Facebook page where fans can keep in touch with your newest items?

Financial Projections

The financial section may be the least favorite part of a business plan for everyone except accountants, and yet it is where you actually define your success. What will make all this effort worthwhile? What is it costing you to set up your online selling business? How will you make money, and how much are you likely to make? Follow these guidelines to create accurate projections:

- If you are already producing and selling your artwork at shops, galleries, and fairs, collect your financial data from the past few years. You will want to show income statements, balance sheets, and cash flow statements. Make note of your existing business collateral and the inventory and equipment you already have.
- If you are just starting a business, you will need to find industry information about similar businesses and project this into your business profile.

After talking about the recent history and the current state of your business, you now need to carefully predict your future financials. What is likely to happen as you move ahead with your new business plan? Make monthly projections for the coming year, then quarterly projections for years two through five. What will expenses cost as you grow? What will your sales income be? Be realistic in your outlook. While you may hope to become an overnight sensation, a gradual but steady growth is much more likely. Don't be too conservative, either. Most entrepreneurs are motivated by their dreams, so include them in your projections. You have to think success in order to become successful!

If you are completing your business plan for your own benefit, you can be a bit more casual about the financial projections. If you are actually seeking loans, grants, or investors, the Financial Projections are the essential parts of your business plan. You will need to be far more detailed, and include projections of your business income statements, balance sheets, cash flow statements, capital expenditure budgets, and more. You may find it effective to hire the help of an accountant or financial planner to complete these documents. This is another instance where a good small business development center might be able to provide needed assistance.

If you are seeking funding from a bank, an agency, or private investors, this is where you make your appeal. What money do you need to raise right now? What exactly do you need this money for, or how will you spend it? What additional funding will be needed in the next three to five years to insure your continued business health?

ALERT

When projecting expenses, double the amount you initially estimate for marketing and triple your estimate for licensing, legal, and insurance needs. These expenses always seem to escalate beyond the expectations of new business owners.

Your Twelve Monthly Landmarks

As a final, and totally useful, part of your business plan, write down the landmarks you plan to achieve, month-by-month, for the coming year. Look carefully at your plan and boil it down to the key things you will have accomplished by each date.

For example, an earring designer might begin with something like:

- End of Month 1: Set up Etsy shop, create banner, post first 10 products. Register with state sales tax agency and city business license. Purchase QuickBooks Online service. Purchase digital camera. Create 20 new earrings.
- End of Month 2: Etsy shop rolled out with 100 products. Have first 5 Etsy sales. Enroll in digital photo evening class at community college. Create 30 new earrings.
- End of month 3: Sell 10 items per week on Etsy. Increase earring production to 50 per month. Also create 10 pendants for matching earrings. Set up Facebook business page. Set up Twitter account. Start website with WordPress.

Your business plan is a living, changeable document telling the story of your business. It is not simply a homework assignment that you stash on a high shelf and allow to collect dust. You learn a lot as you assemble and write your business plan. You've gone through the process and it has changed you. It has changed the way you look at your industry and your place in the world of online selling, successful artists, and established artisans. If you ever do get to the point where you are seeking a business loan or investors, you are ready.

But its true strength will become clear as you revisit your business plan. Be sure to return to it often. This is an ongoing process. Look at your Twelve Monthly Landmarks every single month. Schedule a business lunch with your partners, or with your spouse and your best friends if you are a sole proprietor (or with whoever is likely to be your best support team). Look at what you predicted would happen by a certain date with them, and discuss what has really happened and why. Are you vastly more successful than you thought you would be, or are you way behind? This is not about how "good" or "bad" you are as a businessperson. This is more about how well you are able to predict the future of your business, a skill that will get better and better with experience. Looking at your landmarks is a great motivator, and helps keep you on track.

Revise your business plan every year. Remember setting that appointment with yourself to initially write your business plan? Schedule that same appointment a year later and revise the entire thing. A year's experience will bring plenty of changes in your business profile, in your understanding of your products and target customers, and in your marketing plan and financials. Update everything in detail. It may take you another full day, but make time for it. Create another carefully planned Twelve Monthly Landmarks list, and then get back to work!

CHAPTER 6

Which Online Shop
Is Right for You?

The Internet offers amazing opportunities for artists and crafters. It has never been so easy to offer handcrafted items for sale online. For instance, there are many different websites providing space for shops and galleries, featured items, and auctions. There are places to easily build your own website. There are shopping cart systems for online selling. There is so much available on the Internet, in fact, that it can be hard to know where to begin. What sort of online system is best for your particular artwork and lifestyle?

An Overview of Online Services

The services for selling art and handcrafts online can be loosely gathered into four categories:

- Marketplace websites with shops for participating artists and artisans
- Auction services featuring arts and handcrafts
- Sites where customized art and craft products are created on demand
- Places to build your own website

There are even more ways to sell online, and there is a lot of overlap within these categories. This book does not promise to list everything available, because if there is one thing you can count on with the Internet, it's that things change all the time. The following sections are just a list. Subsequent chapters will fill in the details, profiling the most popular services within each category, and helping you decide which path to follow to get started on the road to your own successful online business.

FACT

Selling online has become one of the most profitable ways for artists to sell their art. For the year September 2011 to August 2012, 25 percent of polled artists reported that online sales were how they made their best income. In comparison, 22 percent preferred selling from their own studio, 10 percent favored art festivals, and 9 percent found gallery sales most profitable.

Marketplace Sites for Art and Handmade Goods

Marketplace websites allow you to create your own shop or gallery within the site's overall shopping system. They handle the selling transactions, and you will receive all or most of the money you get from sales; you ship your own orders. Buyers come to the marketplace site seeking handmade goods, and can discover your products using a variety of search tools. Your shop is also available for customers who are attracted through your own marketing efforts. There are differing fees for participating in marketplace sites, starting with free, which is a nice place to begin for many artists and crafters who don't have much money to invest up front.

Etsy (*www.etsy.com*)

One of the largest online sellers, Etsy.com averaged over 8 million unique visitors per month during 2012, with traffic that continues to grow. This level of traffic is far beyond the scale of the other arts- and crafts marketplace sites (millions of monthly visitors compared to thousands). The size is also reflected in the number of sellers on Etsy, with over 500,000 active shops competing for this traffic.

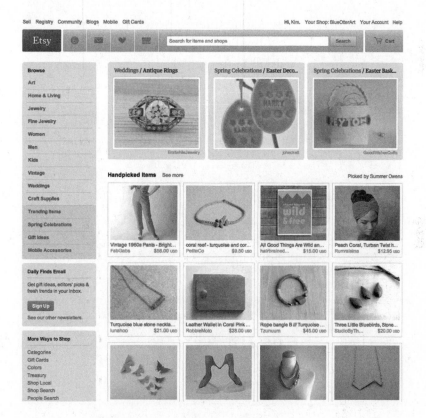

Etsy.com Landing Page

Finding a way to stand out in the crowd is a challenge. Etsy sellers can list handmade items, vintage goods, and arts and crafts supplies. Rest assured that stepping into the Etsy system is not a financial burden, as sellers open a free shop and then list their products for a per-item fee of 20 cents for 4 months. Etsy takes a small percentage of each sale. It's all worth it, though, as Etsy is both a marketplace and a vibrant community, with highly developed tools to help artists and crafters build a successful business.

FACT

In his annual blog message on Jan 28, 2013, Etsy's CEO Chad Dickerson stated: "The Etsy marketplace is thriving as we enter our eighth year. Overall sales by the community in 2012 grew 70.3 percent over the previous year, to $895.1 million from $525.6 million in 2011."

ArtFire (*www.artfire.com*)

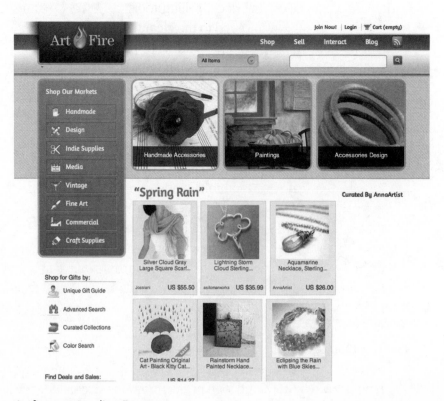

Artfire.com Landing Page

ArtFire.com is a marketplace for handmade goods that averaged 400,000 visitors per month during 2012. While this is only around 4 percent of Etsy's traffic, ArtFire.com is still Etsy's closest competitor in size. ArtFire is gaining in popularity, and offers many attractive features. ArtFire's specific focus on crafts, art, and supplies makes it more an exclusively handmade shop; you won't find any vintage goods here. Visitors on ArtFire can search for things in a variety of creative ways including searching by color, by words, and by style, and can purchase items without the need to set up their own account profile with the site. There are also great tools for listing and promoting ArtFire items, such as the ArtFire Kiosk widget for Facebook pages and applying to become a Featured Artisan.

Many More Marketplace Sites

There are several smaller marketplace websites around, each offering a different philosophy, interface, selling tools, and fee structure. Traffic at these sites is a trickle compared to the gigantic Etsy, but the number of items is likewise much smaller. Simply said, your products have a better chance of standing out in the crowd. Sellers who plan to sell primarily to their own customers (traffic coming from the artist's own website, blog, or gallery) may find the selling tools and community at a smaller venue suits them perfectly.

Here is a list of smaller sites that may work for you:

1. **Zibbet.com** (*www.zibbet.com*)
   Zibbet.com (think "art exhibit" made cool) is a young, up-and-coming marketplace website based in Australia with an excellent handmade look and feel. The enthusiastic Zibbet developers are pleasing both buyers and sellers with lots of new, user-friendly features. There are three different membership plans for sellers, starting with a free option. Traffic averaged 45,000 monthly visitors through 2012 (less than 1 percent of Etsy's 8 million monthly visitors).

2. **ShopHandmade.com** (*www.shophandmade.com*)
   This Seattle-based website has an emphasis on living green. ShopHandmade.com is a free marketplace taking no fee or commission from sellers.

3. **Madeitmyself.com** (*www.madeitmyself.com*) focuses on the hobby seller. The site accepts only handmade items, so no vintage or mass-produced

products compete with self-made artworks. A "negotiable" setting allows sellers the option to entertain offers lower than the list price, and to connect with potential buyers via a unique live chat feature.

4. **Folksy.com** (*www.folksy.com*) specializes in the UK artisan market.

5. **ICraftGifts.com** (*http://icraftgifts.com*) centers its marketplace on handmade gifts, including art, crafts, and fashion.

6. **DaWanda.com** (*http://en.dawanda.com*) features an international focus and an emphasis on the social experience of the customer, making it a popular site for buyers. This is a good marketplace website for connecting with European buyers in general, and German buyers in particular.

7. **Yessy.com** (*www.yessy.com*) averaged 20,000 monthly visitors through 2012. With an emphasis on fine art, it was one of the pioneers of selling art online.

8. **CraftIsArt.com** (*www.craftisart.com*) is a newcomer to the marketplace scene. CraftIsArt.com has a growing number of sellers. Good artwork and crafts would clearly stand out in this smaller crowd! Sellers get shop space for either a commission or a monthly flat fee.

9. **Silkfair.com** (*www.silkfair.com*) was named after the historic Silk Road trading route through Asia. Seeking to provide a seamless transition between selling in marketplace space and selling on your own domain name website, this new marketplace site offers both free shop space (for a 3 percent commission on sales) and completely customizable websites (for a monthly fee).

10. **Facebook shops** (*www.facebook.com*); the world's largest social media platform has recently offered shopping space as part of a business profile. The e-commerce system is not built in (you must use an independent application for selling items), and customers are not yet used to purchasing things on a Facebook page. However, the ability to display products and encourage fans to spread the word about your fabulous items makes Facebook storefronts an attractive additional online venue.

And, yes, there's more. Each year new marketplace sites open with different features, different emphases on a particular handmade niche, and an array of services for the seller. If you want to explore your options even further, take a look at Supermarkethq.com (*www.supermarkethq.com*), eCRATER.com (*www.ecrater.com*), FreeCraftFair.com (*www.freecraftfair.com*),

HandmadeArtists.com (*www.handmadeartists.com*), NotMassProduced.com (*www.notmassproduced.com*), Misi.co.uk (*www.misi.co.uk*), Coriandr.com (*www.coriandr.com*), and Meylah.com (*http://meylah.com*)—and the list just keeps expanding.

Auction Sites

These websites allow you to sell your work online by auction. You set the minimum amount you are willing to accept as an opening price, and customers will bid. For the duration of the auction (which can be several minutes to several days), viewers can increase their bids until the bidding closes and the highest bidder becomes the customer.

eBay

eBay.com Landing Page

Art on eBay (*www.ebay.com/chp/art*) and Crafts on eBay (*www.ebay .com/chp/crafts*) are very popular; the pages had an average monthly traffic of 200,000 visitors through 2012. These sections of the vast eBay website allow you to sell arts and crafts both by auction and by "buy it now" prices, and to set up your own eBay store. Original art, vintage art, supplies, and tools all share this unique platform. Along with artists selling their own handmade works, you will also find antique shops selling the paintings of artists from past generations, eBay fans offering the anonymous art they inherited from great grandma Minnie, and sellers with deals on crafting supplies and machines. Art dealers and resellers also use eBay to offer wholesale lots. Incredible items do really stand out and inspire active bidding, and many artists and crafters use eBay as either their primary platform for selling their work, or as a secondary system to a marketplace shop or their own website's store.

Tophatter.com (*www.tophatter.com*)

Calling itself "the world's most entertaining live auction site," Tophatter .com has a clever interface with themed auctions scheduled throughout the day. Sellers and customers interact via chat as an auction is taking place, with comments, questions, and answers posted for everyone to read. Compelling and personal, the conversations encourage participation.

Buyers are looking for a good deal. Tophatter auctions include vintage items, designer brands, and crafting supplies as well as artwork. Jewelry seems to be the most common handmade product. With a steadily growing audience, Tophatter.com is worth exploring.

Specialized Auction Websites

One example of a specialized auction website is DailyPaintworks.com (*www.dailypaintworks.com*). With 9,000 visitors each month, this auction website offers a good platform for artists wanting to auction their work to a select audience, such as their own fans and collectors. The low monthly traffic allows you to stand out in the crowd, and encourages you to promote your auctions among your own clientele. Selling can be done via eBay or directly through DailyPaintworks.com.

There are auction sites specializing in antique art (get your famous painters of the eighteenth century), famous artists (that Warhol print will go for $2 million), and gallery art (works by emerging artists as well as acknowledged leaders in each media). If your artwork is at this level, you will likely be working with an agent or gallery who can guide you to the best platform.

Products on Demand

Print-on-demand or POD services are a great opportunity for artists to test the market and sell their work without a huge up-front investment. These websites allow you to create a variety of products designed from your own artwork.

Some of these products include:

- Miscellaneous items, such as coffee mugs, cell phone covers, T-shirts, skateboards, and so much more
- Art prints from posters and cards to framed fine art giclées and stretched canvas
- Books of all shapes and sizes; paintings, photography, and instructional books

Most of your orders will come from your own customers and people who are guided to your product space from your website or social media marketing, though the websites also allow their general visitors to see your items through searches and front page promotions. If your designs are clever and appealing, this visibility may result in an expanded clientele. Orders are sent directly to customers, saving you the need to stock inventory, process orders, or do any shipping. Artists earn a royalty on each item sold.

Products on Demand Sites

The following sites allow you to create a dazzling variety of products, from prints and posters to clothing, cases, bags, and much more.

1. **CafePress.com** (*www.cafepress.com*) averages around 5 million monthly visitors. CafePress promises to be the place "Where Art Becomes . . . Stuff," and offers a wide variety of services for individual artists and designers.

CafePress.com Landing Page

2. **Zazzle.com** (*www.zazzle.com*) is (just barely) the leading website for custom products, with an average of 5 million visitors per month in 2012. While it is mainly known for selling T-shirts and posters, artists can use Zazzle to create a huge variety of items incorporating their own designs. Zazzle sellers set up their own store and set their own royalty on each item sold. Their product pricing is adjusted accordingly.

3. **Society6.com** (*www.society6.com*) uses curation to promote the most crowd-pleasing products, which feature artists' designs. As their selling information states, "Selling your artwork as a product on Society6 is as simple as making a Post—except you make money from it." The types

of products you can create include art prints and stretched canvases, greeting cards, iPhone and iPad cases and skins, tote bags, hoodies and T-shirts, and throw pillows. This is an excellent platform if your target customer is young and hip.

4. **RedBubble.com** (*www.redbubble.com*) is an Australian-based product-on-demand site with a pleasing interface and an average of 500,000 visitors per month.

Prints on Demand

While many of the "product-on-demand" websites offer prints as one of the products you can create using your uploaded artwork, the following sites specialize in museum-quality prints, complete with framing services and stretched canvas options.

1. **FineArtAmerica.com** (*www.fineartamerica.com*): With a focus on artists and photographers, this website specializes in museum-quality prints on paper or stretched canvas, with thousands of frame and mat combinations. Website tools allow artists to set up printed catalogs and branded web stores; sell prints on Facebook; sell prints on Amazon.com; create e-newsletters; and much more. Traffic to the site itself runs around 500,000 visitors per month.

2. **Imagekind.com** (*www.imagekind.com*): This fine art print service is part of the CafePress empire, designed especially for artists selling posters, giclée prints, and stretched canvas prints, framed or unframed. The website allows buyers to see what an image will look like when framed or as a stretched canvas, a very powerful visualization tool. Sellers get free space and set their own profit mark-up over Imagekind's base price. In 2012, the site was averaging 100,000 monthly visitors.

3. **ArtistRising.com** (*www.artistrising.com*): This site offers a platform for on-demand art prints and original artwork from photographers and artists. When prints are ordered, the website takes care of the transaction and delivery, with the artist getting a 30 percent commission on the sale. The original painting can also be offered and promoted along with its prints, and the customer is referred directly to the artist if the original sells.

Books on Demand

Books are becoming a popular product for artists, photographers, and even crafters. You can create books with your own images, from compendiums of entire careers to books about specific themes and series. You can also create sketchbook journeys, children's books, and instructional books. Self-publishing is easy with the templates provided by some services. Books can be ordered in small quantities for the artist or crafter to sell through her other channels, and are available for order, one at a time, by customers coming to the website.

Here are some sites to check out:

1. **Blurb.com** (*www.blurb.com*): With 250,000 monthly visitors, Blurb specializes in "beautiful photo books." You can create your book online and sell it in a variety of ways. You can link your Blurb product to your own website, and customers will see a fantastic page-turning preview. They can buy directly from Blurb at a retail price you set yourself, and you earn the mark-up over Blurb's base cost. You can sell an eBook version of your Blurb book in a variety of ways, including placement on the Blurb Bookstore right on the website, submissions to Apple's iBookstore, and links on your own website, blog, and social media posts. And of course, you can order copies to sell yourself (there are bulk discounts).

2. **Lulu.com** (*www.lulu.com*): This POD company produces books, eBooks, mini books, and photo books. Lulu also has channels to merchandise these publications, from the site's Lulu Marketplace to a network of retail partners including the Apple iBookstore and the Barnes and Noble Nook reader.

3. **CreateSpace.com** (*www.createspace.com*): The self-publishing service of Amazon.com offers a do-it-yourself online interface to create and print books, as well as professional design services for a reasonable fee. CreateSpace.com is not a selling platform itself, but since it is very well connected, it is easy to get a book listed and sold on Amazon.com.

Blurb.com Landing Page

Your Own Website

You can confidently elect to start your online career by creating a shop at a marketplace site, but eventually you will want and need a professional website of your own. Fortunately, this is neither difficult nor expensive. Many hosting companies and online services offer templates and systems for creating attractive and effective websites. With the Internet and the computer skills you have developed, it will be easy.

Here are some services to pursue:

1. **WordPress** (*http://wordpress.com*) is the world's most popular system for owner-built and -managed websites. This free open source system is available at a multitude of different hosting companies, and there are plenty of online learning resources and tutorials to help you get started. The WordPress system has the availability of hundreds of different

themes and plug-in applications to add advanced features and functions to a website. It is the best system for integrating search engine optimization, social media marketing, and blogging (since it was actually invented as a blog platform at its inception). There are many other do-it-yourself platforms for creating websites, but WordPress is clearly the best for small business websites, portfolio sites for artists and crafters, and for sites intending to add a blog.

Incorporating e-commerce into a website brings levels of complexity. For example, you can add a simple "Buy Now" button that leads to a PayPal account that links to an integrated inventory management system. There are many considerations when you begin to take orders and process payments. WordPress sites can expand to include a shopping cart in a number of different ways. There are also many systems available for developing your own "store" website.

Example of WordPress Site

2. **BigCartel.com**—"where artists set up shop"—lets you build customizable e-commerce websites. Check out some examples at *www.directory .bigcartel.com.*

3. **Silkfair.com** (*www.silkfair.com*) provides sellers with both a marketplace and custom store websites for a monthly fee.

4. **Shopify.com** is a huge platform for online stores. See examples of websites using this system at *www.shopify.com/examples.*

5. **Amazon Web Stores** (*http://webstore.amazon.com*): This e-commerce giant provides templates so you can set up your own domain website using the powerful Amazon.com technology.

One Site or Many?

The previous list of websites covers the major players and a few of the smaller service providers in the field of selling arts and crafts online. There are many more companies, and new sites will always come along to offer a different approach and a better experience for buyers and sellers of handmade treasures.

So where do you begin? Is the goal to get your items on as many of these sites as possible, or to choose the best one? As always, the answer depends on your business goals. Successful sellers come in many shapes and sizes. It is always your choice to decide how to shape your business to fit the rest of your life.

But let's assume that you really do want to build a business that will support you, one that can provide a good income for you and your family. You want to be your own boss, work from home or from your studio, and have the freedom to do the creative work that you love.

For a professional online business of this sort, you will need:

1. A shop on a marketplace website
2. A business website with your own domain name
3. Possibly a shop on a products-on-demand website, if your artwork lends itself to prints or product decoration
4. Possibly a selling profile at an auction website

5. Business profiles on the main social media websites that your customers use (Facebook, Twitter, and so on)

Yes, this sounds like a lot, but there are very solid reasons for each element.

A Reason for Each Element

First, a good marketplace shop gives you exposure and an easy way to begin selling things that you make. This is often the entry level for artists and crafters new to selling online. The low cost of a marketplace shop lets you dive in and learn! Learn about the people who admire your work. Learn what the competition offers. Learn how to recognize good product photography and copy writing. The selling tools, forums, teams, and discussions at a vibrant marketplace community will become your inspiration. You really need just one good marketplace shop.

Secondly, having your own business website raises the perceived value of your artwork from hobby to professional. Your domain website is the hub for your Internet marketing. It is where fans follow your blog, subscribe to your newsletter, and connect with your real world exhibitions and sales. Your website is where wholesale orders are arranged, where commissions are discussed, and where licensing agreements are reached. Whether or not you sell your retail goods on your domain website, your own website is a key to your success. As noted earlier, it is not expensive, nor is it especially difficult.

Will you create products on demand? It depends on your artwork and your lifestyle. An artist may easily decide that selling prints through a POD website is the perfect solution to time management. Although they receive less money from each sale, they don't have to actually do anything once they've set up their on-demand products. The POD website processes the order, transfers the royalty money to the artist through a bank, creates the product, packs and ships it, and deals with all the customer service. The artist can be off in Hawaii creating more paintings while all this is taking place. What's not to like?

Auctions can be handy for selling extra inventory, moving old items to make space for new stock, trying out new ideas, and selling things that don't quite fit into your branded product line. For some sellers, auctions are the primary venue for selling their work. Auction buyers are often looking for a bargain, and sometimes the bargain price is just fine for your cash flow needs. Keep in mind the other side of auction selling: the bidding war where dedicated fans are offering higher and higher amounts for the right to purchase your latest original. The selling price may far exceed anything you expected. This sort of auction result can inspire you to re-evaluate your own worth and begin pricing your products at a higher professional level.

Lastly, social media is fun. Honestly. As a serious online seller, you need to do this. Customers will only discover your work if you are online telling them about it, giving them reasons to return for more, to share with their friends, and to connect more closely with your world. Social media does not have to take a long time.

The possibilities for selling your artwork online are many and varied. Take the time to look at each of the websites listed in this chapter. Devote at least 10 minutes to each one. Search for artwork similar to what you create. You will be gathering valuable market information on your competitors, their products, and their pricing as you also evaluate the look and feel of the sites themselves. Decide which websites best fit your work and personal style, and then spend several hours on the websites that most interest you. Look into their sales policies and support systems. Read some of the seller comments in forums and discussions. After a few days of research, it will become clear which system is the right place for you to begin, and you'll be ready to start selling online.

CHAPTER 7

Etsy

Imagine a vast shopping mall filled entirely with small artisan craft shops, gift stores, galleries, and quirky antique stores. Imagine that each shop is run by the artist or artisan who creates these treasures . . . friendly, talented people from all over the planet. Imagine shoppers browsing through the shops, collecting lists of their favorite items, talking to the shop owners, putting together collections of beautiful objects to share with their friends, and occasionally buying something. Imagine everyone doing all this from the comfort and convenience of their home, any time of the day or night. Now you have Etsy.com.

Facts about Etsy

Etsy is the biggest and best-known marketplace for artists and crafters. Located in Brooklyn, New York, the website was launched in 2005. The name itself is fictitious. In a January 2010 interview for *Reader's Digest*, originator Rob Kalin named the site Etsy because he "wanted to build the brand from scratch. I was watching Fellini's *8½* and writing down what I was hearing. In Italian, you say 'etsi' a lot. It means 'oh, yes.'"

The marketplace website has grown steadily through the years, constantly improving its web interface and seller policies. Popularity increased, and the first season's sales of $1.7 million dollars had grown to $314 million by 2010, and topped $895 million in 2012. Traffic on the Etsy website dwarfs all competitors, with millions of visitors each month. With Etsy's visibility, easy interface, and low cost, it is the first place artists, designers, and crafters look to find expanded sales and online exposure.

What Does It Mean to Be Etsy-esque?

Etsy.com is certainly not the beginning and end of online success for artists and crafters. But this giant marketplace website is the unquestioned leader in sales of handcrafts, so it is a good idea to pay attention to Etsy's most successful products. The Etsy format shows exactly how many sales a shop has made. Independent sites such as Craftcount.com (*www.craftcount.com*) keep track of Etsy shops with the most sales and share this information in a wide variety of different categories. You'll discover that the shops with the most overall sales are suppliers who sell materials to other crafters. Exclude these suppliers and look deeper into categories where your artwork would fit. Who are the top sellers there? See if you can define what makes their products "Etsy-esque."

Here are just a few Etsy-esque examples of really successful online art and craft products, gathered from the top Etsy sellers in different categories:

- Joyful quotations on high-quality letterpress cards and posters
- Inspirational and often funny quotes on T-shirts and coffee mugs
- Natural fiber clothing and accessories
- Feathers—lots of feathers!
- Sweet little animals dressed as people

- Antique animal engravings printed on old dictionary pages
- Hand-knit baby wear modeled by sleepy infants
- Steampunk style; Victorian science fiction
- Small birds, large birds, ravens, and owls
- Rounded river stones covered with delicate lace crochet
- Anything decorated with pop culture heroes
- Handmade leather journals dyed gorgeous pastel colors

There are thousands of successful arts- and crafts sellers on Etsy. Of course, there are products that sell more than others, but the variety is so diverse that it would be impossible to predict exactly what kind of work will be successful on Etsy. Look at your competition. Search and find sellers who make items similar to your primary product. Then look at each shop's total sales related to the amount of time they have been open to identify the leading sellers in your niche. If your products have a quality, an allure, and a pricing structure similar to these leaders, then you have a good opportunity to sell a similar amount on Etsy.

Features of Etsy

With an interface that has become the standard for marketplace websites, Etsy offers an abundance of features to sellers, such as:

- Your own personalized shop space on the Etsy website
- The ability to sell handmade goods, vintage items, or supplies
- A profile page to share your personal story
- An about page to expand on that story and share photos about your business
- A massive, multifaceted search function (in which your items are included)
- The ability to upload products to your shop for a per-item listing fee
- A description and five different photos allowed for each product
- A fully featured shopping cart system that you can link to your own PayPal account
- The ability to connect your shop with the leading social media websites

- Extensive blogs, video tutorials, and support systems provided by Etsy
- Detailed shop statistics
- Hundreds of special interest teams created by other sellers for collaboration and inspiration
- Live workshops and events, in Brooklyn and throughout the world

Both buyers and sellers alike enjoy Etsy's creative interactive features. Some of these interactive features include:

- A private conversation system for communicating with anyone on Etsy, including fans, customers, or other sellers
- A personal favorites list you assemble with items and shops
- The ability to put together your own circle of Etsy buyers and sellers, and to follow the things they like and share
- A Treasury system that encourages you to assemble and share special collections of items

There's more, too. Etsy has features like gift certificates, Etsy apps for mobile devices, a wedding registry, and discount coupons. It is an amazing collection of selling tools and information available for a very minimal investment.

What Does All This Cost?

There are no fees to open an Etsy shop, and no monthly membership. At the time of this book's publication, it costs 20 cents to list each item, and a listing will last for 4 months. If the item sells, Etsy keeps 3.5 percent of the sale price. The only other possible budget item you'd need to consider is if you wanted to promote your products in the Etsy search tools, an entirely optional and usually unnecessary expense.

It's a good idea to do the math before you set up a shop. Imagine that you keep an inventory of 100 items in your Etsy shop. You'd list these, or renew them, at least every 4 months at 20 cents each. So the cost for displaying those items would cost you a minimum of $80 per year. Then let's say you sell 16 items each month, and your average selling price is $25 per item.

At that level, you have $400 in sales each month, and Etsy keeps 3.5 percent, or $14. Project that out to a full year, and your Etsy shop income would be $4,632, while Etsy will have made $248 from the 20 cent posting fees and its 3.5 percent collection. (There will still be another fee deducted from your income by whichever company you choose to process the credit cards.)

It is a fee structure based on your success. If you do not sell things, this elaborate system costs only the listing fees. Etsy definitely wants you to sell your products, and supports this in every way possible.

Opening a Shop on Etsy

There is no setup charge on Etsy, but there are a few things you want to do correctly from the beginning. Opening an Etsy shop should take you about an hour. Remember that the Internet changes all the time, so if the interface at Etsy is a bit different than what is described in this chapter, just take your time as you go through the process. Visit the Etsy "Help" post at *www.etsy .com/help/article/246* for current procedures.

Register as an Etsy Member

Begin at the *www.etsy.com* home page and click "Sell" in the top left-hand corner, above the red Etsy logo. Read this introductory information, essentially to see if there have been any major changes to Etsy's policies and fee structure. When you are satisfied, click the big blue "Open an Etsy Shop" button.

The next window has two tabs: Register and Sign In. Newcomers should click on Register and complete the required fields: name, e-mail, password, and username. Your recommended username will be provided by Etsy, but you can change this if you wish. This is a permanent identity, so choose carefully. And always, before you submit your registration, be sure you can accept Etsy's Terms of Use and Privacy Policy. Once you click the Register button, a confirmation e-mail will be sent to the e-mail address you specified. You'll need to log in to your e-mail, find this "Etsy Account Confirmation" message, open the message, and click the confirmation link.

Registering with Etsy is the first step.

Create Your Shop Name

Back at the registration process, you'll confirm the country and currency you wish to use, and then finally advance to choosing your shop name. An Etsy shop name can be up to twenty characters long and has no spaces. It should be something original, something that reflects your style and brand, something people will remember—and it must be a name that no one else on Etsy is using. You may have the good fortune to find your ideal shop name is available, or you might discover that the name you want is already taken (the Shop Name screen will let you know). If the name you want is taken, it's time to get creative. Think of other words or ways to name your shop. If "CedarTree" is already taken, try "CedarTreeStudio" or "CedarTreePottery."

ALERT

If you plan to eventually build your own website using the same name as your Etsy shop, be sure you can also register that .com domain name. Search for domain name availability at your favorite registrar, such as GoDaddy.com or Register.com. Sign up for both your Etsy shop name and your .com domain name as soon as you decide the best name available for your business on both systems.

List Your First Item

Once you arrive at a successful shop name, Etsy encourages you to "stock your shop" with several items. You can do this right away, or wait until after you have set up the rest of your shop profile pages.

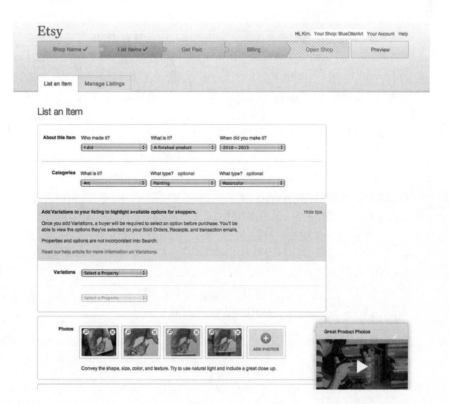

Add a product to your new shop. You can edit everything later, so feel free to explore.

If you do jump right into listing, you'll find that the process begins with information about each item. Use the pull-down menus to answer the questions that appear: Who made it? What is it? When did you make it? Specifying these fields adds your item to its appropriate Etsy category.

FACT

Jewelry is the number-one category on Etsy, but areas like clothing and housewares are quickly catching up. Furniture was the fastest-growing category on Etsy in 2012, growing 134 percent from the 2011 numbers.

Next, you can specify any variations that make sense for this particular item. Do you carry that T-shirt in small, medium, and large? Does the candle come in vanilla, cinnamon, or mint? Don't stress out over any of these choices. The pressure is off. It's easy to return and edit.

You can add up to five photos for each item. The photo in the first (left) spot will be the default photo. Simply click the Add Photos button and navigate through your own computer folders until you find the image you want to use. Once the first image uploads, you can add a second, and so on.

Complete the Item Title and Description fields. Follow through the optional choices for Shop Section, Recipient, Occasion, and Style. Tags are words that describe your item, and are important for showing up in search results. You'll learn much more about tags as you get into working your Etsy shop. In the beginning, just type words that make sense and click "Add" until you get thirteen descriptive tags. For example, if you are selling seashell jewelry, you'll use words like "shell," "pearl," and "scalloped." In the next field, add the materials that are used in your item.

Set your price and the quantity that you have available. Etsy will only charge you for items one at a time. If you set a quantity of ten items and sell one, you'll be charged another 20 cents when that listing then changes to nine items available, then again when it goes down to eight. This is a recent Etsy policy change, and is much kinder than getting charged for all ten items at once.

Next, set the shipping information. Keep in mind that processing time lets buyers know how long it will take you to get the item sent. You can also set individual item shipping charges here. Click the blue Preview Listing, and finally, the Save as Draft button.

Setting Your Payment Gateway

As delightful as it is to see your products online, there is still so much you need to do before your shop is open to the public. Setting up your payment method is the next step. A Payment Gateway is where credit card numbers go to be processed, and where money is taken out of the customer's bank account and moved into your bank account. Yes, there is a fee for this service, for every merchant everywhere. Fortunately, Etsy gives you pretty reasonable rates.

There are two primary Payment Gateway systems for Etsy shops, and clicking Get Paid on the top navigation bar advances you to a page where you will choose which system you want to use. The most prominent option is Etsy's internal Direct Checkout system. This is incredibly easy to set up and simply requires you to provide routing information for your bank account. Clicking the Sign Me Up button brings you to a page with the Terms of Service and financial details. At this writing, the processing fee is 3 percent of the order total plus 25 cents per transaction.

The other Payment Gateway is PayPal, which becomes visible when you expand Additional Payment Methods back on that first Get Paid page. If you have a PayPal account, you can simply enter the e-mail you use for Pay-Pal, and Etsy will make the connection. The processing fee is essentially the same (2.9 percent plus 30 cents per transaction). PayPal, however, is independent from Etsy and can be used in multiple locations, including on your own website or in your studio and at craft fairs. This is why so many sellers prefer the PayPal option.

Remember to pay your Etsy fees! The Billing tab has you enter your own credit card. Each month you will approve a charge to pay your Etsy fees, depending on how many items you have listed and renewed, and how many sales you have made.

Complete Your Profile

Finally, you will advance to the final section on the Open Shop tab. You are nearing the grand opening, but you still have a banner to upload, and some information and policies to complete. Clicking Add Shop Banner takes you to an Info & Appearance page with lots of information you will need to complete.

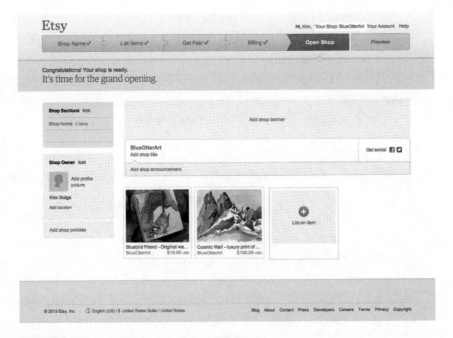

Adding your Shop Banner is next. If you don't have a banner image ready, you can add it later.

As you are filling out this information, remember that your shop title is your tagline, not your shop name. In a few words, what is it that you sell? Search engines pay attention to these words, so use powerful search terms such as "Glassmaker of artisan-fused and handblown collectibles." If your name is recognizable as an artist, be sure to include it in the tagline you write here. The other sections you'll need to fill out include:

1. Your shop banner image. The banner is a little bar, 760 pixels wide by 100 pixels high, that lives on the top of your shop's home page. Simply

select the banner image file from your computer, assuming you already have one. If you do not have a banner image now, you can always make another banner later. You can update it any time you want to. If you use a graphic design program like Photoshop, it is pretty easy to create your own banner. You can hire a graphic artist to create a banner for you. You can even shop for a banner on Etsy—simply type "Etsy shop banner" into Etsy's search box to find designers selling banners and matching avatars.

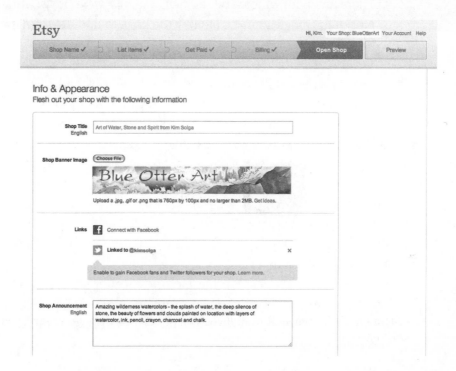

This simple banner was made with typeset words on top of a product detail.

There are several independent websites offering free banner generators:

- EtsyBannerGenerator.com (*www.etsybannergenerator.com*) has dozens of "scrapbookish" backgrounds for you to choose from. Type in your shop name and then your tagline. Select your desired font and one of the backgrounds. Adjust the size and color of your selected font until the banner preview at the top of the page is what you want, then click Save—and there it is, ready to be downloaded to your computer and installed on your new shop!

- Another free banner generator is found at *www.shopvaluecalculator .com/free-etsy-banner-generator*. This system pulls the first four items from your shop to create a photographic banner featuring those products. Make sure you have four great items listed before you build a banner here.

- There are many other services available. Just type "Etsy banner generator" into Google.com and follow the links to find a system that works for you.

2. The Links section will connect with your Facebook and Twitter accounts and will put small icons onto the top of your Etsy shop page so visitors can easily "friend" and "follow" you. Be sure you already have business profiles set up on these websites, and are actively signed into those business Facebook and Twitter accounts as you click to connect.

3. Your Shop Announcement appears at the top of your first shop page and welcomes visitors. You'll want to type two or three sentences to clearly describe your products.

4. Type a short Message to Buyers that will appear on order confirmations, and click Save Changes.

5. Add your Shop Owner's profile picture, location, and a short description about yourself. You can use a smiling photo of yourself, or a shop avatar—a small image, 170 pixels tall by 130 pixels wide, that blends with your shop banner.

Open for Business

When all is complete, simply click "It's time for the grand opening." Etsy will confirm that you want to list your initial items at 20 cents each, and your shop is open. Congratulations! You have a unique web address at etsy.com/shop/YourNewShopName. And you can immediately begin selling the items you have listed.

ESSENTIAL

Etsy added 10 million new members in 2012, nearly doubling the total number of members to 22 million around the world. By mid-March of 2013, the number had grown another 3 million. An exploration of Etsy's shop search page reveals that there are currently over half a million active shops.

Your Shop

Now that your shop is open, you have access to the extensive Etsy shop management pages and support systems. Your next step is to explore each of these links and learn your way around. Here's an overview of what is available.

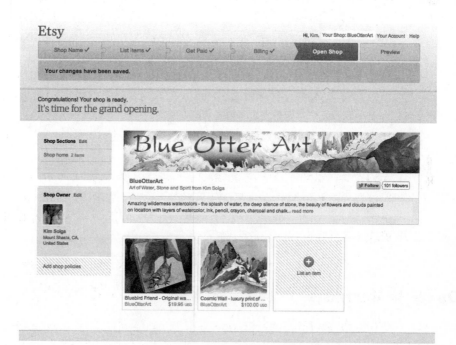

A simple Etsy store with two products, ready for the grand opening.

The Main Menu Bar

Across the top of every Etsy page for all users is a gray bar opening on the left with the red Etsy logo. Clicking the red Etsy logo takes you to the Etsy home page. The items on this page change all the time, selected from treasuries that users have created. You will see all the Browsing links that lead to different categories and ways to shop, featured sections created by Etsy staff and the Etsy blog, your own recent browsing history, and more.

The second icon, a small ringed circle, will display your activity feed. Here you will see the recent activity of the friends you follow and the people who have favored items from your shop or featured them in a Treasury.

The little envelope icon leads to your conversations, called "convos," with other Etsy users. This is Etsy's internal and private-mail system. The heart icon takes you to all the items, shops, and Treasury lists that you have favored. The house icon leads always to your shop home page.

A shop's main page is similar for all Etsy sellers.

Management Pages

The links to your management pages are the top right side of your new Etsy shop page, above the search button and shopping cart tab. Holding your cursor over the second Your Shop link will show a variety of sections for you to explore. Click any of these links and you will enter the management area. The left sidebar menu expands the following possibilities:

- **Add New Item** opens a new listing page, the process that you experienced when you first set up your shop. You will do this again and again as you put new items into your shop.
- The **Listings** page shows all of the products you have listed. You can edit any product at any time: change the photos, the title and description, the tags, and the price. Each listing lasts for four months or until the item sells. Once a listing expires, the item appears in the Expired tab until you renew it. You will also see tabs for Draft, Inactive, Sold Out, and Featured items.

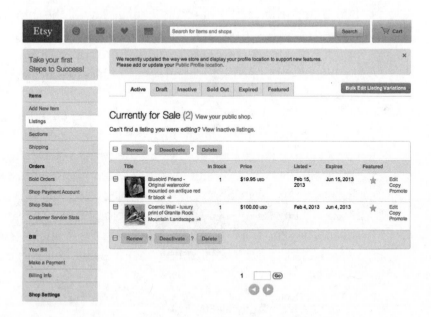

Your shop management section is a large collection of resources.

- **Sections** help you organize your products, and appear on your shop page as links on the top right side. Set up sections if it would be convenient to customers to have your items categorized into smaller groups.
- **Shipping** provides a simple view of the shipping rates you specified for each item as you listed it. If you set up different shipping profiles for your products, you can easily apply these to individual items here.
- **Sold Orders** will be where you see your incoming orders, get shipping information, and communicate with buyers.
- **Shop Payment Account** connects with Etsy's internal Direct Checkout system, if this is your payment gateway choice.
- **Shop Stats** and **Customer Service Stats** will accumulate a vast amount of information on how people are finding and looking at your products, and communicating with you.
- The three links in the **Bill** section show your current Etsy fees—they give you an easy interface for paying these, and for managing your personal credit card information.
- **Info & Appearance** allows you to change any of the information you entered as you set up your shop. You will also see tabs for setting up an About page, describing all of your shop policies, and changing your shop name (not recommended unless really necessary) and language.
- **Shipping & Payment** is where you can define shipping profiles, or click tabs to change your payment method, specify sales tax you need to collect, and change the currency for the prices you display.
- **Options** brings you a variety of controls. You may initially want to use the Rearrange Your Shop option, or place your shop on "Vacation Mode" when you are not available to ship orders or respond to messages. The other tabs in this section relate to advanced tracking and record keeping systems. Just note that they are here so you can find them later if needed.
- The **Promote** section is where you may wish to purchase Search Ads on Etsy, learn about the free Google ads that Etsy uses, set up coupons for use in your shop, or download graphics or widgets to use on your own website that link to your new Etsy shop.

- **Resources**, at the bottom of the left menu bar, lead to the rich support materials offered by Etsy. The links at the very top left of each page also lead to Etsy resources. Explore these at your convenience.

A Few Final Startup Steps

While Etsy has provided your new shop with its grand opening, there are still a few tasks to complete.

1. Set your sales tax. In your management section, at Shop Settings/ Shipping & Payment, click the tab for Sales Tax. Choose the area for which you must collect sales tax, and specify the tax rate.
2. Describe your shop policies. In your management section, at Shop Settings/Info & Appearance, click the Policies tab. Not sure what to say? Links in the introduction will take you to Etsy's Dos and Don'ts, Terms of Use, and ideas on writing shop policies. You can view the policies that other shop owners have written by clicking the Policies link in the left side menu on their pages.
3. Get ready to build your About page. Another tab in Shop Settings/Info & Appearance leads to the About page. This is a new feature at Etsy and is certainly not required. There are many shop owners who have never gotten around to completing their About page. But as you look at successful shops on Etsy, note the ones with an About link in the left side menu on their pages, and check out what different sellers have done with this page, especially the fabulous slideshows created from their uploaded photos.
4. Add more products. Your shop should have at least thirty different products to begin, and eventually 100 or more. Learn the strategy of renewing your items, even before they expire, to get them back to the front of a category. Just as listing new items brings your shop and products more views, so does renewing an item. Track and see what works to increase sales.
5. Encourage your friends, family, and supporters to visit your new shop and buy a product. This gives you experience filling Etsy orders and lets your shop show a few sales right from its earliest days.

Running Your Etsy Shop

Opening a shop on Etsy is fast and simple, but it is merely the tiniest tip of the iceberg. Becoming successful as a seller on Etsy is a long and complex process. Etsy has a huge number of shops, and yours will be essentially invisible unless you actively promote your work and participate in the online community. Fortunately, there are plenty of techniques for doing this. Here's how to get started.

Read Etsy's Seller Handbook Articles

Move your cursor over the Blogs button on the top left of any Etsy page, then click Seller Handbook in the links that appear. The articles that appear are written by the Etsy staff, each providing insights on how to sell successfully. There's no particular order. You can simply start at the most recent and work backward, or cruise through the pages listing articles and read the ones that catch your eye. Or use a handy index at *www.etsy.com/blog/en/2012/the-seller-handbook-archive*. You'll discover interviews with successful shop owners, tips and techniques, bookkeeping hints, and business tools to use with your Etsy shop. Make it a habit to read an article every day. One article per day while you are getting started will provide you with more than enough information and ideas to think about, while allowing you plenty of time to do all the other tasks required for your new business.

I Heart It!

Start collecting your own set of "favorites." As you work on your Etsy shop, pay attention to items at other shops and watch the products displayed on the Etsy home page. Whenever you notice an item that you really like, add it to your own personal favorites.

On that item's page, just click the Favorite button on the right side. You can "favorite" a single item, or if you like everything, go to that shop's front page. Find the Add to Favorites link in the left menu, and click to favorite the entire shop. As you gather your favorites, you can view them via the heart icon in the menu bar. You can see other people's favorites on their profile pages. Shop owners get notified when you favorite one of their items. They will often visit your shop to see who you are, and the valuable process of social networking on Etsy begins.

Follow Your Customers

Etsy encourages users to follow one another. This increases enjoyment and interactivity, and makes shopping on Etsy more fun. On an Etsy activity feed, people will see the recent activities of the people they follow . . . what items they have favored, what Treasuries they have created. Sellers can gain valuable insight into their customers. Whenever you make a sale, visit the buyer's profile page and click the blue Follow button. It is also important to pay attention to your activity feed to gather data about your customers. Notice the items and shops they are adding to their own favorites. Look for patterns. What styles are they drawn to, what colors, what trends? The information you can gain from the customers you follow will inform your future business decisions.

Pay Attention to Treasuries

Building Treasury lists is one of the most popular activities for buyers and sellers alike. Etsy makes it really easy to create a special collection of items, up to sixteen of them, and share this with your friends. Having your products included in Treasuries will be one of the main ways new people discover you on Etsy, so understanding Treasuries is a great first step.

Look at the Etsy home page. The handpicked items displayed there came from a Treasury that caught the eye of Etsy staff and was chosen for the home page. A particular Treasury stays on the home page for a short time, usually an hour or so, and is then replaced with another. To view all Treasuries, simply click See More next to Handpicked Items. Looking at Treasuries gives new sellers a wonderful sense of the Etsy community and what people like.

Then it's time to join the fun! Build your own Treasury lists. Start by looking at any Treasury from the See More link, and notice down in the left column beneath Curator Tools a link called Create a List. Clicking this opens a page with blank spaces for you to fill in your own Treasury's title, description, tags, and images. Good treasuries are designed around a theme. The products are added, one by one. To do this easily, open a second browser window to view product pages from many different Etsy shops. Find a great product, copy its page URL, and then return to your first browser window. Paste what you have copied into one of the sixteen spaces.

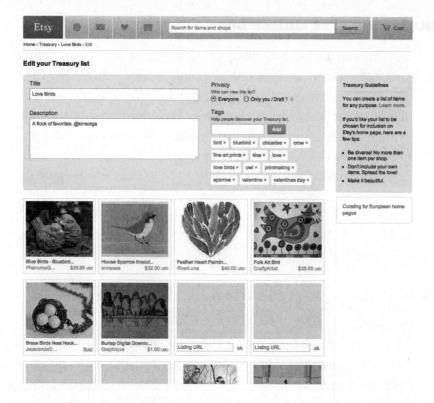

A Treasury list under construction.

Once you fill all the spaces, it is easy to move items around—just drag boxes until your arrangement looks good. Save your Treasury to publish it. While each of the shops you have treasured will see a notification, it is also appropriate to "convo" each of the artists in your new Treasury, personally notifying and thanking them. They will probably come view your Treasury, and many will leave a comment. Some will then visit your shop to see who you are. You can announce your Treasury on Twitter and Facebook, pasting its URL to encourage visitors. You will discover that the more Treasuries you create, the more your products will be treasured in return. One thing to remember, though: It is considered bad form to put your own products into the Treasuries you make. As Etsy says, "Don't include your own items. Spread the love!"

Watch Videos at Online Labs

Among the top-left links above the red Etsy logo is Community, and holding your cursor over this reveals a link called Online Labs. There is a ton of awesome information here, mainly videos of training sessions sponsored by Etsy at their Brooklyn headquarters. There are currently eighty-six hour-long videos in the library called Etsy Success. Watch one every week if you can.

Use All the Tags

When you list or edit an item in your shop, you can add up to thirteen tags. Those are thirteen ways for people to find your items when they search for things. It's to your advantage to use all of the tags you are allowed. Each tag is a marketing opportunity. Think like a customer and try to imagine the words they would use if searching for products like yours. Describe your item using different terms (handbag, purse, clutch bag, shoulder bag, travel case). State its main color, and include color synonyms (blue, sky blue, baby blue, azure) as well as trendy colors (aqua, teal, mint green, peach). Put material into the tag field as well as in the materials field, especially if that material is popular and likely to be used by a buyer in a search (sterling silver, copper, organic cotton). Include your own name if you are a recognized artist.

Get to Know Your Shop Stats

On your Shop Stats page, simple graphs and lists show you exactly how people are finding and looking at your shop items. To see your Shop Stats, pull down on the Your Shop link in the top menu bar until you get to Shop Stats (also located in the left side menu on all Your Shop pages). The default setting for showing your stats is "Last 7 Days," but you can adjust for a variety of different time periods, from a specific day to "All Time," which shows your stats since you joined Etsy.

The data boxes and the cool graphs (click the tabs to see different graphs) display:

- Views—how many people have looked at your shop homepage and at individual listings
- Favorites—how many people have clicked the heart button to favorite your shop or items in your shop

- Orders and Revenue—how many things you sold and how much money you earned
- Traffic Sources—this shows you the sites that sent people to your shop. Etsy.com will be at the top of this list, but these stats will also show traffic that came from your own blog and website, from Twitter or e-mails promoting your items, visitors who found you with a search on Google or other search engines, and any other blogs or websites linking to your Etsy pages.
- Keywords—This section tells you exactly what words folks used on the different searching tools (Etsy, Google, or others) just before they clicked and entered your shop. Click each keyword and it will show you the page that searcher landed on.
- Pages Viewed and Listing Favorites—shows you the basic popularity of the items in your shop. By clicking each listed item, you discover a detailed report on the activity for that particular product.

Your stats page has an awesome amount of information and will help you learn how to promote and expand your shop for maximum Etsy success. View your Shop Stats often! Learn more at *www.etsy.com/help/article/541*. Read the Etsy blog article "Shop Stats: How Shoppers Find Your Listings," (*www.etsy.com/blog/en/2012/shop-stats-how-shoppers-find-your-listings*).

Join a Team

Etsy is all about connections. Being part of an Etsy team is one great way to build relationships. Teams are created by Etsy members and listed at *www.etsy.com/teams*. There's also a search function to find teams that appeal to your interests. Click on any team name to visit, check out the members, and read the current discussions. If you decide you want to be a member, click Join This Team. Some teams are open to everyone; others have specific requirements and might require approval by team leaders. You can belong to several different teams, and these will show up on your personal Etsy profile page. Team activities begin on their discussion boards, where members post questions and answers, comments, and conversation. Projects will be planned, challenges issued, and collaboration inspired. Get involved! Begin by reading the discussions for a few days until you get a sense of what is going on. Then jump in!

Forums

A huge amount of information is shared on the Etsy Forums (*www.etsy .com/forums*). You can learn by simply reading the questions that others have posted, and the answers they get from the community and from the Etsy staff. Any time you wonder about a certain system, how it works, how to fix a problem, etc., just go to the appropriate forum and ask. Within an hour or two there will be plenty of answers. You can even subscribe to weekly tips from the Etsy Success Newsletter at *www.etsy.com/emails/success*. Yes, it's free.

Discover the Apps

Learn about Etsy Apps (*www.etsy.com/apps*), the many useful and interesting tools built by independent programmers for use in Etsy stores. A few of the most popular apps include Outright, Craftopolis, StitchLabs, and Etsy on Sale.

Words of Wisdom

There are blog articles on Etsy and pages all over the Internet packed with ideas on how to succeed as an Etsy seller. In fact, there is so much advice you'll never run out of ideas. Pay particular attention to what the successful sellers have to say, sellers such as David Joaquin of *Painted Moon Gallery*.

David is a very skilled painter, creating works of vision and dreams. For years, David pursued traditional gallery outlets for his work, including running his own gallery in New Zealand. In 2009, he and his wife MoenJu discovered Etsy.

"I had no idea Etsy existed, but it seemed ideal, easy to use, and not expensive. We wanted to be able to sell online as an alternative to gallery sales, where 50 percent or more of the selling price for a painting is kept as gallery commission," says David.

David's Etsy shop is called *Painted Moon Gallery*. "It has definitely been a success. Between 2009 and 2013 we have had over 56,000 people looking at my work, and our revenue from the Etsy sales in those years has been over $90,000. Etsy has become one of our main 'muscles.'"

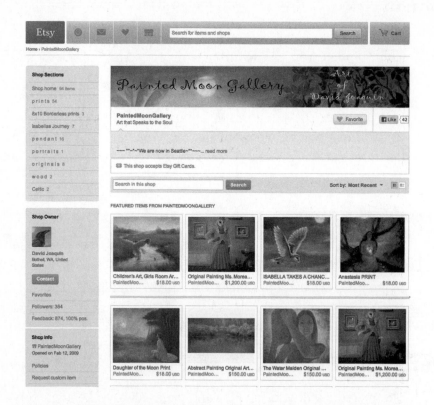

David Joaquin's *Painted Moon Gallery* on Etsy. Art that speaks to the soul.

"It is important to home in on the taste of the people who hang out on Etsy, alternative folks with alternative lifestyles," explains David. "My most successful pieces on Etsy appeal to the spiritual, the mystical, the lovers of Celtic mythology, and owls and Native American legend. I also pay attention to what is fashionable on Etsy, what colors and themes are popular. For example, if I paint the same subject in different color tones, it is the painting where I used tiger-eye pigment that sells so much more easily than the others."

David suggests having plenty of small items for sale on an Etsy shop. For a painter, this means inexpensive smaller paintings as well as prints. "I call these 'foot in the door' pieces. Buyers can't see and touch the reality of your work online. They can only see photographs. You need to offer affordable small pieces so they can easily get something into their hands, to begin to love and trust your work. Only then will they return to purchase that large original painting."

Things change on the Internet all the time, and Etsy is no exception. As David explains, "The way we promoted our shop within Etsy has changed, even in the past year. There is a much larger emphasis now on using social media sites to attract new viewers. But that's the essence of being an online seller. You have to be flexible as a shop owner so that when rules change you change too. And it's so worthwhile. Even if an artist is using Etsy purely as a portfolio site, it is a great way to showcase a body of work."

Etsy has been the source of unexpected opportunities for David. "Perhaps the best thing about Etsy has been the direct feedback I get from customers and fans. It is so easy to have a dialogue with followers on Etsy, and to grow my own work as a result of listening to what people have to say." Etsy provides a great platform for being discovered. "I have collaborated with other Etsy sellers and designers, been contacted by writers and bloggers who want to share my work. The Brush Dance Calendar folks found me on Etsy and have published calendars with my images for the past couple years. Gallery owners contact me to see if they can carry my work. I am even writing a book about Isabella because customers collecting the prints began to say 'Hey, this should be a kids' book!'"

Find David at *www.etsy.com/shop/PaintedMoonGallery* and *www .twohawkstudio.com.*

Opening a marketplace shop on Etsy takes a bit of work. You will spend a significant amount of time there. Like any other marketing path, it takes planning and a large amount of attention to reach the goal you have set for your success. However, both the Etsy support staff and the Etsy community are honestly committed to helping each seller do their very best. Ashley, owner of *Adam Rabbit* (*www.etsy.com/shop/AdamRabbit*) on Etsy, says it best. "Although I always had the desire to create and sell what I make, I am really shy. It took lot of courage for me to even open an Etsy shop. The thought of being judged terrified me. Once I joined Etsy I was able to connect with hundreds of different artists in the forums. They were extremely encouraging and supportive. They gave me advice on photos, shop policies, new items, pricing, branding—any question you have, at least a handful of people will be there to support you. Etsy is a truly inspiring place. There are so many talented people who actually want to help you."

CHAPTER 8

ArtFire

ArtFire.com is a marketplace website with a loyal following among the artists and crafters who sell on the e-commerce platform. ArtFire was founded by John Jacobs, an experienced crafts seller who developed the website after years of selling jewelry supplies on eBay. Seeking to create an optimal experience for both customers and merchants, the Tucson, Arizona–based website opened in 2008 with a secure e-commerce platform for selling handmade goods, fine art, vintage items, designed items, supplies, and media. Although ArtFire has less than 10 percent of Etsy's traffic, it is the second largest arts and crafts marketplace venue online.

Selling on ArtFire

Sellers on ArtFire get their own shop space where they present products and tell their story. Unlike other marketplace platforms, there are no listing fees or sales commissions on ArtFire. Instead, ArtFire sellers pay a flat charge. Currently a Pro Seller account costs $12.95 USD per month. For artists and crafters who want to list a lot of items, the unlimited listings feature is attractive. For those who sell more expensive works, it is clearly an advantage to have no commission deducted from sales. Arts businesses can simply budget $12.95 per month and calculate exactly what their marketplace space will cost each year.

Shop space on ArtFire can be customized in a number of ways, creating a look that is unique for each business. Although each shop keeps the basic ArtFire layout, the colors of top bars and display fonts can be changed. Different decorative fonts are available for the text in the navigation bar, section titles, headlines, and shop name. Each seller can upload a decorative banner and shop avatar. Paying attention to color scheme, banner design, and placement of the Seller Information widget can result in a very handsome website feel. There are a number of ways to include social media, such as using share and follow icons, integrating with Amazon.com, and creating a tag cloud for the tags you apply to your items and featured products.

ArtFire Features

ArtFire distinguishes itself from other marketplace websites with expanded selling tools designed to appeal to the creative independence of artists and artisans, including:

- ArtFire Themer is the easy-to-use design tool that allows sellers to create their own page theme. The Fusion Studios tool takes the customizing process a step further. The tools are simple, intuitive, and always available.
- ArtFire shop space has a Blog tab incorporated into each shop. Sellers can use this part of their shop to post news for their ArtFire visitors. Your ArtFire Blog posts are search engine friendly and can attract new visitors to your ArtFire shop. The Help Center offers all sorts of tips and tricks for beginning bloggers: what to write about, how often

and how much to write, how to include photos, and how to edit articles you might have on other blogs so you don't post duplicate content. Sellers are also encouraged to "micro-blog" on Twitter.

- There is also a Gallery tab in each shop space, where a large collection of photos can be displayed. Most sellers use this to showcase past work—items that have sold but still serve to provide a portfolio of an artist's product line. The captions on Gallery photos invite requests from buyers to contact the artist for an item created in the same style. Sold products, or items created on consignment or for other sales venues can enhance your ArtFire business as long as you keep them in your Gallery space.

- Connecting your ArtFire shop to the rest of the Internet is encouraged. The Find Me Online widget provides icons that link your website and blogs, Facebook, Twitter, and more. The Share This Item widget lets viewers click links to post the item photo, item link, and their own comment on their Facebook, Pinterest, Wanelo, Google Plus, Delicious, StumbleUpon, and Twitter accounts.

- Managing products is easier on ArtFire than on other marketplace websites. Tools like the Merchandiser let you control the way your products are displayed, and the Global Product Editor allows you to modify items in categories as well as one-by-one. You can easily increase or decrease prices by percentage or dollar amount, add tags, change shipping profiles, and do a variety of edits to whole groups of products. ArtFire provides tools that allow you to import your products from other marketplace websites and spreadsheets.

- ArtFire allows sellers to set up all sorts of special offers and discounts to promote their sales. Shop management tools streamline the process of creating sale prices, coupons, percentages off, dollars off, free shipping, and free gift with order. Customers can search ArtFire specifically for special deals, which provide a popular way for new customers to discover your items. There's even a Make an Offer button available. If a seller is open to using this feature on specific product pages, he essentially invites bids from potential customers for that item. It is always the seller's choice to accept a bid or reject it, but this feature certainly opens communication with potential customers.

- Products can have up to ten photos, which are displayed in the main photo area with simple forward and back controls. This gives sellers a wonderful opportunity to show product details, as well as post photos that show items in use. There is a unique section where you can share the Inspiration/Story Behind the Product, and where viewers can leave comments about the artwork at the bottom of each product page. (This discussion shows up for all viewers.) Bulk import tools allow sellers to import products from other websites or via database files.

- ArtFire provides several options for your payment gateway. ProPay is fully integrated into the website, and allows buyers to complete the purchasing right on your shop pages without having to advance to a third-party website for checkout. PayPal and Amazon Payments accounts are also available.

- You can also use the Add to Amazon Wish List tool. With this tool, a simple click lets viewers add your ArtFire products to their wish lists on Amazon.com. The item shows up on their Wish List page with a small photo, title, price, and a link back to the ArtFire product page. Since many consumers use the Wish List service at Amazon.com as a gift registry or a "what I want for the holidays" list with family and friends, the ability to have your handmade artwork included is a distinct advantage.

- ArtFire integrates with Google Shopping (*www.google.com/shopping*). With a simple click of a button, you can activate the automatic feed that lists all your items within the popular Google Shopping search. Your ArtFire product is displayed along with similar items that Google pulls from Etsy, eBay, and other websites.

FACT

Google Shopping, the comparison shopping section of Google.com, consistently had the highest conversion rates through 2012. Statistics show that 2.78 percent of clicks resulted in orders at merchant websites, more than with any other Internet shopping guide.

- Facebook Kiosk is a fantastic ArtFire widget. This simple system connects your ArtFire shop to your Facebook business pages. Your shop banner and all of your products can be displayed on Facebook in an attractive catalog grid. It becomes easy for your Facebook fans to view and purchase your products without ever having to leave the Facebook site. You can also embed a similar widget to display a grid of your linked ArtFire products on your personal website or blog.

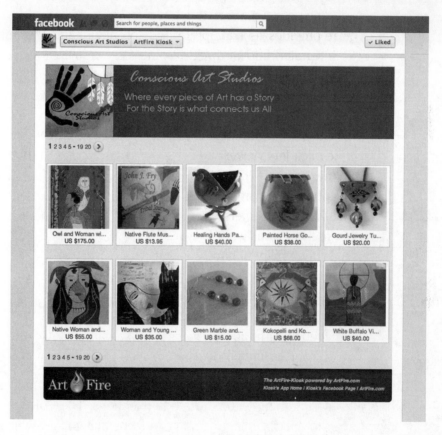

Conscious Art Studios uses the ArtFire Kiosk on their Facebook business pages.

- ArtFire's internal search feature keeps track of visitors search history, and displays their frequently visited shops more often. If someone visits your ArtFire shop and looks at your pieces, and then returns to ArtFire days later and searches for similar items, the ArtFire system will display your shop items again within their first results. It gives your products a slight edge, another chance to impress the customer and inspire a purchase.

- The ArtFire support system is extensive and easy to follow. You'll learn how to optimize your items for search engines (both ArtFire's internal search function and external websites like Google), how to blog, how to write product descriptions that really engage the customer, and much more. The instructions for managing your ArtFire space are clearly written and lavishly illustrated. If all else fails, there's always telephone support.

- ArtFire emphasizes handmade craft products, and the home page always opens with Handmade as the top market. Other market sections include Design, Supplies, Vintage, Fine Art, and a huge Commercial section. Many ArtFire sellers departed when the website opened its platform to commercial merchants, not wanting to compete in the ArtFire search with retailers who have imported thousands of manufactured products.

ArtFire for Customers

The purchasing experience on ArtFire is smooth, which enhances your sales opportunities. Customers do not have to set up an account in order to make a purchase. They can enter ArtFire, search and find a great gift, and check out quickly. It is, however, easy and free to set up a profile as a customer and gain access to special features, such as the ability to save HotLists of favorite items and shops, and to create and share curated collections.

Customers have multiple ways to search ArtFire. Categories can be searched with increasingly specific filters. Gifts can be found using keywords and by searching within curated collections. The Color Search tool allows buyers to select a color and name the type of item they want to locate, and the ArtFire search displays a wide variety of appropriate products. On every search page there's a price filter link that engages a sliding minimum/maximum price-selecting tool, thus displaying only items within a specified range. Shoppers love the Find Deals and Sales tool, where they can search for items with free shipping, products on sale, and shops where sellers are offering coupons and bargains.

ArtFire also prominently displays the number of sales each shop has made, and a rating according to the customer feedback that shop has received. The information does not, however, include the amount of time that seller has been on ArtFire. One ArtFire feature that is pleasing to buyers but perhaps pesky for sellers is "Last Checked In" options. This announces, front and center, when the shop owner last logged in and checked their Art-Fire pages. "Today" and "1 day ago" give viewers the impression that the artist is readily available and customer service will be fast and efficient. If they see something that says "8 months ago," it may cause a potential buyer to look elsewhere.

Opening an ArtFire Shop

The process to open your shop on ArtFire is simple. As ArtFire promises, you can open and stock your online shop without any knowledge of coding or advanced computer skills. ArtFire's design tools make the process easy.

1. Click the Sell button on ArtFire's top navigation bar. Read the next page. Remember that the Internet changes all the time, so make sure you understand the current terms and conditions. In 2013, the monthly charge was $12.95 with no fees ever, and a prominent orange button promised "Start Your FREE Trial Now. No fees, No Commitments."

2. Clicking that button gets you to the registration page. Here you specify the type of shop you are setting up, your desired shop name and a password, your e-mail, and your credit card details. Yes, you need to provide your credit card. ArtFire will not charge your card for 14 days, since you have a free trial, but they will begin automatically charging you after 2 weeks, unless you have canceled your subscription before then. Agree to ArtFire's terms of use, and click Create My Shop.

3. Now you can view the My ArtFire dashboard, the launch pad for managing your account. There is a handy Studio Setup list with links to Help Guides. To begin designing, simply click your name in the upper right links, and begin by uploading your banner and avatar. Click Toggle Banner On/Off. Create your images ahead of time. Your shop banner can be up to 1,000 pixels wide by 200 pixels tall. You can make one yourself, hire a graphic designer to make one, or use one of ArtFire's twelve

attractive generic banners to begin. Your shop avatar is 140 pixels by 140 pixels. Spend some time looking at other ArtFire shops to see the different choices sellers have made for their banners and avatars. To upload your images, simply double click the little gear icon in the banner and avatar areas.

4. Now click Toggle Themer. ArtFire Themer is the main design tool for customizing the look of your shop with color, font, and layout choices. Clicking it again will turn Themer off when you are done. The interface is simple and intuitive. Choose colors and fonts to blend with your banner and avatar graphics. The Merchandiser tab is where you control the layout of your shop. This will make much more sense after you upload a few products, so ignore it for now. When you finally arrive at a shop design that you like, be sure to click the Save Theme button, and then Toggle Themer again to get out of design mode. Relax—you can return any time you want to make changes.

A new ArtFire website after initial Themer design steps.

5. Listing a couple of products is your next step. Click MyArtFire in the upper-right links to return to the dashboard. Then click the plus sign

icon to List New Item. Follow the simple steps to upload photos and complete each of the data fields. Your new products will show up under the Items tab at the dashboard and on your shop page (though it seems to take a minute or two for new products to show up there).

The Merchandiser in the Themer tools allows you to arrange your products.

6. Back in the dashboard, you will set up your Payment Options, your Shipping Profiles, Sales Tax, Google Shopping, and your Artisan Bio and Studio Policies. There are abundant instructions for all of these steps in the ArtFire Help Center, (*www.artfire.com/modules.php?name=help_center*).

Words of Wisdom

Opening a shop on ArtFire is pretty simple, but turning it into a successful business takes effort and planning. Jeanne and John Fry are the artists behind *Conscious Art Studios* on ArtFire. This husband-and-wife team work from North Carolina in the historic Blue Ridge Mountain region of the eastern United States, creating colorful and creative works of art in many different media. Jeanne makes folk art and spirit dolls, and is also a painter. John creates Eastern woodland style flutes and music, and intricate gourd art. Their shop has been on ArtFire for nearly two years, and they consider it an easy and affordable platform for selling their work online.

Conscious Art Studios on ArtFire.

Jeanne opened the online shop with paintings, flute music, and art dolls. She explains, "I always prefer showing my art in person, but for health reasons I needed to find an outlet for selling that would be gentler on me. I chose ArtFire because I preferred the business model of paying one low set fee each month, and not being charged listing and commission fees. Whether I have ten items or 200 items, my fee is always the same."

Paintings are consistently good sellers at ArtFire. Jeanne's originals are acrylic on canvas in the Contemporary Folk Art style, incorporating bold and vibrant colors, symbols, and themes of personal growth, cultural stories, and inspiration. High-quality prints of the paintings are available at the prints-on-demand website FineArtAmerica.com (*www.fineartamerica.com*). "Along with paintings, gourd art bowls and masks, hand painted wooden ornaments, and folk art dolls are our bestsellers," says Jeanne. It is a diverse product line, yet consistent themes and colors pull everything together perfectly.

"ArtFire has given us a very easy and affordable platform for offering our artwork. Artists and crafters who are thinking about opening a shop on ArtFire need to keep in mind that it is very different from Etsy. It is not so much a 'community-circle'–based marketplace with large numbers of customers coming to visit and buy. Rather, it is a platform for you to create and market your own shop. You need to spend time learning about Internet searches, keywords, and driving your own traffic." ArtFire is a good source of information on what to do. "There are very active forums with a good community of sellers who are willing to help critique and problem solve. ArtFire Marketing offers many tutorials and other assistance, especially when new features are added to the venue."

The Frys work the Internet seriously. They have a popular Facebook business page where they have embedded the popular ArtFire Kiosk. They have a website and a few blogs, and they update their Twitter and Pinterest pages on a regular basis. "The majority of traffic to our shop comes from our own website, blogs, social media, and Internet searches." Visit *www.artfire.com/ext/shop/studio/ConsciousArtStudios* and *www.consciousartstudios.com* for more information.

Is ArtFire Right for You?

Now that you have taken a close look at Etsy.com and ArtFire.com, how do you decide which is best for you? Will your journey to success be better served by the vast traffic of Etsy, or will your products find their niche on a smaller venue? Ultimately it is your own intuition that will provide the answer, but here are a few suggestions for evaluating these options:

- Make an informed decision. Spend some time on Etsy and ArtFire, as well as the smaller marketplace websites. As you get down to your top two or three favorites, look even more deeply into these systems. You will be investing a significant amount of time setting up a shop on the marketplace platform you choose, so choose carefully.

- Look at items that are similar to the products you make. Are the items of high quality? Are your items of an equal quality? Are they priced in the same range? In other words, how would your items fit into this website? It won't do you much good to offer shabby chic earrings on a website filled with highly polished, sophisticated jewels. The viewer expectation will be to find silver and gold, precious stones, and elegance. You'd waste your energy promoting tarnished copper and repurposed thrift shop beads here. But equally true, if your products are markedly superior to everything else in your genre, you could simply be lowering the perceived value of your own work.

- Large venue or small? This is often the crux of the matter. Do you join Etsy.com because its traffic is so much higher than other marketplace websites? Or will your artwork simply get lost in that crowd, while a smaller venue will allow your pieces to shine? On a large system, your items will be competing with hundreds of other pieces. Will your products be able to stand out and capture the attention of viewers? Is your market segment on a website saturated with shops similar to yours, or does it feel like there is room for your unique artwork?

- How will the competition affect your sales? Since you will be promoting yourself widely online and sending traffic to your marketplace shop, will these people stay on your pages—viewing, loving, and purchasing your work? Or will they tend to get lured away from your shop to look at other artists? It may be more likely that viewers will stay on your shop pages if there are fewer competitors. In this case, setting up shop on a smaller venue may work in your favor, leading to a greater number of sales from the traffic you generate. On the other hand, a larger venue will have much more overall traffic, and in itself will become a major source of new customers for you.

- Are sellers finding success? Look deeper into the people who sell products that are similar to yours. Look at their work, click on their bio pages, and make note of how many sales they have had. If possible, look at when they opened their shops. Once you have identified artists or crafters who have the sort of sales success you hope to achieve, examine their shops. How many different items do those successful sellers carry in their shops, and do you have enough product to match that level? Are your prices in line with theirs? Try to discover a marketplace website where your artwork fits comfortably among the top sellers in your genre.

- Is cost a factor? How much does each site charge to set up a shop per month? How about per listing? How often do items need renewing, and what does that cost? Does the site charge a commission, and if so, what percentage of each sale? Project your shop into full professional mode by estimating a healthy level of inventory and sales, and then run the numbers. You might project, for example, that you will that you will maintain 150 different products and sell thirty items each month at an average cost of $40 each. What will that cost you on the different websites you are considering, and is the cost difference meaningful in the big picture?

- Will your items be displayed well? Does the product display allow you to show off your products? How many photos are you allowed, and how large can they be? Is there a zoom feature that lets potential buyers enlarge the photo and see details? Remember that the photos are the only "reality" an online customer has to make a purchasing decision. Along with learning how to take the best possible photographs, you need to choose a selling venue that lets you use those yummy photos to their best advantage.

- Are your target customers likely to be on the website looking for work such as yours? Mandy Budan, a Canadian painter, sells her unique abstract landscapes on a variety of different sites. She recommends that artists know their market first, and then find the venues that support it. Budan lists full-sized originals on her own website, small originals at *www.dailypaintworks.com*, and prints on Etsy. She also sells on *www.cargoh.com* and *www.dailypaintworks.com*. Though the reach is smaller on these venues, the content is more specifically fine-art based. (*www.budanart.com*)

- How many marketplaces will you use? Could setting up a store on a new venue help expose your products to a new crowd? The more places your name and your business name show up on the Internet, the easier it will be for people to find you. Search engines such as Google.com will have more links to display for your name (assuming that you do not use duplicate content on different websites). In addition, traffic on the different websites you use will be able to discover your products.

ESSENTIAL

Pay close attention to sales and tracking statistics on the websites where you sell. If they are making you more money than they are costing you, keep them. It's that simple.

- Read the forums. Every marketplace website has a support system with discussion boards that are used by sellers. Find these and follow them over several days. What are sellers saying? Are they generally favorable, or disenchanted with the platform? Can you picture yourself among them? Do any websites stand out as particularly well suited to your own personality and philosophy?
- Look at the support systems. Read some of the how-to pages and check out what learning resources are offered. Is there forum, e-mail, or live telephone support?
- Do some Internet searches to find opinions outside of the websites themselves. If, for example, you are trying to decide between Etsy and DaWanda, go to Google and search, "Etsy or DaWanda," and "which is better Etsy DaWanda," and "selling handmade pottery Etsy DaWanda." Ask the question in different ways and follow the most interesting links.

Finally, try them out. Most marketplace sites allow you to set up a shop at minimal cost. Go ahead and sign up with your favorites. Don't roll out your entire product line and don't go through all the financial setup details at first, but do get to the point where you can list a couple of items and see what your shop space will look like. You should be able to do this in a few hours for a handful of different websites. Once you actually see your items in place, and are able to experience the management interface, you will be amazed at how easy the decision will be. One marketplace platform will emerge as your clear favorite, and that will be the place you stick with to build your new business.

CHAPTER 9

Auction Sites

Many artists and crafters begin their online selling career at an auction website, listing and selling a piece of their artwork or handcrafted goods to the highest bidder. An auction is an easy entry point for Internet sales. It requires only a single item and the willingness to sell it. In addition, auction websites have been around far longer than the handcraft marketplaces or print-on-demand venues. The granddaddy Internet auction is eBay (*www.ebay.com*), one of the earliest online selling platforms. It continues to be a popular place to sell "direct from the artist" artwork and handcraft, by auction and through Buy It Now standard shopping. The Tophatter (*www.tophatter.com*) auction site is a newcomer to the field, specifically selling handcrafted items through a clever system that allows sellers and buyers to interact during the sale.

eBay

eBay is the most well known of all auction websites. Beginning in 1995 as a small section of its founder's personal website, eBay surfed the wave of Internet growth. By 1996 it hosted 250,000 auctions. By 1997 there were 2 million auctions. By 2008, the company had expanded worldwide with hundreds of millions of registered users.

Everything is sold on eBay, except for items prohibited by eBay's terms of use. One clear advantage to selling work on eBay is that visitors to the site are usually not just looking around, connecting with their friends, and admiring nice work . . . they are there to buy something. A bargain, usually. And your handcraft or artwork may be exactly the bargain they are looking for.

FACT

Millions of collectibles, décor, appliances, computers, furnishings, equipment, domain names, vehicles, and other miscellaneous items are listed, bought, or sold daily on eBay.

Items being offered for sale on eBay are placed in an appropriate category and tagged with searchable words, making it easy for buyers to find products to fit their particular interests. A buyer can browse categories, such as eBay Art (*www.ebay.com/chp/art*) or even more specifically, eBay Direct from the Artist (*www.ebay.com/sch/Direct-from-the-Artist*) to view items being auctioned. If buyers are interested in handcrafts, they could visit the Handcrafted and Finished Pieces in eBays Crafts section (*www.ebay.com/ sch/Handcrafted-Finished-Pieces*). Or from any page of the eBay website, a buyer can simply type a keyword into the search box to see items that match their query. "Handcrafted folk art dolls" brings up a page showing handmade dolls, sock monkeys, and dollhouses in many different categories including Dolls, Antiques, and Collectibles, as well as Direct from the Artist. eBay Stores offer yet another way for customers to find your products.

Selling an Item on eBay

Selling on eBay is open to anyone, and millions of people list things for sale each year. Go to *http://pages.ebay.com/help/sell/selling-basics.html* for complete and current information. Sellers register as an eBay user and then create a seller's account. Once their account is set up, they can immediately begin listing the items they wish to sell. These can be offered as auction-style listings or as fixed-price products from their eBay store. There is often a fee for listing an item, depending on its cost and type of offering. The basic listing fee is anywhere from free to 50 cents each. When an item sells, eBay charges a commission on the amount of the sale, basically 9 percent for auction items and 11 percent for fixed-price items. There are many other promotional opportunities requiring small additional fees. You can post multiple photos on a listing, have your listing displayed in bold font, add a subtitle, purchase promotional advertisements, and more. All of these are optional and you can decide for yourself if they are worth the cost for different items you sell.

When you are setting up a seller's account, your phone number is required and is used as an authentication method. You can specify that your seller's fees be taken out of PayPal transactions if you also sign up with PayPal to accept payments for sales on eBay. This is seamless, since PayPal is owned by eBay. You can also submit your personal credit card number or bank account information if you prefer to sell without a PayPal account.

Once you have an account set up, it is easy to list an item for sale. Just follow these steps:

1. On any eBay page, click the Sell link at the top right. Pull down to Sell an item, then on the next screen click "Start Selling."
2. Type in a couple of keywords describing your item, and eBay will display one or more possible categories where such an item might fit. Choose the one you want, but be aware that different categories have different eBay options. You'll get familiar with the best categories for your work as you gain experience.

Each category will have different item specifics to complete.

3. Now you will arrive at the listing page. This is where you write a title for your product. Since the title is also a searchable field, include all the main keywords for your item. Thus your title would not simply be "Annie Doll," but "Handmade Prairie Cloth Doll Americana Folk Art Primitive OOAK." Always make each word count. Next, upload your product photos. Currently, twelve photos are allowed at no additional listing cost. You should have your images sized to the recommended 1,600 pixels on their longest side, which allows the eBay zoom feature to let customers get in close and see details.

OOAK is online shorthand for "one of a kind," a way to indicate that your product is an original with no copies, and therefore more unique and valuable than mass-produced items.

4. Write your product description. There are text formatting tools and themes you can use to make your description eye-catching, and you can use HTML to further dress up your description, but really what you write in the first sentence is probably the most important element. Include everything important about your product—all the details a viewer might want to know before deciding to buy the piece. Later on, you can stream-line the writing process by setting up standard information as inserts.

5. There are two ways to list items on eBay: You can list your item as an auction item, or you can list it using the fixed-price tab. In either case, you decide the starting price or the fixed selling price. Your auction item can also have a fixed Buy It Now price. Check the listing fee; you will be charged different amounts by eBay depending on the method of selling that you choose.

Decide if you will sell your item by auction or with a fixed price.

6. You also set the duration this item will be listed, from 3–10 days, or until you cancel (for fixed-price items). As you sell more items, you will dis-cover the best amount of time to set for your auctions. You want to be able to publicize the auction, and have enough time for people to dis-cover it and make a bid. Most bids happen on the final day, in the last hours, or sometimes in the last few seconds of an auction. Adjust the start time of your auction so your listing ends at an optimal hour. Sunday nights are good, or most weekday evenings. You certainly don't want

your auction to end at 3 A.M. your time zone, unless your ideal customers are night owls who will be up and online at that hour.

7. Specify how you will be shipping the item. It is easiest to select the appropriate default shipping costs suggested by eBay.

8. As you preview your listing, note that eBay will automatically connect with your PayPal account if you already have one (your e-mail address is the identifying factor here). PayPal is a good choice for payment, unless you wish to take the risk of fraud with checks and money orders. You'll be advanced to PayPal.com to confirm your new connection with eBay. If you want to use a different payment method, click the Advanced Tool option in the links above the menu bar. There are many other details you can add on the Advanced Selling Tool page, some of which will add small charges to your listing fee.

Quick Listing Tool view provides the basic selling information. More options are available by switching to Advanced Tool at the top of the eBay screen.

ALERT

As a small business, you are required to remit the appropriate sales tax that might apply to the sale of your item, and to accept returns if buyers are not satisfied.

9. When everything on the form is completed, click Continue. Check out some more optional promotional services, buy any you wish or none at all, and then click List Your Item. It will immediately appear on eBay. You can find and review what you have just listed by clicking My eBay on the top right of the webpage, then scrolling to view your own Active Selling list.

Watch your items as they go through their auctions. You can see how many bids have been made and what the current bid price is. If anyone sends you a question about the item, be sure to answer them immediately; if the information is important, go back and put it into the description. When the item sells, send a confirmation message to the buyer with your thanks and the expected shipping/delivery details.

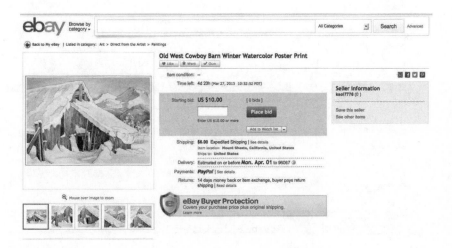

Your item is now available as an eBay auction. Good luck!

Stores on eBay

One popular option for regular sellers is to open an eBay store, where buyers can view and follow all of your products and learn more about you as a seller. A basic eBay store costs $15.95 per month, plus additional fees for both auctions and fixed-price listings. See *www.pages.ebay.com/help/sell/ stores.html* for current information.

Words of Wisdom

Holdman Studios creates stained glass and hot glass from their shop in Lehi, Utah. Founded twenty years ago by Tom Holdman, who opened a stained glass studio in his parent's garage, the studio's projects now include stained glass installations in churches, temples, and private and public spaces around the world. Glass artists Treavor Holdman and Vicente del Campo also produce amazing hot glass creations from lighting and sculpture to large blown glass platters and bowls. Many of their creations are sold on eBay at *www.stores.ebay.com/Holdman-Studios*.

Holdman Studios sells hand blown, hot glass platters and vases at their eBay store.

Holdman Studios began blowing glass in 2005, and within a few years had started using eBay as an online selling platform. "We list a new platter or vase every day, auctioning it for a 10-day period," explains Amilia from Holdman Studios. "So unless we miss a day, we generally have ten active listings. There have been times in the past when we have tried two auctions a day, but that seemed to saturate the market, and final bids ended up being lower. Ten listings seems to be our sweet spot."

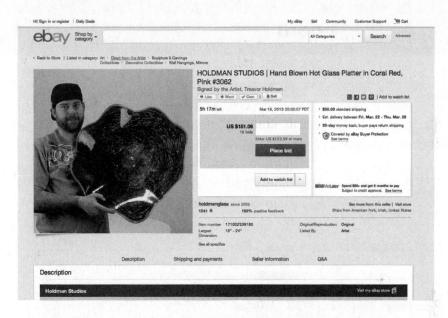

A typical Holdman Studios listing shows the artist holding his creation.

All pieces are listed using a photo of the artist holding the platter or vase. Additional photos are included in the product description. The photo adds personality and scale to the product, showing both the smiling glass artist and the scale of the glass platters, which are huge. By repeating this photo format, the Holdman Studios shop on eBay takes on an attractive unified look.

Items are listed in various categories, such as Wall Hangings and Decorative Plates and Bowls. "There are several different categories that work for our artwork. We rotate which categories to use on individual auctions so that we can attract folks browsing in different categories to our store. We use as many search words in our titles as possible. We use our name in all of the titles." A typical listing title might be "HOLDMAN STUDIOS | Hand Blown Art Glass Platter in Red, Yellow, Green, Blue," and Holdman always chooses to add the subtitle "Signed by the Artist, Treavor Holdman" or "Signed by the Artist, Vicente del Campo," a fantastic artisan touch.

A look at the eBay feedback page for Holdman Studios (100 percent positive), the selling price for platters seems to run between $100 to $300 and upwards, depending on the size of the piece and sometimes simply the activity on eBay when the auction closed. "We usually have a good idea of which listings will do the best, but sometimes something will surprise us, something will do even better than expected." Auctions rarely close with lower than expected bids, though it does happen.

Customers also become collectors on eBay. Repeat sales are not uncommon. "We encourage repeat customers by sending a 15 percent off coupon out with all of our shipments." Although the Studio sells through its own website, eBay is its main online sales arm. "We started selling glass on eBay as a way to get our name out. We think of eBay as an advertising tool. Several of our long-term customers and large custom orders originated with people who found us through eBay."

Visit *www.holdmanstudios.com* and *www.stores.ebay.com/Holdman-Studios* for more information.

Is eBay Right for You?

Searching for items on eBay is a great way for sellers to get to know their own market possibilities using this site. Simply use search terms that describe the kind of artwork you create, and see what is being auctioned each day. Not only can you view current auctions, you can click the Sold Listings tab to see what has recently sold, and each item's selling price. A few appropriate searches will give you a good idea whether your work fits into the eBay platform, and if you are willing to accept the average selling price for items in your niche.

Think of your own inventory of products as you look at the recently sold items on eBay. Do you have work that will do well here? Does your work fit into any of the themes you have noticed selling well on eBay? Do you have stock that has not sold in your marketplace shop or elsewhere that you'd like to move along to new owners? You may get a little less than you would have liked, but if it means you don't have to store all your winter items until next fall, it may be worth it.

Tophatter

While eBay might be the largest and most established of online auction websites, with categories for arts and crafts "direct from the artist," Tophatter. com (*www.tophatter.com*) is one of the newest and most innovative auction platforms for crafters and artists. An animated graphic creates each auction, complete with an auctioneer, various sellers with items up for sale, and a crowd of avatars representing the people on the webpage—at the auction—as it takes place. There are usually several auctions going on at any given time. Items come up for sale with a minimum bid. The seller, who is encouraged to attend, can say things about their item by typing into the chat field. People in the audience can chat back and make comments as the bids increase. Each sale takes about a minute, and then goes to the highest bidder. Soft sounds keep the viewers engaged as the avatars chat and available products ascend the list to the auction block.

To sell on Tophatter, you only need to have a Tophatter account (which you have already set up to look at the website) and a PayPal account. Tophatter items can be sold by individuals and commercial distributors, as well as by handcraft artists themselves. You describe your item, upload photos, and set your minimum bid—the lowest price you will be willing to take for the item. The first time you list an item for sale, the Tophatter staff will check it out and help you get featured in one of the upcoming auctions. Once you have become an accepted seller, you can freely join upcoming auctions as you wish, or even host your own auctions. There is a scheduling fee for each listing you make.

Each successful sale is between you (the seller) and your buyer. They pay you their winning bid via your PayPal account. You then ship the item to them. Tophatter, in the meantime, takes a commission of 10–13 percent out of the selling price. Sellers have a profile page on Tophatter that you can populate with information about yourself and links to your social media sites and other online selling venues. Tophatter encourages you to use auctions and your social media sites to collect fans and customers.

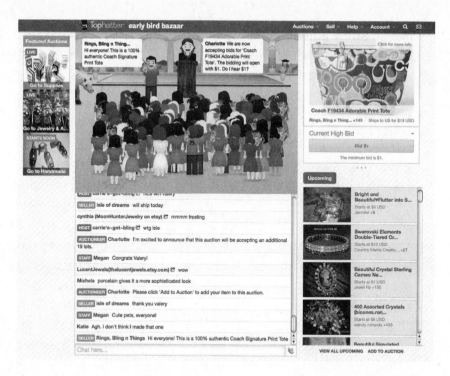

TopHatter.com Landing Page

The most common Tophatter product is jewelry. Also popular at auctions are handbags and fashion accessories, soaps and lotions, crafting supplies, and a mix of other handcrafted and art items. Spend a bit of time on Tophatter, watching a few auctions and getting a feel for the action to decide if you want to step in.

To Auction or Not to Auction?

If you feel that your items would get exposure on an auction platform, give it a try! Selling single items is easy on both eBay and Tophatter. You have nothing to lose. The audience at eBay is potentially larger, while buyers who participate at Tophatter are far more involved. Try a few sales on each venue, and analyze your experience to decide which platform is best for your work.

When you list an item for auction on either website, be sure to promote it widely through your Facebook and Twitter business profiles. Encourage your fans to share with their friends. You never know when someone who has passively admired your work in a gallery or on your marketplace shop will get caught up in the excitement of an online auction. And yes, auctions are exciting! The sale is made to the "winning bid" as if the customer just earned a rare treasure, a bargain that other bidders missed out on. Auctions may not work for your handcrafts or paintings, but then again you might be surprised at the results, and gain a new customer in the process.

CHAPTER 10

Products on Demand

Print-on-demand (POD) products are an innovative way to promote yourself as an artist and make sales in the process. Modern printing technology has made it easy to upload your designs and use them on a wide variety of items. You can then offer those products for sale through your shop space on the print-on-demand website and on your own website and blog. The products are created when they are ordered, and they are shipped directly to the customer. You do not have to pay for inventory ahead of time or even stock and ship things yourself. You simply create and market your items, and get paid a royalty on sales. There are many different great print-on-demand websites where you can create everything from T-shirts to cell phone cases, books to calendars, and board games to fabric.

POD websites make it so easy to sign up and create products that they have thousands and thousands of shops and individual artist galleries, and millions of possible products. Although the sites allow all visitors to browse and purchase products, it is highly unlikely that a new shop will attract much attention. Think of POD websites not as a significant sales venue in themselves, but as a platform to create products that you can promote and sell to your own fans and customers. You will need to generate pretty much all of the traffic that comes to your POD shop space.

Products on Demand: An Overview

Launching its website in 1999, CafePress was one of the first companies to provide products on demand. Along with the popular CafePress.com website, the company also has several other sites specializing in fine art products. CafePress has dozens of different products available for sellers to customize and sell. Zazzle.com is the other main print-on-demand service, with similar features for artists.

A typical POD success story begins with an illustrator who creates clever and appealing artwork. Her designs are humorous, quirky, or otherwise compelling to a wide group of admirers. The artist uses the Internet a lot and has a well-known blog and a Facebook page with lots of followers. She sells original artwork and fine art prints on her website and at her marketplace shop, but fans keep asking for more! So one afternoon the illustrator goes online, sets up a shop on CafePress, and uploads artwork to create a branded line of T-shirts, hoodies, and pajamas with a coffee mug to match. These products become even more widely successful, and all her original artwork is suddenly worth much more. The items are available to the Cafe-Press traffic, but almost all of the sales come from her links at Facebook, from her blog, and through the continued sharing of her posts by fans and their friends.

FACT

With over 300 million unique products available, CafePress.com shipped 7.8 million products in 2011.

What Kind of Work Is Successful on CafePress?

A search of the current bestsellers in various product categories reveals popular trends for the CafePress traffic as a whole, including:

- Tote bags with clever sayings and designs about knitting
- Shower curtains with colorful water-themed paintings
- iPhone cases printed to look like vintage cameras
- Pop culture, TV, and video heroes
- T-shirts with tribal or petroglyph-style figures
- "Rock on" birthday cards illustrated with photos of beach pebbles—35 pebbles, 36 pebbles, and so on
- Coffee mugs decorated with grumpy cats
- Contemporary tattoo artwork on pajamas
- Mexican sugar skull characters on pillows
- Geek and science gear
- Designs celebrating popular YouTube videos, such as the honey badger and bacon

The ability to expand your product line without investing in manufacturing, warehousing, and shipping is a pretty irresistible attraction. If you have a clever idea, a creative design, and a style of artwork that is colorful and graphic (along with a loyal following of fans who will buy and help promote your work into popularity), then CafePress might be an excellent choice.

ESSENTIAL

While CafePress is best known for funny sayings and popular causes, there are thousands of artists and designers using the CafePress product-on-demand services to create items with amazing works of art.

Selling Your Designs at CafePress.com

There are two basic levels of services if you wish to be a seller at Cafe-Press. Design and List is the simplest, requiring nothing but a free account and the properly formatted uploaded work. You'll need to read the image guidelines and make sure your digital file is correctly prepared. You can upload, title, describe, and tag a design in a few minutes. By uploading your design, you still retain your copyright and ownership of the image, but you grant a nonexclusive license to CafePress to allow them to print and ship your products to your customers.

Your design then becomes available on all of the standard products (T-shirts, mugs, totebags, and such). You can view these products and decide which items you want to make available for sale. You can link to these products on your blog, your website, in e-mails, and however you wish to promote your CafePress gear. The tags you add when you upload an image enable CafePress visitors to search and locate your products. CafePress completes each sale, processes the payment, makes the item, and ships it to the customer. They keep 92 percent of the item price. This means you earn an 8 percent commission on the sale of products at CafePress standard prices.

Or, you can open a CafePress shop. This will give you your own shop space, customizable with your header bar, colors, fonts, and of course, with your products. You earn money in several different ways once you have a CafePress shop.

1. You can mark up the prices of items in your shop, and you earn the markup. For example, if you offer a T-shirt with your design, and the basic CafePress cost for that shirt is $16, you can set your selling price at $23. When someone buys the T-shirt from your shop page, you keep the $7 mark-up. The base retail price for CafePress items is already on the high side of retail, so don't plan on adding huge markups unless you have designs people simply can't live without.

2. On top of that, you earn a monthly bonus depending on how much your CafePress shop is selling. You will earn 10 percent of sales if you are between $100 and $500 in sales that month, 15 percent of sales you earn above $500, 20 percent if they rise above $1,000, and so on to a maximum 30 percent for sales over $5,000 a month. Note that there's no royalty for shops with less than $100 in sales each month, so if you are selling at that level, your only profit will be your markup amount.

3. You yourself can order your products in bulk at a discount, and then sell them in person at your studio, craft fairs, and events. For example, a standard coffee mug with your design sells at the base cost of $11 each.

You order 12 of them from your shop for only $9.89 each, plus shipping. Then you can then sell them for whatever retail price you want.

Having a shop at CafePress costs you a monthly fee. There are a couple of ways to pay for this, depending on whether you wish to pay up front, or pay as you go. But none of them are very costly. The least you would pay is $5 per month if you pay a year in advance. The most you would pay would be $10 per month if you chose the no-upfront-costs option.

ALERT

While the shop templates at CafePress give many design options, CafePress also allows template customization. Shop pages can be designed to look very much like your own website or blog. It is even possible, with the use of independent scripts, to integrate your Cafe-Press shop directly into your independent website. You may wish to get help from an experienced web programmer to make design changes of this magnitude.

Open an Account on CafePress

Opening an account at CafePress won't take you more than a few minutes. It is easy and worth the time. Follow these steps to open your account:

1. Simply click Sell at the top of the CafePress opening page, click the Learn More button beneath Shops, and then read all the details and current terms. Remember that the Internet changes all the time, so be sure you understand and agree with everything that is being offered at the time you are signing up. If you want to proceed, click Create My Shop.
2. CafePress then has you register for a free account with your e-mail and a password of your choice.
3. Now you can "Open a Shop in 4 Easy Steps!" First, enter a shop name and some basic information.
4. Select a theme for your shop. There are many themes offered, from simple to fun, retro, or romantic. Choose a framework that seems to match your own website or artwork. You can change this or add customization later.

5. Choose a product set for your shop. These will be the products upon which your designs will be placed. CafePress has several sets recommended, or you can build your own set from their 398 different items.
6. Uploading your first image is next. Have your digital file ready, following the CafePress submission guidelines.

You can choose a product set, then later delete unwanted items and add new ones to customize your shop.

ALERT

Product design tags and category placements let your items be found by general CafePress visitors. Carefully writing product titles and descriptions with keywords will help your CafePress products be discovered by search engines.

7. Now your shop is open. The next page is your Account Management page. There's a link at top right to Visit Your Shop where you will see the template you have chosen and the product set with your first image.

8. Be sure to completely fill out your Payee Information, so CafePress will be able to send you royalty checks when your products sell.

9. Explore the Additional Settings and Tools on your Management interface.

   • The Basic shop settings allow you to edit the information in your shop profile, to change to different templates, to see what is the best look for your new CafePress shop, and to manage your products one by one.

The Manage Your Shop interface at CafePress.com.

   • Customize your shop with Colors and Fonts Tools, and Display Features. These tools are not the easiest to use, but the CafePress Learning Center will help if you need it. (*www.cafepress.com/cp/learn*)

- You can Bulk Add or Remove products so your shop is displaying exactly the products you want to sell, and quickly change prices as long as you intend to make the identical change to all products.
- Additional tools help you handle your payment agreement with Cafe-Press; add Google Analytics to get usage information on visitors to your shop and get sales reports.

10. Finally, look at the Share Your Shop! resources in the right column of your management page. This is where you will generate link images and widgets to place on your own website and blog, and generally connect with all of the social media things you do.

A simple little CafePress Shop for the Bluebird of Happiness.

Are shop owners required to buy any of their CafePress items?
Most artists order a few of their own items so they can check out how their designs look after printing. Having a product in hand allows you to take more interesting product photos to use on blogs and websites to promote CafePress items. Shop owners pay only the CafePress base price when logged in and ordering from their own shop.

Words of Wisdom

Brandon Bird (*www.brandonbird.com*) is a phenomenon among today's pop culture artists. He paints figures from history and popular culture such as Edward Norton, Chuck Norris, and Abraham Lincoln, in absurd situations. His best-known oil portraits include TV icon Michael Landon lamenting the death of a Humboldt squid, film actor Christopher Walken tinkering with robots in his garage workshop, and philosopher Noam Chomsky strolling through a shopping mall parking lot toward his funky 1970s van with custom "Chomsky" paint job.

Brandon sails among the stars of contemporary art today, but he jump-started his career by pleasing followers with a banquet of print-on-demand products from CafePress. "I sold shirts, prints, metal buttons—I basically took paintings and images I had at the time and slapped them on whatever products CafePress offered. There was no upfront cost, so no risk or investment," says Brandon.

It was a great marketing technique. Customers loved the weird Brandon Bird designs they could wear and display. His CafePress products became prized possessions. "Years down the road, I'd meet people at conventions or hear stories through e-mail about how their favorite shirt from my original CafePress shop had faded or crumbled and they had no way to get a replacement," he says.

CafePress items were not cheap. "The way their pricing worked, each item had a base cost, and you could add on to that whatever profit you'd like to make. But the base cost was nowhere near what you'd think of as wholesale. I remember a T-shirt being $17.50, so if you wanted to make $5 per shirt, you had to charge your customers $22.50 + shipping for a white T-shirt. And in 2003 people weren't used to paying that."

Pop culture iPhone cases at BrandonBird.com are POD products.

Because of his artistic genre, Brandon occasionally ran into conflicts with the print-on-demand services. "CafePress and Zazzle both have zero-tolerance copyright infringement policies. As a pop-artist, I use images of celebrities and famous people. It's all fun and humorous and perfectly acceptable fair use. But a couple of my images were yanked with no explanation (or an image would get pulled from one product but not others). I think it was randomized, automated policing, but it makes sense from their end—if someone does object or threaten a suit, they as the publisher would have to spend the time and money to deal with it, not you the artist."

Eventually Brandon migrated to more traditional wholesale production methods, where he has greater control over the quality of products and can get a better retail mark-up. He produces his own archival prints. "I walked into a computer store and saw that the Epson 2400 existed. For the longest time, if you wanted an archival professional inkjet printer you needed $4,000 and a lot of floor space, but suddenly there was a smaller version of the same thing for around $700. I realized I could make one not-so-risky investment in equipment and do all my own printing, and flip the profit margin in my favor. I could charge $40 for a better-quality print, and all of that would go to me, instead of 80 percent to CafePress. I could actually start to make a living selling my stuff," he explains.

"I still use a third-party POD service for my cell phone cases. I get wholesale pricing, and they take care of fulfillment, but people can order them straight through my website. And POD lets me offer a lot more image and case style combinations than if I were ordering them in bulk."

Brandon encourages artists and designers to consider print-on-demand services as a way to test the marketplace and expand their product line. "You have literally nothing to lose. It's not really a feasible long-term solution (unless you somehow do very high volume), but it's very useful for testing the waters and seeing what, if any, demand there is for your stuff. When I finally got around to buying my first printer, I knew that it wasn't really a risk, because people were already buying stuff from me."

Along with Mr. T Christmas cards, Nicolas Cage iPad covers, and the "Law and Order" coloring book, Brandon's latest offerings include a new book titled *Brandon Bird's Amazing World of Art*. "In Fall 2013, Chronicle Books will publish a collection of my work, including slick color reproductions of some of my paintings, plus stickers, postcards, and a sizable coloring section (you know, the usual art book stuff)."

Other Stores

Zazzle.com runs neck-and-neck with CafePress in both services and traffic, so be sure to compare both systems before you open a shop. Look at the type of products you can create, the look and feel of the website, and the finances of selling on each platform. Check out Spreadshirt (*www.spreadshirt.com*), RedBubble (*www.redbubble.com*), and Pikistore (*www.pikistore.com*) to see if these smaller venues might work better for your target audience. Especially of interest to the arts and crafts industry is Spoonflower (*www.spoonflower.com*), where you can create and sell fabric with your own designs.

Prints on Demand

A niche of the POD market that is particularly appropriate for artists are the websites delivering high-quality prints on demand. Many artists find these services fit their needs perfectly, allowing them to focus on creating art rather than purchasing prints in quantity, finding safe storage space for inventory, and packing and shipping orders.

The POD websites do it all! After uploading high-quality images of their work, artists can sell prints on a wide variety of surfaces, from premium matte paper to glossy posters and stretched canvas. The prints can also be purchased with different matting and framing options. It is easy to upload images and organize them into different galleries. You will need to have high-quality digital files, because the prints will look only as good as your images allow. Working with a professional photographer or scanning service is essential.

FineArtAmerica.com Landing Page

Many artists have become accustomed to FineArtAmerica (*www .fineartamerica.com*), one of the first websites to provide high-quality art prints. Despite the name, this website is a worldwide service with artists from every nation. Individual artists get their own gallery site and artist profile space at no monthly cost. They can upload and organize their artwork, post regular news in the Events, Blog, and Press Release areas of their profile, and see a listing of customers who have signed up to follow their work and be informed of new releases. Artists set their own print options and prices, and earn 100 percent of the markup over FineArtAmerica's base price for any given product. There's also a royalty paid if a customer also purchases additional services such as framing.

The other print-on-demand websites work much the same. Please check the exact terms of service as you explore each of these options. Imagekind (*www.imagekind.com*) is one of the CafePress sites for fine art prints. Other services include CanvasOnDemand (*www.canvasondemand.com*) for photography, GreatBigCanvas (*www.greatbigcanvas.com*) for even more wall art products, and InvitationBox (*www.invitationbox.com*) for cards. DeviantArt (*www.deviantart.com*) is a popular, somewhat more innovative platform for fine art prints and other products. ArtistRising (*www.artistrising.com*) pays a 30 percent royalty, offers free membership for artists with fifty images or less, and $50 per year memberships for artists with up to 300 uploads.

Books on Demand

Another POD niche for artists and crafters to consider is in the self-publishing genre, with websites that allow you to create books online and sell both printed copies and e-books on demand. While these services appeal primarily to writers, they can also be used to create art books and instructional books.

Here are just a few possibilities for the arts and crafts market:

- A collection of an artist's work on a particular theme, such as goddess collage or the boats of Cape Cod
- A Year's Work, the annual work of an artist or designer
- Adventures in Stain Painting, or any title featuring works and instruction in an unusual media

- Thirty Years of Baskets, a retrospective of a master crafter's work
- Hot Glass, the work of a fused glass crafter
- How to Paint Koi, an instruction in traditional Japanese brushwork
- Grand Canyon Journal, with the sketch journal of a river rafter
- Scrapbooking for Kids, by a multimedia artist with lots of parenting experience

QUESTION

Is print on demand popular in the publishing industry?
Far more new books are created using print-on-demand technology than using traditional publishing methods. Today annual POD titles are almost eight times the amount of traditional titles, though there may be only a few copies of each self-published title printed.

Blurb (*www.blurb.com*) is a typical self-publishing books-on-demand platform. An artist or crafter would simply need a good computer, high-quality digital files of their artwork, and the words to create a book. The website provides the rest. Books can be assembled online using a variety of templates, or with software that can be downloaded to work on your own computer. There is a good support system to help you learn the ins and outs of book design. Once your book is completed and you have purchased at least one copy at the basic price for that type of book, you can add your title to the Blurb Bookstore. You then set your retail price, and when a book sells, you will earn any markup that you have specified over the base price. You can promote your book as widely as you wish. Your customers will go to Blurb to order the book, and Blurb will print and ship it to them.

FACT

Since its inception in 2004, Blurb has delivered more than 6 million books created by more than a half million customers.

E-books are also available at Blurb.com, and you earn a whopping 80 percent of the retail price for any e-book downloads that are sold. If you anticipate that the book you are writing might become a popular e-book product, be sure to research the best template to use, especially the size and shape that will keep your desired look and feel when an electronic version is viewed on a reading device.

You could possibly get sales from general visitors to Blurb.com, but it is far more likely that all of your sales will come from traffic you generate yourself. Two other major books-on-demand sites with similar features are CreateSpace (*www.createspace.com*) and Lulu (*www.lulu.com*).

The Internet obviously provides amazing opportunities for creative artists and crafters. As long as you understand that it is up to you to promote yourself, the right print-on-demand services can expand your product line, increase your income (while not adding responsibilities of inventory and order fulfillment), and expand your reputation in unexpected ways.

CHAPTER 11

Your Own Website

All successful online artists and crafters desire to have their own websites. Your own website, using your own domain name, is an essential piece of your online identity. It is the hub from which all your other Internet activity is linked and coordinated. Some folks begin with their own website and work outward, developing their social media channels, their marketplace shop, their auctions, and newsletter. Others create their own website as the final step that ties together all of the other platforms they use. Whether you start here or end here, setting up your own website is essential.

There is no reason for any artist or crafter to put off building a website. It is no longer necessary, or even advisable, to pay big bucks for a professional web designer to set up an elaborate site. Those clunky, overly designed websites are not very effective anyway. With the systems available online these days, you can create your own attractive, efficient website in less than a day. You will be in complete control, able to edit your own web pages, add current news and photos, and interweave all of your online locations. It will cost you very little, and will be far easier than you imagine.

Why Have a Website at All?

With the abundance of free and inexpensive Internet platforms for sharing and selling your artwork online, why even bother to have a domain website? Isn't it enough to have an Etsy shop, a Facebook page, and eBay auctions? The short answer is "no." The long answer is, "These other platforms are merely the satellites of your Internet solar system. You need your own website around which all these rotate—a home for all your online marketing efforts."

Successful artists and crafters have their own business websites, and here are ten good reasons why.

1. **Credibility.** Having your own website tells the world that you are the real deal! It shows that you take your work seriously, and that you are not a hobby artist dabbling in the field; you are a dedicated professional with your own domain name.
2. **Branding.** You can set up your website to communicate the look and feel that is uniquely yours. You are in complete control here, not limited by any other website format or logos. Using colors, fonts, and images, you create a branded image that can be carried consistently throughout your business.
3. **The hub.** Your website is your central point of connection with fans and followers who have been attracted to you from different social media and marketplace platforms. People who discover your Pinterest boards are able to find your marketplace shop and click to follow you on Twitter. Folks who know your shop on ArtFire can easily discover your blog. Everything comes together on your own site, and as links and URLs

change (which is inevitable with the Internet), you can easily update what's on your website.

4. **News!** On your own website, (especially a website on a system where you have complete editing control), you can easily feature your newest works. Followers who are collecting you may be inspired to make an immediate purchase. You can list upcoming events, fairs where you will be selling, gallery openings, open studio hours, and items you have on auction. You have one location to keep all of your followers in the loop with the latest information.

5. **Blog.** Successful online artists and crafters blog regularly. Writing a blog helps increase search engine visibility for your name and brand, keeps followers interested and engaged in your work, and lets you have fun sharing insights and ideas. If your website is created with WordPress, you have a blogging system built in, ready to go.

6. **Wholesale.** If you are interested in connecting with shops and galleries to sell your artwork, your website serves as information central for wholesale relationships. Retailers who discover your work online can easily get to your website and see that you welcome their inquiries. Galleries love to see artists with websites because they know the artist or crafter is actively promoting herself, and will help attract visitors to the gallery door.

7. **Real-world promotion.** With a simple domain name, you can easily include your web address on all of your packaging materials, press releases, hang tags, group exhibitions, booth banners at fairs … basically every piece of printed information that you appear on. Your domain address never changes.

8. **Media.** Your website provides a place where magazine writers, newspaper reporters, TV hosts, radio personalities, reviewers, and bloggers can easily get information about you and your work. A media page on your website attracts attention and lets writers know that you are newsworthy. When last-minute deadlines approach, and there is simply no time for a writer to contact you personally to ask questions, a good media page on your website could assure that you are featured in reviews and articles.

9. **Keep in touch.** Collecting your own circle of followers is part of an overall marketing plan. Setting up a simple, free account at MailChimp (*www .mailchimp.com*) gives people the opportunity to give you their e-mail

address and say, "Yes, I want to keep in touch." Your website is where the sign-up form lives.

10. **Search engines.** As you become well known, new people search for you or your business name using Google or other search engines. The more places you show up, the better your chances of attracting new customers. Having your own website gives you a higher level of credibility with search engine systems, as well as another prominent link for them to display.

What to Look for in a Website System

Building your own website is an excellent investment—mainly an investment of time as you learn how to manage each step. But it is time very well spent, and will pay off handsomely in the future. You will be in total control of your website, as you are with all other aspects of your online presence. Control means you will update your site often, and you will use your website the way it's meant to be used; doing so will add significantly to your online success.

There are many ways to build your own website these days. Here's what you should look for:

- A system that you can manage yourself, online, from any computer anywhere in the world, without having to hire help for every change and addition
- A system that lets you set up web pages that are attractive and contain a lot of photos
- A system that lets you customize the main search engine fields on each page
- A monthly hosting fee that is $10 or less; no huge up-front charges; no hidden fees
- A hosting company that offers free tech support by phone or live chat for the system you are using
- A system that lets you use your own independent domain name for all your website pages
- A system that you can backup, archive, and move to a different hosting company if you ever choose to do so
- Fast server space and no significant time when your website is offline

At this point in time, the system that best satisfies all of these requirements is WordPress. This independent, open-source platform is available for free at hundreds of different hosting companies. WordPress was originally developed to be a blogging platform, and in recent years has become the standard content management system (CMS) for building small business websites. There are numerous tutorials available for WordPress, and the best hosting companies will support you fully, answering your questions as you build your WordPress site.

FACT

WordPress is currently the most popular system in use on the Internet. As of August 2011, 22 percent of all new active websites were created using WordPress.

There are several basic steps you will take toward creating your new website. Even if you decide to go with a system other than WordPress, many of the initial tasks are the same.

Your Domain Name

You need to have your own .com domain name, a name that you have registered yourself. It can be as simple as your own name with "art" or "studio" tacked onto the end: *BillJonesArt.com* or *MarySmithStudio.com*. It can be your business name for a more professional feel . . . *HarrisonIslandTextiles.com* or *NovemberWind.com*. You can only use a domain name that no one else is using. Many common names are already taken, so searching for possibilities and being creative is the first part of the process.

Online domain registry companies have a search box where you can type in your name ideas and see if that particular string of letters is available. Find a domain name ending with .com. It is the standard extension for commercial websites, and the one that people will automatically use when they are trying to find your site. You can buy the other extensions if you wish—*BillJonesArt.net* and *BillJonesArt.org*. This effectively keeps anyone else from using those sites, but find a .com name for your main identity.

ESSENTIAL

Domain registry is not difficult and costs around $20 per year or less for each domain you sign up for. Do this process yourself. Don't let anyone else—a web designer, a hosting company, or your brother-in-law—register your domain for you. You want to be in complete control of this essential part of your online business.

Many different online companies provide domain registration services. Work with a company that has a good management interface and telephone support in case you ever need help. GoDaddy (*www.godaddy.com*) is the leader in the field, with other options including Network Solutions (*www .networksolutions.com*), Register.com (*www.register.com*), and many others. Most of these companies will gladly sell you dozens of services besides the simple domain registry—privacy, security, hosting space, and more. Some are pretty pushy about it, but remember that you can always add services later.

ALERT

Product design tags and category placements let your items be found by general CafePress visitors. Carefully writing product titles and descriptions with keywords will help your CafePress products be discovered by search engines.

At the beginning, simply find a domain name that works for your business, and buy only a basic domain registry for one or more years. Purchase this in your own name and use your most stable e-mail address as you check out. You can initially leave the domain name parked with the registrar company. At this point, when you type your new domain name into a browser, you should see some sort of "parking" page from the registrar company you used. The entire registration process, after you finish brainstorming and finally arrive at a domain name that is available, should take 10 minutes. The brainstorming part takes days sometimes, depending on how lucky you are and how inventive you need to be to find a domain name that will suit you.

Hosting Space

Once you have a domain name, you need to rent space somewhere to build your website. Hosting services are provided by the registrar companies, but these deals are not especially the best options. Using a popular service such as Bluehost (*www.bluehost.com*), HostMonster (*www.hostmonster.com*), or HostGator (*www.hostgator.com*) can cost less each month and give you more features. Call each company's sales number and ask questions. You are looking for a hosting package that provides free WordPress as part of a basic hosting package. Your hosting company should have free 24/7 technical support by phone or live chat, and they should be willing to help you with WordPress questions as well as other hosting concerns. None of this is particularly expensive. Excellent hosting packages with all of these features currently costs $4 to $9 per month.

Once you decide on a hosting service, sign up online. Just purchase basic hosting. You do not yet need any special services, and you can always get them later if you want. You already have a domain name, so choose that option. When you've finished, you will get at least one e-mail with all the information you need to manage your hosting space, including the nameserver information you will use to get your domain name pointed to your new hosting company. Once you decide which company to use, signing up should take 10 minutes.

ALERT

Keep track of your username and password at your hosting company, so you can easily log in later to install WordPress and manage e-mail and other server functions.

Point Your Domain Name to Your New Hosting Space

Remember keeping track of your username and password at your domain registrar? Good. Now use that to log into the management system there and edit the nameservers for your domain name. You will indeed have questions on how to do this, so call the registrar's help line. This is why you must choose a company with 24/7 phone support. Their friendly support folks will walk you through the process. This should take 5 minutes (not counting the time you wait on hold, which is a wonderful incentive to do these things in the middle of the night when tech support is not too busy). Once completed, it will take up to 24 hours for the Internet to update itself. At this point, when you type your domain name into a browser (and remember to click the refresh button) you will see some sort of "parking" page from your hosting company. Once this change happens, it's time to get to work.

Install WordPress

Now that your domain name is pointed to your hosting space, you can install WordPress. This is done through the control panel. You will have questions on how to do this, so call the hosting company's tech support. Remember, you chose a company with great support who said they would help you with WordPress. Now is the time. Have their friendly support folks talk you through the process of installing WordPress to use for your entire domain website.

The easiest installation process will use Fantastico or SimpleScripts. (Well, actually the easiest will be if your tech support operator says, "No problem, I can do that for you"—but they are more likely to direct you through each step, with you working on your computer while you talk with them.) It will be an excellent learning experience for you. Once WordPress is installed, when you type your domain name into a browser (and remember to click the refresh button), you will see the generic initial WordPress page, titled "My Blog," saying "Hello world!"

ALERT

Keep track of the username and password WordPress generates so you can log in to the WordPress dashboard. You will use this over and over again as you change and expand your website. If your installation process assigns "admin" as your default user name, learn how to set up a more secure user name with administration rights and delete the too-obvious "admin" user.

Learning WordPress

Now that you have WordPress available, it's time to learn how to use this amazing platform. Because it is such a popular system, there are many online tutorials and videos to help. You'll find free help pages to read, free videos to watch, and there are complete learning systems available for a fee.

The official free tutorial for WordPress can be found at *http://codex .wordpress.org/WordPress/Lessons*, the beginner's section at the central website for all things WordPress.

For more free options, go to Google and search "WordPress tutorials." You can also go to Google and search "WordPress tutorials YouTube" to discover all sorts of videos. Watch those made on more recent dates, since the WordPress format changes frequently.

You'll get more complete training if you pay a bit. Check out Lynda .com (*www.lynda.com/WordPress-training-tutorials/330-0.html*) and look at WordPress Essential Training. Several of the videos are available for free. The entire set costs $25 for a month's access. A more comprehensive system for Internet marketing, which begins with online marketing basics and includes building a small business website step-by-step with WordPress, is found at the Take Control of Your Internet Marketing website (*www .TakeControlOfYourInternetMarketing.com/art*) for a mere $5 per month.

Classes and workshops on WordPress are often available from community colleges and small business development organizations. Also, keep in mind that many professional web designers are skilled with WordPress and can be hired to give you some basic lessons and support. Make sure you check the WordPress sites they have built and talk with some of their former clients before you hire anyone.

ESSENTIAL

Although your hosting company may agree to help you get WordPress installed and answer basic questions, it is unreasonable to expect them to teach you how to use WordPress. You are responsible for finding the learning resources that will best help you get up to speed with the WordPress system.

Customizing WordPress

WordPress creates the framework upon which you build your website. The theme you use creates the look of your site. Widgets can also help you make your website into a one-of-a-kind destination for your customers and fans.

The theme you choose will give a basic look and feel to your WordPress website. (*www.solga.com*)

Themes

Choosing a theme will be one of your first decisions after you've watched some tutorials and played around a bit with your own basic WordPress installation. You are already using a theme, probably the Twenty Twelve theme, or whatever the default is when you install. There is no reason you can't keep on using this theme, but a new theme will give a completely different look to your website. All the basic information stays the same. The pages you have created are still there, but a new theme decorates them in an entirely new way.

Each theme has its own special features, so before you get too deeply into building your website, find a theme that you want to use. Independent programmers design themes and make them available to the community of WordPress users. Some themes are free, others cost money. You want to find a theme that:

- Looks great for your artwork
- Can be further customized with your own colors, fonts, and graphics
- Gives you the functions you want for your website
- Is actively supported and regularly updated by the programmers who created the theme

FACT

Commercial themes that cost a bit of money are far more likely to be updated and supported than free themes.

Go to *www.wordpress.org/extend/themes* and begin exploring theme options. You can also go to the Themes section of your WordPress control dashboard—Appearance/Themes/Install Themes/Featured—and see all sorts of free themes to preview. You can search Google for "WordPress theme art gallery" or "WordPress e-commerce theme." If a theme catches your eye, check out its support pages and return again to Google to search specifically for that theme. See what people have to say. How many downloads have there been, and what sort of rating have users given it? Is the theme responsive, or in other words, does it have the ability to change itself depending on whether people are viewing your website with a big computer or a tiny smartphone? Make sure the theme you select is well used and well liked by lots of other users.

Once you decide on a theme, simply go to your WordPress control dashboard, search for and find the theme you want, and install it. When installed, it will become one of the available themes to activate in the other dashboard Themes tab, the one called Manage Themes.

ALERT

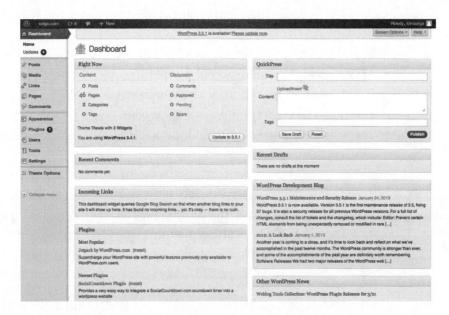

The WordPress Dashboard is the control center for all edits and additions to your new website.

Plug-ins

Along with thousands of independently designed themes, there are thousands of plug-ins that expand the function of your WordPress website. There are plug-ins to create forms for accepting e-mailed inquiries, to make slideshows from uploaded images, to help you with Search Engine Optimization, to add social media icons, to easily backup your entire Wordpress website, and to save archives in case you want to move or if there is a server error.

You'll discover many plug-ins as you proceed with your adventures with WordPress. Or, you won't use any. But know that they are all listed at *www.wordpress.org/extend/plugins*, and you can install the ones that will help you do what you want your website to do. A few favorites to check out include the following:

- **NextGEN Gallery** builds amazing photo gallery displays and slide-shows, and lets you watermark images.
- **All in One SEO Pack** helps you tweak your pages for search engine relevancy.
- **SI CAPTCHA Anti-Spam** creates the little "type what you see in the box below" field that allows real people to send comments, but blocks robot spam machines from doing the same.
- **Google XML Sitemaps** helps search engines index your website.
- **Gravity Forms** makes forms so people can e-mail you with specific information included.
- **Table Press** allows you to arrange words and photos in neat rows and columns, a task otherwise difficult with WordPress, which tends to simply let paragraphs wrap around photos.
- **AddToAny Subscribe Button** provides subscription options for folks who want to be notified whenever you post something new.
- **Share Buttons by Lockerz/AddToAny** creates little social media buttons that let people easily share your post on their Facebook pages, pin your photo on Pinterest, e-mail your article to friends, and lots more.
- **Limit Login Attempts**, a simple security plug-in that prevents robotic spammers from attempting to log into your website.
- **BackupCreator** is an inexpensive plug-in that lets you easily archive your WordPress website so you have a secure back-up in case anything ever goes wrong. (*www.backupcreator.com*)

Stats

A good hosting company will have a system to track and display your web stats. Ask the tech support people how you view your stats, and learn as much as you can about the information collected there. If the stats provided by the server are not easy and complete, open a free Google Analytics account (*www.google.com/analytics*) and connect your website. The free Google system will keep track of the traffic on your website and create all sorts of interesting reports for you to look at each month. You can discover how many visitors you have, where they are coming from, what pages on your site they are looking at, and how long they stick around. You can see what site they were on just before coming to your site, and thus see which other places on the Internet are sending you the most visitors.

Do you have a paid banner ad on another website? Analytics will tell you how effective it is. Do you see unexpected traffic from other sites who have promoted you, mentioned your artwork, and linked to your website? Link back to and cultivate those connections. You can discover where you are making the most impact, and use your web stats to make all of your major online marketing decisions.

The Elements of Your WordPress Website

Depending on the theme you decide to use, a typical WordPress site will have these areas for you to populate:

- **A header image.** This is similar to your header graphic on a marketplace shop. Design this carefully to establish your unique identity. Remember the importance of branding your work, using a unified theme of color, font, and images. Keep your header image short— as wide as your web page, but not very tall. The top of a web page is valuable online real estate, and you don't want to use it all up with a header bar that takes up too much space.
- **A menu bar**, with top level tabs and pull down tabs that appear beneath the top tabs when the cursor moves over. Plan your site navigation carefully so your top level tabs, the main sections of your website, fit comfortably across the page on a single bar.
- **One or two sidebars.** These skinny columns are great places to put navigation links for your website pages, your contact information, and the various little icons for your social media pages such as Facebook and Twitter. You can include forms and widgets from other websites, such as a sign-up form for your newsletter, or a small display of items from your ArtFire or Etsy shop.
- **The main page content**, which is the largest area on your WordPress layout. Your use of keywords in each page title and in the paragraphs

on the page will make a huge difference in the way search engines will be able to find and link your website.

- **The page footer,** a narrow area at the bottom of each page with the small WordPress link. Put your contact address and e-mail down here and be sure to add your copyright notice.

Northern California artist Lauri Sturdivant uses a WordPress website with all of the traditional elements. (*www.lauristurdivant.com*)

Blog

The WordPress system can create both pages and posts. Pages are simply web pages, like the pages of a book. Each one is filled with whatever words and pictures you want to put there, and they are connected to one another with links (as in "Click here for page 2"), or as tabs on your navigation bar. Posts, traditionally much shorter, are news postings, and in their simplest manifestation, they show up on a blog page of your website. This page displays the most recent four posts, or six, or ten—you set the number. Whenever you write a new post, it appears at the top, pushes the older ones down, and the last one falls off the display. Most blogs are set to allow comments to be added by readers, always a popular option and under your full control. Comments don't show up on the website until you approve them. Fans love blogs and will return often to see what new adventures you've been up to.

Adding a blog to your WordPress website is as simple as creating a new page and designating it to be your posts page (Settings/Reading), then writing your first post. Ta da! You are a blogger. You can blog as often as you wish, but you should try to write a new post at least once a week. Keep your posts short and sweet. Write as if you are chatting with a good friend. Blogs are a conversation with your readers. A blog post is usually just a few paragraphs long, 400 words or so, with a photo to illustrate. If you have more to say, break it down into several different posts over a couple of days. If you are off on vacation, you can create a series of posts ahead of time, then schedule them to publish themselves on future dates.

Carol Jenkins uses a WordPress theme that easily creates online galleries for her vibrant abstract paintings. (*www.caroljenkinsart.com*)

ALERT

Visit the blog for this book at *www.SellingArtsandCraftsOnline.com* to see an example of the WordPress blogging platform and to have the opportunity to get your own website featured on the "Inspired" pages.

Selling Your Products

You can sell your products on your website. You certainly don't have to if you are working a marketplace shop where everything is already for sale. You can simply link to your marketplace shop and send customers there. For example, you can link to your print-on-demand profile so your customers can easily go order prints of your artwork, or you can link to your eBay store to share your current auctions. However, there are several persuasive reasons to sell your products right on your own website:

- No distractions. On marketplace websites, your customers may be just as likely to begin surfing to look at other artists and crafters. There's no guarantee they will stick to your products. On your own website, there are no competitors to confuse buyers. You keep all the attention yourself.
- Better branding. You can totally control the design of your website pages, and present your work exactly the way you want to be known.
- It's simpler for your customers. No need for them to go to a different website or set up a buyer's profile with another system if they can easily purchase things directly from you.
- No fees or commissions taken out, except of course the inevitable credit card processing fee charged by your payment gateway.
- You control your own destiny. No corporate decision by another company will ever close your shop down. As unlikely as it is that Etsy, ArtFire, CafePress, or ImageReady will go out of business, the fact remains that if you are selling only on their websites, you are completely dependent on them to stay in business. By designing your own shop within WordPress, a system you can move to any number of different hosting companies, you increase your options and your control.

The simplest way to take online orders is to use PayPal as your payment gateway and create "Add to Cart" buttons. On PayPal.com, you log in to your account and build a button for each of your products. PayPal provides a little chunk of HTML code for that button. You copy that code, and then when you return to your own website, you paste the code on a webpage so that "Add to Cart" button shows up next to the appropriate product photo. Buyers click the button and the free PayPal shopping cart goes into action, with a checkout page specific to your business. It's secure, customers can use any credit card, and you are notified when there is an order to ship. The money (less PayPal's usual percentage for processing the card) gets credited to your PayPal account, and you can transfer it into your bank account.

This individual button system works pretty well if you have just a few products, but gets pretty cumbersome if you are selling dozens or hundreds of one-of-a-kind items. At that level of inventory you really need a more sophisticated shopping cart with a management interface that lets you set prices, display items in categories and on individual pages, and easily add new items into a database of products.

There are shopping cart themes and plug-ins for WordPress that will do all of this and more. Search *www.wordpress.org/extend/plugins* for "shopping cart" to discover your options, including WP Marketplace, Simple Ecommerce Shopping Cart, TheCartPress, WP e-Commerce, and many others. Or search Google for "WordPress shopping cart themes." Each of these plug-ins and themes has been developed by an independent programmer, and most will have their own website and support system. Some may be free; others may cost money. Still others may be "shareware," which means that if you try it and end up using it, you should play fair and make a donation to the programmer who developed it. Look for a system that has been used widely, has lots of downloads, and has good ratings from its users.

Search Engine Optimization (SEO)

SEO stands for Search Engine Optimization, and is the art and science of getting your website to show up in search engines for your key search terms. Despite the reputation, SEO is mainly common sense. Know your key search terms, and use them in your website. That's basically it.

Specific to using WordPress, there are two areas where it is really important to use keywords: in your page title and in the hidden meta description tag on each page. Search engines are gigantic robot systems that work by "reading" the code that creates each webpage on the Internet. It's hard to imagine how many pages that would be . . . billions and growing every moment. The search engine machine is programmed to build a database out of the words on each web page and to assign more significance to words that appear in particular spots. The page title is a very important spot. Back to common sense, the page title *must* be what a page is about, right?

If someone goes to a search engine such as Google or the internal search engine used on the Etsy website and types in "encaustic art," that machine is programmed to return web pages about "encaustic art." The top results will be pages where those words are part of the page title.

Your job as webmaster is to make sure that the title you write for each of your web pages contains the most powerful search words for that particular page. Thus the "about" page on your website should not be titled "All about Me"—it should be titled "Artist Mary Smith Encaustic Wax Painter." Those same words should also be repeated in the paragraphs on that page. Yes, the search engine robots check this. "This page says it is about 'Artist Mary Smith Encaustic Wax Painter'—but is it really? Oh yeah, there are those same words down on the page, too. It really is." You are allowed up to seventy characters (letters and spaces) for a title. Use them well. "Artist Mary Smith Encaustic Wax Painter" only uses thirty-nine, so if Mary was especially well known within the encaustic art movement of Boston, she might add "Boston" to her title. That way, if someone searched for "Boston encaustic artist," her title would have all those words and her page would meet their needs perfectly.

Meta Tags

Meta tags hold instructions for Internet browser programs. The meta description field is a hidden part of a webpage and is meant to be a clearly written sentence or two that tells precisely what this particular page is about. This 160-character field is indexed by search engines and sometimes used to describe your web page when the list of suggested links is returned to a searcher. Some WordPress themes give you a box where you can specify the meta description tag. Other themes do not. If the theme you choose for your site does not have this field on the editing interface for each page, you can install a plug-in such as "All in One SEO" to add this editing field. Again, use your most powerful search words in this sentence, and write it so that a reader can see at a glance what your page is about.

ALERT

Sign up for the free Google Webmaster Tools (*www.google.com/webmasters*). You will learn everything you need to know about SEO with the videos and articles offered in Webmaster Academy.

There are many more factors to search engines and how they rank websites, but all searches begin with page titles and descriptions. Use these two fields correctly. It will make a positive difference in how your new website shows up.

Words of Wisdom

Jenny Hoople makes the most amazing river rock jewelry, turning smooth pebbles into necklaces, earrings, and other pieces of wearable natural art. She assembles matched stones to create "rainbow" necklaces, with the colors of the rocks moving through a subtle spectrum from gray through gold, from deep purple through delicate lavender—all with undyed, natural pebbles. "I've always been the sort to pick up interesting stones and carry them home with me, so much so that I minored in geology in college," says Jenny. Jenny sells her products on Etsy, and offers both retail and wholesale on her own website at jennyhoople.com.

Jenny has branded her business clearly, with natural colors, brown paper, clear product photos on white backgrounds, and a handwritten logo that carries all the way through to the notes she includes with packed orders.

The Authentic Arts website is sophisticated and includes a full-featured shopping cart. "My current site is a couple generations in. I started with a free Google site that was really simple and linked to my Etsy shop. Then I built a WordPress site using a theme that I quickly outgrew. It wasn't versatile enough! I did a lot of searching for best e-commerce WordPress themes and picked the one that I use now," Jenny explains. "It had excellent features and customer service and simply looked the best!"

The flexible WordPress platform allows Jenny to have web pages, a shopping cart system for her products, and a blog. "The shopping cart is built in. My site uses a very inclusive theme, so self-contained that it actually can't work with most plug-ins." In her Authentic Living Blog she writes and posts great photos about geology, her passion for nature, lifestyle and urban homesteading, her own travels and adventures . . . and her products. It's a wonderful example of a blog that is not all about selling things, and yet inspires and enhances every sale she makes.

Learning WordPress is no simple task. "I learned everything online just searching around! It took *so* much energy to learn the basics of dealing with website host companies. I did it all myself for the first WordPress site I set up, but that theme was very simple. I had a programmer set up the current theme, and then I uploaded my photos, customized the backgrounds, wrote the copy, and so on."

The Authentic Arts website has a blog that readers can subscribe to, a newsletter signup for, and a link making it easy to share pages and products on social media websites.

The importance of carefully selecting the theme for your WordPress site is explained here by Jenny's experience. "Get ready to learn . . . *a lot*. And get ready to have the company that made your theme suddenly disappear and stop answering your e-mails when you need help with the next WordPress update. (Yes, this really happened to me just this year!) My site still works for now, but I can never again get tech help with my theme and I can never update to newer versions of WordPress. It is possible to switch a WordPress site to a new theme and keep most of your website content intact, but it depends on the theme. When I switched between the first, simpler theme to my current one, I had to redo everything from scratch because the themes were so different! I'd say that self-hosted WordPress sites are great to get you off the ground and rolling quickly for little investment. But they are not a permanent solution if you're serious about your business!" Visit (*www.jennyhoople.com*) and (*www.etsy.com/shop/ AuthenticStone*) for more information.

Beyond WordPress

WordPress is a fantastic system for creating and managing your own simple website, but it is certainly not the only system available. There are many other options, some more simple, some far more complex. From GoDaddy's Website Builder to Homestead.com (*www.homestead.com*), Wix.com (*www.wix.com*), and Webs.com (*www.webs.com*), there are hundreds of online systems that will allow you to build a simple website. In most cases you'll be signing up and staying with the company that provides the platform. You won't be able to archive your website and host it somewhere else later. If you are considering any of these services, check out the hosting fees, startup fees, and any limitations to your space. Ask if you are able to optimize SEO fields. Ask which payment processing systems are supported and if there are additional costs for shopping cart features. And be sure you can use your own domain URL, one you have registered and control yourself, on all of your web pages.

ALERT

You can point your domain name to wherever you build your website. Do it yourself by editing the nameservers on the management interface at your domain registrar. Never transfer your domain name management to a hosting company.

When you are ready to expand to a full-features shopping cart website, you might wish to consider the platforms specifically designed for selling arts and crafts online. These systems provide templates to create a professional online store with your own web address, custom look and feel, and shopping cart system. A few of the options include:

1. **BigCartel.com** "where artists set up shop," lets you build customizable e-commerce websites. "We provide clothing designers, bands, jewelry

makers, crafters, and other artists with their own customizable store to sell their stuff online." Find plenty of examples to check out at *www .directory.bigcartel.com*.

2. **Silkfair.com** offers completely customizable websites, as well as a marketplace shopping area.

3. **Shopify.com** is a huge platform for online stores. See examples of websites using this system at *www.shopify.com/examples*.

It is customary on the Internet for successful companies to redesign their websites every few years. The business grows and the Internet changes. Selling art and handcrafts is no exception. But the good news is that you do not have to begin with a fully featured shopping cart website. Keep it simple. Artists and crafters entering the world of online sales should plan to start with a small website that they can easily edit themselves, and expand it as they grow.

CHAPTER 12

Writing for the Internet

Successful online artists and crafters understand how to talk about their artwork, including the words they use to describe themselves and their products on the Internet. They know how to weave together the mystery and the facts to create a compelling story. They understand how people read text on the Internet and how to present their writing in the best possible format. Successful artists and artisans have learned how to be their own best marketing agents and encourage readers to enjoy, experience, and buy their artwork.

Whether you are writing about yourself for the Bio page of your website, or guest blogging for a colleague, or writing product descriptions for your marketplace shop, your words should inspire readers to connect with you. To do this, you first need to catch their attention!

Write Text That People Can Read at a Glance

To write good website copy, it is important to understand how people read the Internet. Webpages are not read like books, magazines, or newspapers. On the Internet, people jump around from place to place, site to site, sometimes barely glancing at a web page before moving on. You have a few seconds to catch their attention, and the way you put words and sentences onto your webpages plays a huge part in whether viewers will stick around long enough to read your message.

Internet expert Jakob Nielsen found that most Internet users do not actually read web pages. Instead, they scan the text, picking out individual words and phrases as they look at a webpage. (*www.nngroup .com/articles/how-users-read-on-the-web*)

Website copy that can be easily scanned by viewers is broken down into short, easy-to-read bits. The elements of good copy include:

- Meaningful subheadings
- Short, one-idea paragraphs
- Bulleted lists
- Fewer words

Here's an example of the difference between old-style copywriting and the new, concise Internet style. Which is easier to read? Which gives more information?

Conventional Promotional Writing—73 words:

This striking necklace has antique parts that glitter and shine as you move. It will bring you plenty of admiring comments, without fail. Fastened securely in this steampunk-style pendant are an old watch mechanism (from 1920) on a filigree backing, a skeleton key, a dangling jewel of clear quartz, and a little moon and star cut out of brass and tarnished for an aged look. The clunky chain has a curly clasp.

Concise Internet Writing—65 words:

Handcrafted Steampunk Watchworks Necklace "Time Gone By"

- Pendant features clock movement reclaimed from vintage 1920 wristwatch.
- Sturdy assembly on 2-inch Victorian filigree setting.
- Neutral golden tones with silver highlights.
- Embellished with brass moon and star charms and tiny antique key.
- The pendant is finished with a sparkling quartz crystal gem.
- 18-inch ladder chain with handcrafted spiral clasp can be resized for perfect fit.

Internet users want to get clear, simple information. They want to get it fast, in text that is short and to the point. They do not want to read boastful statements or advertising copy. They want to get the straight facts. Good Internet writing gives viewers exactly what they want . . . honest, friendly words arranged in easy-to-read bits that can be scanned and understood quickly.

ESSENTIAL

"People do not buy products, but meanings. People use things for profound emotional, psychological, and sociocultural reasons, as well as utilitarian ones. . . . Look beyond features, functions, and performance and understand the real meanings users give to things."
—Roberto Verganti, in his book *Design-Driven Innovation*

Product Descriptions

The most important Internet writing you do will be your product descriptions. Your words will inspire viewers to add that item to their shopping carts. Remember that customers buy benefits even if they think they are shopping for features. They buy products because these items help them feel good about themselves, enhance their enjoyment or comfort, and communicate their style. When you write about your products, speak in terms of the benefits your item will bring to the buyer.

For example:

- Handcrafted sterling silver earrings dangle at just the right length, sassy with jeans and boots, amazing with your best slinky black dress.
- Pack this gourmet chocolate assortment in a boutique-style gift box wrapped with a silk bow for elegant gift giving on both personal and business occasions. Happy to include a gift card with your personal greeting!
- Soon to be your favorite footwear, these handstitched leather moccasins will cradle your feet in triple-sole comfort for years of dependable use, indoors and out.
- Artisan reading lamps with ivory rice paper shades bring soft, golden light and relaxation to your library corner.

Write to Your Audience

Speak directly to your perfect customer, the typical person who buys most of your products and probably accounts for 80 percent of your sales. When you write product descriptions, keep this customer in mind. Write with the words and the phrases that he would use to talk about the wonderful handcraft he just purchased from you.

Visitors to your marketplace shop or website are as curious about you as they are about your products. They have sought out handcrafted work because they value the creative process. Share yourself. Use the "I" word, and write as if you are talking to a friend.

Here's a great example from Jenny Hoople's Authentic Arts website for the product she calls "Natural Slate Cairn Necklace handmade with New York Beach Stone":

"I handmade this natural slate cairn necklace from smooth, grey slate rocks that I gathered on the shores of Seneca Lake, NY and drilled myself. Cairns are important. I bet the first way a human ever shouted out 'I'm here and I matter!' was by building a cairn! (The beach pictured is the one these slate stones came from!)" (*www.jennyhoople.com*)

What to Avoid

Online customers are clear about what makes them decide to not buy from an online shop or website. Here are a few of the major buyer turnoffs, as seen on recent online discussion boards at Etsy:

- Really long descriptions that contain information not at all pertinent to the item.
- Really short listings that tell nothing at all.
- Descriptions that do not tell how the item was made, especially for pieces of art.
- Not explaining the dimensions of an item or what materials were used.
- Misleading terms that are used in a description.
- Errors in spelling or grammar.
- Sellers who don't bother to include shipping prices for other countries.
- Too many links in a description.
- Terms and conditions written in a hostile tone.

Testimonials Are Powerful

Customer comments or "testimonials" are great tools to promote your products. Believable comments from real-life customers add credibility to any message. It could be a comment about the quality of your products or how someone has used one of your art pieces in a special way. It could be a note on how fast shipping was or how delightful it felt to open your clever packaging. It could be a specific thank-you for service above and beyond the call of duty. It might be a note of satisfaction from someone who commissioned you to create a special product.

People tend to trust the word of another customer, even if it's an opinion from someone they have never heard of and will never meet. It's a basic human trait to listen to what others have to say. But to positively influence a potential customer's buying decision, a testimonial must pass these tests:

1. It must be conversational and believable. If a testimonial sounds like "marketing fluff," it will have the opposite effect and turn your potential customers away.
2. It must be specific. General comments such as "Carrie makes great soap!" won't have anywhere near the impact as a comment like "My husband loves your Sage Pinon Soap. Thanks, Carrie, for creating a scent for both of us."
3. It must come from real people your customers can relate to.

Gather and save the good things your customers have to say about you and scatter their comments around on your web pages. You can even include short testimonials in your product descriptions.

Words of Wisdom

Christina from Cardiff, Wales, in the United Kingdom creates all things shiny at *Jackdaw* on Etsy—pendants, rings, pins, and earrings. "I love making jewelry. I am so happy to have it as a hobby. It provides me with a creative outlet and a way to relax after a hard day at the office. My office work is mostly administrative/computer based, so I love to come home, put on some trash TV, and just sit and make some new pieces. It gives me a real buzz when

I see my work being sold at gift shops, displayed nicely in their glass cabinets," she says.

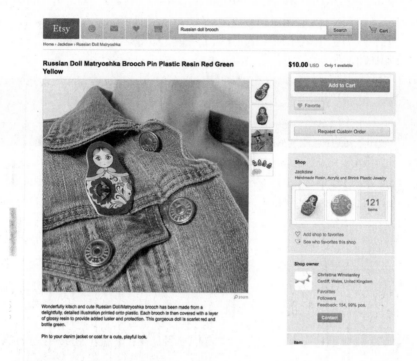

Jackdaw's product names are descriptive and contain the keywords that help customers find Christina's clever jewelry. (*www.etsy.com/shop/Jackdaw*)

Christina uses all of the best Internet writing practices in her product descriptions. From title to item tags, the information is presented in an easy-to-read format so viewers can see, at a glance, the features of the product. In the product description for her Matryoshka Brooch, Christina includes:

- A three-sentence explanation of a matryoshka, giving the opportunity to use additional searchable words such as "Russian nesting doll," "babushka dolls," and "grandmother doll."
- The pin's measurements and materials.
- A packaging section that clearly suggests how perfect the product is for gift giving. "Brooch presented on a Jackdaw branded cloud card. All orders come gift ready, wrapped in gift wrap and finished with decorative ribbon."

- Instructions on how to care for the brooch, further emphasizing the attention to detail that goes into her products.
- Short testimonials. "What people are saying about Jackdaw: Adorable!!! Impossibly fast receipt of product (came all the way from Wales . . . HOW did you do that?!?)! Beautifully packaged!"
- Shipping prices, an invitation to contact the artist, and Christina's professional copyright. "All designs are the property of Miss. Christina Winstanley ©2013 Jackdaw."

Although she calls herself a part-time Etsy seller with another career, Christina's products and presentation are clearly professional. "I love running into people that wear my work. This happened just recently at my full-time job. I was discussing a project with a colleague and looked up and happened to notice she was wearing a pair of my earrings. She had purchased them at a craft fair I had attended over Christmas. Small world!"

Visit *www.etsy.com/shop/Jackdaw* for more information, and to see Christina's work.

Good Internet Writing Uses Power Keywords

When someone searches on the Internet, whether she is using a major search engine such as Google or she is searching within a marketplace site like Etsy, she uses a search box to type what she wishes to find. Your ideal customers are typing words to search for your artwork, though they may not yet know that you exist. What words are they typing? Those exact words need to appear on your web pages in order for search engine systems to "find" you and return your site to searchers as an appropriate link.

The very words on your page are part of the search engine's calculations. And when keywords are included in headlines and in page titles, search engines consider them even more relevant. So collect your power keywords and use them. Make sure your product names and the headlines on your web pages are packed with words that count.

Keywords in Titles

When you add a product to a marketplace shop, you give your product a name. When you write your blog page, you give your post a title. When you create a new page on your website, you name it something. Make these titles count! Write titles with the most powerful keywords for that page, the words that your ideal customers will be using to locate such products or information.

Headings and Subheadings

As you write copy on your blog or website, break the text up into simple, scan-able chunks. Separate your paragraphs with headings and subheadings—simple little three- to seven-word phrases that are bold and a bit larger than your regular words. Subheadings should contain the most essential words about your topic or your product. They should be written using your power keywords.

You can probably guess many of your keywords and key phrases. They will be the terms you use as you talk about your artwork. There will be other keywords you can discover from talking with your customers and in your shop or website stats. You can also use the Internet itself to discover search terms and keywords that you may not think of yourself:

- Go to Google.com. Search for one of your key phrases, something you clearly know is a term for your artwork. Then scroll down to the bottom of the search results page and look at the related searches. These are suggestions from Google for other ways to search for the information you seek. For a business owner, these related search terms may reveal important keywords that can be incorporated into your web pages and product descriptions. For example, searching Google for "wilderness paintings" reveals several related searches, including "sunset paintings," "bison paintings," and "outdoor artwork." All of these phrases are frequently searched for on Google by the same people who searched for "wilderness paintings." Use these terms to spark a new blog post, to write a new description or title on an existing product, or simply to work into your current website copy.

- Pay attention to the "suggested" terms that Google offers as you type into the search box. Go to Google.com and begin slowly typing in any of your power search words. Notice the drop down list of suggestions that shows up as you type. These are statistically the most common things that people will be typing in next. Google is providing them as a shortcut. Find the ones that are relevant to your website, then make sure you use those words in titles, in headlines, and on pages. Give the people what they already want.
- On your stats reports, you can see the actual words that people were searching for when they clicked through to your web page from a search engine. This tells you which words are already working for your website. It can give you a good idea of what people are seeking, and what trends and phrases are being used by the people who have proven themselves to be curious about your website.

Writing Your Own Profile

As tough as it is to write good product descriptions, it is much harder to talk about yourself. To capture your own personality and talents in words suitable for the general public can be intimidating. And yet, who you are is one of the main reasons people will come to your website and end up buying your work. You are the face behind the handcraft—the human part of the sales experience. So turn your focus inward and write a profile piece for your marketplace shop, and another version (not the same words) for your website, and edited versions for other online locations that call for an "about the artist" page. Here are a few ideas to get you started:

1. Say hello. Greet the reader. Write directly to them.
2. Where do you live? Where are you from? How has your location helped form your artwork?
3. What other influences mean the most to you? What people, styles, and eras, and events in life?
4. How did you start your craft? What were your first learning experiences?
5. What do you create? What sort of items do you make?
6. Why do you create? How is your work important in your life?

7. What is the process like? Describe your studio space. Provide a snapshot into your life as an artist or artisan.
8. What materials do you use? How are they special?
9. Why do people love owning the things you make?
10. Tell stories. Can you share any funny or sweet anecdotes about one of your pieces or your life as an artist or crafter?
11. If you've won important awards, mention them, but please don't list too many. A few, perhaps, and in the context of how you walk in the world as an artist, not as a bragging list.
12. How can people see more work? Link your marketplace shop, your social media profiles, your blog, and your e-mail.

To get the creative juices going, start with a flow-of-consciousness exercise. Write about yourself for 10 minutes without taking the pen off the paper—not editing, not pausing. Then, using this as notes, carefully write the profile you will further edit and eventually put online.

More Internet Writing Tips

When you write the copy for your web pages and product descriptions, you become your own marketing department. Take your job as seriously as if you were a corporation hiring an advertising firm to launch a worldwide campaign.

- Write with a simple text-editing program. If you'd rather use a full-featured program like Microsoft Word, remember to remove all fancy formatting before you paste things onto web interfaces.
- Look at your web pages with different browser programs. Fancy quotation marks that look fine on Internet Explorer might have all sorts of strange errors in Firefox or Safari. Try to get your text formatting down to the simplest and most basic characters.
- Avoid exclamation points. Let your readers feel the excitement by themselves—don't force it.
- Keep sentences short. As you look over your writing before you put it online, separate long clunky sentences into two or even three short

sentences. A sentence should be no longer than one line across a web page column.

- Assume the sale. Write something like: "Contact me to see mat colors and frames recommended for your new print."
- Learn the proper way to use their, there, and they're. Learn the use of it's and its. And "a lot" is two words.
- Use headlines and bulleted lists.
- Do not ever use ALL CAPITAL LETTERS.
- Include your brand name often in your writing. "Your skin deserves soap from Anderson Soap Company!" begins each description at Dennis Anderson's successful Etsy shop. Get your name out there and known. (*www.etsy.com/shop/AndersonSoapCompany*)
- Communicate everything essential in the first short paragraph, and then expand the details in subsequent paragraphs. If someone only reads the first paragraph, he should have a solid idea what your product is, what it does, and why he should own it.
- Mention dimensions and materials in benefits-oriented statements. Features are important, but take advantage of each opportunity to suggest the emotional reasons for owning your products.
- Plain language is always the best practice. Use words that most of your readers will immediately understand. Always try to think of a shorter way to explain something, or a shorter word to use.

The Internet is a very forgiving place. You won't have the same pressure you feel when writing copy for a book or catalog, where you will commit to thousands of copies the moment you send the project off to the printing company. On the Internet you can log in and change what you wrote yesterday, easily and immediately. So do not hesitate to get your writing out there. You will improve your skills with practice, and can always return to make things better.

CHAPTER 13

Effective Online Photography

Photography is the one element that will have the most impact on your success as an online arts and crafts seller. Your photos essentially are your products in an online store. If you have poor product photos, your items will not sell well, it is as simple as that. No matter what else you do; no matter how well your real items are made, how often you blog, how many marketplace sites you create, how well you integrate search terms into your product titles and descriptions, how often you tweet . . . your product photos must be clear and beautiful for your artwork to be successful on the Internet.

Large retailers can hire professional photographers to take exquisite photos for the store website. They are planning on selling thousands of each item. Investing in professional photos is an easy budget decision for them. Handmade businesses are selling one-of-a-kind items, yet competing in the same market. The wonderful photos they see on large retail websites already establish customers' expectations. They unconsciously expect to see the same at Etsy and ArtFire, at eBay, and on artisan websites. But hiring a professional to take multiple pictures of every scarf or teapot or basket is far beyond small business budgets. Artists and crafters must come up with the skills and equipment to create their own excellent product photos.

Happily, with today's great digital cameras and the many fine examples of product photography seen on handmade blogs, websites, and marketplace shops, it is not impossible to learn how to take your own good product photos. A good sense of design and creativity helps, but these are attributes that artists and artisans have in abundance.

What Makes Great Product Photography?

A good product photo is crisp and focused. At a glance, the viewer can clearly see the detail and texture, how well the item is made, and all of its unique handcrafted goodness. A good photo will communicate as much as possible about the real product, everything that an online customer needs to know.

The Right Details

Alyssa photographs her intricate polymer clay sculptures on a white surface, then uses Photoshop to create a subtle reflection effect to catch the viewer's eye (*www.etsy.com/shop/ClaydeLys1*). In a good product photo, the lighting is bright and natural. The exact colors of the product show up clearly. This is essential to online sales, because the photos must honestly represent the item that will eventually get shipped to a buyer. But beyond that, if photos are not taken with proper lighting, an ugly yellowish or gray tone can totally cheapen the feeling of the photo. Full spectrum light bulbs and natural sunlight help get the brightest, most realistic colors.

This sculpture is photographed well, with good lighting, and accurate color. (*www.etsy.com/shop/ClaydeLys1*)

In a good product photo, the lighting is smooth. There are no hard shadows cast by flash lighting, and no glaring "hot spot" reflections from direct spotlights. The light is bright, but not harsh. Learning how to photograph with diffused or reflected light is the key here.

Good product photography gets up close and personal. Detail photos show the quality of a handmade object, the hand stitching on a leather wallet, the bamboo buttons that fasten a shawl, the luxurious fiber of handspun yarns.

A good product photo shows the product against a simple background that enhances the item being pictured. The setting does not compete with the product. The item stands out clearly as the centerpiece of the photo. A white background with the softest possible shadows is a classic setting for product photography. While black velvet may be the classic surface for showing fine jewelry in person, it does not make a good product photo.

Stay light! Other great backgrounds for handcrafts include weathered wood, stone, and flat beige or tan walls.

Knitware from *The Knotty Needle* is photographed to communicate all the luxurious details of yarn, pattern, and wrap. (*www.etsy.com/shop/TheKnottyNeedle*)

Show Variety

With good product photography, multiple photos show different angles. When an item is presented on a website or marketplace product page, there are several photos to look at. The viewer has all the information she needs to know the product inside and out, as if she had been able to pick it up and turn it over in her hands.

Along with photos of the item on a plain white background, good product photography will also show the item in a natural setting, giving the viewer an idea of how it will look in her home. A common object can be included to communicate the size of the product, such as apples in a pottery bowl, cut flowers in a market basket, a framed watercolor leaning on a stone mantle with a single leafy twig. Placing a small, brightly colored object alongside a handcrafted product of neutral color tone can "pop" an otherwise bland photo.

Deb photographs her ceramic colander with strawberries to suggest the item's use and size and to add a sparkle of color. (*www.blueskypotterycolorado.com*)

Your photos should also suggest the different ways a product can be used, and the different needs that buying the item can satisfy. If your product is a popular gift item, for example, use one of your product photos to show it in full gift-wrapped glory.

Include at least one shot with a model wherever appropriate. A hand-knit baby sweater can be photographed on a background, with close up details of sleeves and ribbon tie. But the photo of the sweater worn by a precious smiling baby will make the sale. Show necklaces on attractive necks, shawls draped over shoulders, hats on interesting faces. Observe how the very expressions and posture of models can help set the tone for an item. There's nothing like the human form to draw the eyes of viewers.

Some one-of-a-kind items are perhaps best not shown on a model. Many buyers do not like the feeling that anyone else has worn the item they want to buy. Instead, show earrings hanging from a driftwood stick or seashell, or held up next to the model's ear. If you photograph a model wearing your lacy undies, make sure the item description clearly states that the undies being shipped will be brand new and not the ones shown in the photo.

Take time to prepare and arrange products carefully to get the best product photographs. Carefully iron clothes and fluff fiber items, buff pottery and polish finished woodwork. Create pleasant arrangements. This is your stage! Drape that silk scarf in graceful swirls to show off the handpainted design. Fan out the plant markers. Stack the bowls in a rainbow. Hang colorful little onesies on a line to show variations. A good product photo communicates care and attention to detail from beginning to end.

Tana of *PrairiePrimitives* showcases her folk art pieces on a background of rustic weathered wood. (*www.etsy.com/shop/PrairiePrimitives*)

If your product is part of a set or series, include at least one photo that shows the entire collection. A pottery soup bowl, for example, may be the product, but one photo can show an entire place setting of matching dishes, the bowl perched on salad plate and dinner plate, with coffee mug on the side. Customers can see the extent of your skills and may be inspired to purchase more than one item.

The composition of a great product photo is interesting, with an artful arrangement of foreground items and background space. Photocomposition is often done with editing software, cropping down to the best section of a larger photo, and angling the photo to create interesting negative space around the product.

Good product photography is an essential part of the identity and branding of your work. Develop a particular style that becomes your signature. Use similar lighting and color palette to tie all of the items you create into a unified body of work. Your backgrounds don't have to be the same for every product, but they should all work together to set a consistent tone. You will end up with favorite backgrounds you use over and over again—perhaps a panel of old boards, a blond wooden tabletop, or a smooth river stone upon which you arrange jewelry. These standard props help to set the atmosphere of your studio and your online shop.

Learn to Take Good Photos

You don't need to be an expert photographer to take great photos of your products. You just need to be patient and have an eye for detail. Use your creativity, and don't be afraid to try different things.

Inspiration

Your first step is to get acquainted with good product photography. Spend time online looking at the best examples you can find for products similar to the artwork you create. Whatever your art or craft, seek out the websites of the top retailers in your product line. For example, if you create handcrafts that are used in homes, go to websites such as Pottery Barn, Crate and Barrel, Williams Sonoma, Martha Stewart, and Ikea. Simply spending time looking at the photos that get displayed on Etsy's home page will give you a fantastic introduction into good product photography done by artists and crafters just like yourself. Imagine your own items in the photos and settings that you admire there. Then begin to plan how you will duplicate those photos yourself.

Camera

Invest in a decent digital SLR camera. This will be the best money you spend for your online business. Consider the following before purchasing:

- How much power? 3-megapixel to 6-megapixel cameras are fine for Internet images, which are displayed at a relatively low screen resolution. But if you also plan to use your product photos for print media such as magazines and high-quality catalogs, then move up to a 7-megapixel resolution or higher. Printed images need much a higher resolution to look good. In a nutshell, if you have the money, invest in a point-and-shoot digital camera with a minimum of 7 megapixels, a good auto focus, and a 4× zoom.
- Macro focus is the ability to focus close-up. Your digital camera should have a lens made to focus as close as an inch from an object. If you make small items like jewelry, you'll want some extreme close-up detail shots. Any time you are picturing things "larger than life-size," you'll appreciate the clarity that a more powerful, higher megapixel camera will provide. Even if your items are large, you will still be taking detail photos.

ALERT

Even the smallest movement can cause a blurred photo when taking ultra-close-up shots. For best results, use a tripod and set the timer to shoot the picture so even the simple act of pressing the button won't shake the camera.

- Being able to fully control the flash function is essential. You want a camera with a flash that can be turned off so you can use studio lighting. Adjustments that allow fill flash and let you adjust flash intensity will come in handy for location shots.

- Your camera must have a built-in viewing screen so you can look at the shots you've just taken and see if you need a few more. It takes significant time and energy to set up for product photos. You want to make sure you have all the views, angles, and close-ups you need before you clean up and move on.

- White balance is a fantastic feature on new digital cameras. This high-tech setting helps the camera compensate for different lighting situations and record the most realistic color possible. It really helps when you are taking indoor photos, which will be most of the time. Set your white balance and ISO to automatic.

FACT

ISO settings handle how your camera reacts to different light conditions. Low settings work for bright scenes, and increased values are for darker situations, while a good automatic setting will adjust for you.

- Get to know the size settings on your camera. You may not need to take your photos using the largest file size available, but be sure your images are between 1MB and 3MB in size. The more digital information you have, the better. You will end up reducing the size of your photos for use on the Internet, but it helps to start with large images.

- After you decide on the camera you want, a backup battery and extra memory cards are great additional investments. You don't want to run out of power or memory in the middle of a complex photo shoot. Take lots of photos. You should have dozens of each product so you can view and select the best. It's a digital camera, remember? No film to buy, no developing costs. Don't hold back. Get a camera case too, so you can easily take your camera with you on location shots, like photographing your new jewelry on the neck of your cool surfer friend out at the beach.

- Get a camera that feels comfortable in your hands, since you will be handling it a lot. This means that you should actually shop at a camera store or the camera department of a large electronics store so you can handle different cameras and discover how each weight and shape feels.

- Should you get a tripod? Many of the latest cameras are so good at image quality for handheld shots that amateurs often sidestep getting a tripod. And for many types of product photography, this is fine. But professionals understand the value of a tripod, and would certainly encourage this addition to your photographic equipment. A tripod also becomes a really useful tool so you can be in the picture too. A camera with a timed shutter release on a tripod allows you to model that new scarf or hold that tiny animal totem sculpture yourself.

Lighting

Consistent lighting is the key to easy product photography. Do not rely on the camera flash. Continuous light will make the biggest difference between a good photo and a poor one. Although the intensity of continuous light is lower than a flash or strobe, your product "subjects" generally hold still, so a lower-light shutter speed works fine. Buy several inexpensive clip-on utility lights at the hardware store, and fit them with full-spectrum, daylight-balanced bulbs. Experiment with 30- and 60-watt bulbs before you buy stronger versions. The qualities of balanced light will show the true colors of your handcrafted work to the best advantage.

Set up a photography corner in your studio. Clip the lights to cupboards or walls to illuminate your photo space. Direct the utility lights at your product through diffuser screens to get soft, clear light. Or you can point lights so they shine on white sheets of foamboard that then reflect the light back onto the product, thus avoiding hard shadows. If you photograph models indoors, you will want a large white or light-colored backdrop, and you may wish to invest in a softbox diffusion light (only around $30).

Many photographers get the best results with natural sunlight. For small objects, set up a curved sheet of white poster board next to a bright window—bright but not in direct sunlight. The curved paper creates a seamless white background, while the natural light brings out the best in colors and details without harsh shadows.

Eclectic earrings made from old vacuum tubes by *MadScientistsDesigns* on Etsy are a challenge to photograph, but so much fun to wear. (*www.etsy.com/shop/ MadScientistsDesigns*)

If you don't want to wait around for sunlight, build yourself a light box. This is a container lined with white poster board, with sides covered in lightweight white fabric through which your spotlights can softly shine. Simply go to Google and search for "DIY lightbox" for examples and instructions.

The advantage of developing your photography skills indoors with spotlights is that you can take photos of new products easily and immediately. If you make one-of-a-kind items frequently, the sooner you get them online, the better. There's no profit to be made in work that is sitting on a shelf waiting for photos.

You will shoot some of your product photos outdoors. Models wearing garments can be just too much for a small indoor photo corner. Try photography outdoors on an overcast day (good light but no direct sun). Shoot in the full shade of a large building on a bright day. Experiment with photos taken late in the afternoon, just before dusk, a magical time loved by many photographers. Look for simple backgrounds that won't compete with the figure being photographed.

Learn Online

Watch the short video called "Product Photography for Beginners" at the Etsy support blog, *www.etsy.com/blog/en/2011/etsy-success-product-photography-for-beginners*. Whether you plan to sell on Etsy or not, this little video provides a great introduction to the learning curve ahead of you. You should then start searching Google for additional "how-to" tutorials, both on the general subject of product photography and also on specific issues as you run into challenges. There is an amazing wealth of free advice available. Sign up for a digital photography class or workshop at a nearby community college or art center.

More than anything else, practice! Take lots of photos, do your best, and be ready to photograph things again as you learn. One great feature of marketplace websites like Etsy and ArtFire are the discussion forums, where sellers offer advice to one another. It is common for a new seller, a brave and serious new shop owner, to post "Please critique my photos!" on team or support center discussion forums. The feedback is immediate and valuable. Experienced sellers will be generous and honest with opinions and suggestions.

Editing Those Photos

The photos that come out of your digital camera are the raw material for your online photos. In almost every case, these camera photos will need to be adjusted with a photo editing program before you upload them to product pages. You will use a photo-editing program to:

- Simply look at the dozens of photos you have taken, and decide which ones are the best to keep. (Feel free to delete the rejects.)
- Resize the photos so they are the optimal size required by your selling platform.
- Save images in .jpg format for the Internet.
- Crop the edges so the most interesting part of the photo is used.
- Rotate a photo if it is not quite level.
- Adjust brightness to lighten up a photo that turned out a bit too dark. This only looks natural if you are making a slight change in bright-

ness; if a source photo is much too dark, go back for a new camera shot.

- Sharpen an image. Just like brightness, this only helps if the needed change is quite small. If your source is too blurry, there is simply no digital data to bring things into focus, so once again, go take a new photo.
- Tweak the color so the photo shows the most realistic color tones possible. Never enhance color beyond what is real in the actual object. You would merely disappoint your future customer who believes he is buying what he sees in the photo.
- Many programs have automatic tools to give "the best" levels or contrast. Try them out, but trust your own eye and intuition. Sometimes the auto tools can go too far.
- Remember also to organize your digital files in a logical system so you can return to your archives and easily find photos in the future. Many online sellers rename their photo files, discarding the automatic numbers that came from the camera and using their own naming system to integrate with their inventory. Back up your growing library of photographs regularly, on an external hard drive or an online backup system in the cloud.

If you have photo-editing software on your computer, such as Photoshop or Photoshop Elements, more power to you. Photoshop is the industry standard, and is a fantastically powerful program to learn and use. Many computers come with a simple photo editing system built in, such as Preview on Mac and Windows Photo Gallery on PC. You can also download free editing software like Picasa, GIMP, or Paint.net. Or, you can learn to edit your photos at a number of free online sites . . . so many, in fact, that you have no excuse not to fall in love with one of them.

Software to Download

Here are a few products to check out:

- **Picasa** (*https://picasa.google.com*) is a free photo editing program from Google, and one of the easiest and most intuitive to use. You can download a version to work on whatever computer you are using.

- **GIMP** (*www.gimp.org/downloads*) is a free and powerful program for editing digital images. It runs on the Mac OSX, the operating system on any modern Mac computer. Many online tutorials can be found by searching Google for "gimp tutorials."
- **Paint.net** (*www.getpaint.net*) is a similar free program that runs on Windows XP/Vista/7. It also has a variety of online tutorials provided by independent programmers. You would download this program to use on your PC.

Online Photo Editing

Instead of downloading software, you can just edit your photos online using these services:

- **Google Plus** has a free online editing system called Picnik built right into *https://plus.google.com*. If you have signed up with Google for any of their free services, you can also use Google Plus. You will find the photo tool on the left sidebar. It is simple to upload photos to different albums, and edit them with the free editing system. Another advantage is that all your photos get saved online in your Google Plus albums, creating a handy backup system for your valuable image files.
- **iPiccy** (*www.ipiccy.com*) is a lovely free service where you can upload a photo, crop, retouch, then save the edited file as a new image.
- **PicMonkey** (*www.picmonkey.com*) is another free online service for photo editing.
- **Pixlr** (*www.pixlr.com*) offers an editor for advanced work, Express for efficient image editing, and Pixlr-o-matic for fun.
- **FotoFlexer** (*www.fotoflexer.com*) is yet another good online photo editing website.
- **FotoFuze** (*www.fotofuze.com*) is a simpler photo enhancement system that can integrate automatically with Etsy shops. While it does not offer the crop and rotate features that are often needed, it certainly has the ability to enhance product photos with the click of a button and make them look great.

Words of Wisdom

Heather Jessica, owner of *Papertique* on Etsy, does her own fine product photography. Her products are handcrafted cards and paper tags, delightfully designed, and dyed to create delicate color tones with an antique look. Her photographs display *Papertique* products at their best, carefully arranged on a neutral background with appropriate props such as champagne bottles (with gift tag attached) and pure white gift boxes (awaiting those tags).

Heather has long been a photographer as well as a graphic artist and designer. "Photography was a part of my design course load in college, but has been a personal interest that I have casually pursued since I was young, toddling around with a rainbow Polaroid One-Step around my neck, taking pictures, often without film even loaded into the camera!"

Lighting and arrangement help create the unique look of *Papertique* photos. "For me, natural light is the key," she says. "There are sellers who use a lightbox, which is a good fit for producing product shots with the clean white background that so many shops covet. However, my personal preference is to focus on photographing an item beautifully in a visually interesting environment as well. I feel my creative clientry appreciates the artistic presentation of my paper goods in addition to simply showing the size and color of an item."

Heather adds, "My studio is filled with windows, which lends itself wonderfully to my photography style. Shooting in natural light, plus a bit of Photoshop tweaking, brings out the organic texture of my hand-inked goodies, with a warmth that I believe is hard to reproduce using artificial light. This does mean I am influenced easily by time of day and weather conditions, but the outcome is well worth the additional planning for that one perfect shot." (*www.etsy.com/shop/papertique*)

http://papertique.etsy.com

Heather Jessica creates artful arrangements of her hand-inked, rustic paper goods and tags for photographs in her shop, *Papertique* (*www.etsy.com/shop/papertique*).

Keep Your Learning Curve Going

Excellent product photography is definitely a skill that mixes art with technology. There are plenty of resources to help you learn, and the obvious benefit of being able to take your own excellent product photos is well worth the effort. If you start to feel frustrated, simply take your camera and walk away from your products for a while. Head out to the park, the beach, or your favorite shopping center and simply play with your camera. Take random close-ups of plants and door handles, rock textures, and the kids' shoes. Have fun. You may discover new ways of using your camera, which may then inspire a new angle for a photo back in the studio and lead to your best product photos ever.

CHAPTER 14

Pricing to Make a Profit

Pricing your work is an important part of your online success, and is often a source of anxiety for new business owners. If prices are too high, sales will drop . . . or simply not even begin. If prices are too low, you'll find yourself unable to continue making new items. There's a sweet spot between these extremes—a price that is just right for your product line.

The Formula

There is a simple and elegant calculation that will bring you close to knowing the "right" price for your products. It has been around for decades, and has been the backbone of many successful businesses. The formula goes like this:

Materials + Labor + Overhead + Profit = Wholesale price
Wholesale × 2 = Retail price

Here are the definitions of each of the elements in this pricing formula.

- **Materials:** Everything that goes into your product. If you are sewing elf dolls, it's the cost of fabric, stuffing, buttons, ribbon, and yarn. Remember to include little things like the cost of thread. It's often handy to calculate this cost in a batch—buying everything you'll need to produce 10 items—then dividing to get the materials' cost per item.
- **Labor:** How long does it take to make the item, and how much is this time worth per hour? Be sure to calculate this at a fair wage. You don't want to base your business on "sweatshop" wages, whether for yourself or anyone else. Conversely, if you value your time too highly, you will soon price yourself out of the market. Be fair but don't be greedy.
- **Overhead:** This is a "per item" amount figured by adding up everything it costs for you to be in business, and then dividing that by the number of items you intend to sell. What do you spend on your business that you would not otherwise need to pay for? These costs are things like office supplies, packing tape for sealing shipping boxes, website hosting fees, the cost of your business bank account, rent for studio space, the fee your tax professional charges . . . and so on. Long-term costs should also be factored into this; for example, a new computer every few years, or repair on the sewing machine.

    When a small business first opens, there tend to be expenses the owner does not include. If you are working out of your home, in a spare bedroom perhaps, you might choose to ignore expenses like rent, electricity, and heat. After all, you're living there and would need to pay rent and utilities anyway. But remember that such costs are a legitimate part of doing business. As you grow, you may want to add these costs in anticipation of the day you will need to rent a larger studio and office space.

The number of items you sell each month should be an honest guess if you are just starting out. After a few months of sales, you will be able to track and project the real number. So . . .

Overhead total ÷ number of sales = the per item amount

- **Profit:** So what is your personal genius worth? This is the value you put on your investment of energy, your creative spark, or your unique talent. Accounting for profit now will give you a wholesale price you can live with. Some people double the price at this time, saying that "materials + labor + overhead × 2 = profit." Other folks add much more, while yet others set their profit far lower. The profit figure is yours to set and to change as time goes by. Only you can decide what it should be.

The Formula in Action

Here's an example of the pricing formula in action:

Ellen is a printmaker selling 6" × 9" prints made from her beautiful hand-cut blocks.

- **Materials:** Her materials include printing ink, high-quality paper, and linoleum blocks. She also adds a small annual amount to reflect the cost of her antique printing press. She figures the yearly total for cotton rags, carving tools, latex gloves, cleaners, and other studio expenses. Since she creates 50 prints from each carved block, her per-print cost comes to $4.25 in materials.
- **Labor:** Ellen has carefully tracked her time, and it takes a full 8-hour work day to produce a new run of 50 prints, from initial sketch through carving, printing, and clean up. This comes to 10 minutes per print. She's also found out that it takes her 10 minutes to package and mail each order when she batches her orders out twice a week. So her time investment is 20 minutes per item, one third of an hour. Ellen figures a

fair wage is $12 per hour, so with $12 divided by 3, the labor for each print comes to $4.00.

- **Overhead:** After figuring all of the costs for her website, her Etsy fees, her PayPal fees, the packing materials she needs to ship prints, office supplies, shelving needed to store her prints safely, and every other business detail, Ellen has a monthly overhead cost of $240. Her studio is in her home, so right now Ellen is not including rent or utilities into her overhead. She also has a computer and Internet access for personal use, so she's not counting that cost either. She averages 2 print sales a day, which comes to 60 sales per month. So $240 divided by 60 sales means each print sale needs to cover $4.00 of Ellen's monthly overhead
- **Profit:** Ellen adds $5.00 profit to each item.

Ellen now has her wholesale price: $4.25 materials + $4.00 labor + $4.00 overhead + $5.00 profit = $17.00 wholesale cost.

Doubling this brings a retail price of $34.00, a high-end selling cost for this size print on Etsy, but Ellen's work is charming and quite popular. She's sticking with her price, and with her 2 sales per day, for now.

Why Wholesale and Retail?

Many newbie sellers look at this formula and think, "Hey, why the retail markup? I feel okay with what I make on labor and the profit is already figured in, so how come I shouldn't just sell my stuff for the wholesale price? Wouldn't this be a great way to get lots of customers?"

The answer is no. You should always sell your products for their true retail price, and here are a few reasons why:

1. You will want to sell things to resellers like shops, galleries, and catalogs as well as at your own websites. Resellers need to buy items at a wholesale price, and need to be able to add their 50 percent markup so they can stay in business. You must have a wholesale price where you can comfortably make money (i.e., your "profit" figure). Also, you cannot sell online for less than what your galleries are charging. They'd soon discover you were undercutting their prices and drop you in a hurry. Your

retail must match what your galleries and shops charge for the same items. So plan for success from the beginning and sell at a true retail price.

2. If your retail prices are significantly lower than similar products online, customers will wonder what's wrong. Is your work so cheap because it really isn't handmade, because you are using cheaper materials, because it's just not as good? Your price is part of the story you tell with each product, and if you value items, so will your customers. In fact, they may feel better about an online sale when the price is higher.

3. It's far easier, more sustainable, and healthier for you as an artist or crafter to sell fewer items at a good price than many more items at a lower price. After all, you have to make everything. Running a success-ful online business is hard work, but it should never be drudgery. Hold on to the joy of what you do. Handmade is not about volume; it is about unique, original luxury.

4. You always want to have wiggle room to offer bundled items and sales. Bundling allows your customer to buy multiple items in a set at a dis-counted price. Sales and specials are used to attract new customers, reward loyal customers, celebrate holidays, or simply to clear out old products. With a true retail price set, you always have the ability to gen-erously discount.

Tweaking the Figures

You may follow the pricing formula and come to the sinking realization that your selling price is simply too high. Perhaps you look at similar items on websites and Etsy shops, and you discover that other successful sellers have prices consistently lower than yours.

You have a couple of excellent ways to solve this problem without aban-doning the tried-and-true pricing formula: You can add value to your items, or you can figure out how to make your items for less.

With the first solution, make sure you are comparing apples to apples. If your products are indeed better than the lower-priced items, don't reduce your prices. Instead, make sure that your product descriptions and photo-graphs adequately explain how superior your items are. People will pay more when they understand what they are getting. Know your worth and have confidence in it.

QUESTION

What price range is reasonable with online buyers?
Sales research shows that buyers will pay 8–12 percent more than the normal price if they think the particular product is the highest quality. If your product photos and description can convince them that your product is the best, and you stay within that price range, customers will consider your price competitive. If your product price is completely outside that range, you must define your item as an entirely different product so it is not compared with lower-priced items.

If you are convinced that your items are pretty much the same as the lower-priced competition, then take a good look at how you can lower your manufacturing costs rather than abandoning the pricing formula. Since labor is the main cost of a handcrafted item, brainstorm how you can create the item more quickly. For instance, make ten quilted handbags at once rather than one at a time . . . lay out and cut the fabric in stacks, pin all at once, sew all at once, steam finish all at once. Your time per bag is bound to be faster and enable you to price the item more reasonably. Look into buying materials in bulk at reduced rates. Make sure you have a reseller's number and are buying wholesale rather than retail.

The pricing formula has been used by countless businesses through the years. It is a key to success as your business expands.

CHAPTER 15

Successful Online Marketing

The way people use the Internet has inspired an entirely new philosophy of marketing: attraction rather than the traditional interruption marketing. Online business owners who understand this new approach are thriving. Old-fashioned broadcast advertising techniques do not work very well online. Large corporations and major brand names are struggling to adapt to this reality and trying to incorporate new marketing practices—no doubt upsetting their embedded publicity departments along the way and only ever so slowly getting the Internet-style message. The good news is that the practice of attraction marketing, which really does work well on the Internet, is absolutely perfect for online hand-craft sellers. It requires creativity, personal attention, and friendship—attributes that artists and crafters have in abundance.

Target Your Efforts

The essence of successful online marketing is to know your ideal customers so well and so specifically that you can focus all your attention on activities that attract them to you. Step away from what you do and begin to think about the people you sell to. Who are your customers? Look at who currently buys your work.

ESSENTIAL

In traditional interrupt marketing, a "spray-and-pray" technique was the norm. A business would spray their advertisements in as many places as they could afford, and pray that someone would trip over the ad at exactly the time they were ready to buy. It was very expensive, inefficient, and unlikely to lead to success online. In modern attraction marketing, a business focuses on building trust and offering benefits to exactly the audience most likely to be interested in their products and services. Potential customers are attracted to the business and want to learn more.

Understanding Your Customer

The more you know about the people who buy your art or handcrafts, the easier it is for you to become successful. What is it about your customer that draws her to your work? What is it about purchasing your artwork that makes her feel good?

If you are a landscape artist, for example, who paints scenes of the wilderness while on backcountry expeditions, you may find that all of your customers likewise love the outdoors. They are hikers, hunters, boaters, and fishermen. They are people who also canoe and raft down the rivers and hike through the mountains that you picture in your paintings. Some have traveled to the very locations you paint, but more often your customers simply wish they could travel to those distant wilderness settings. They intend to get there someday, and meanwhile are delighted to own a landscape painting that was created at that location. They value conservation, the beauty of nature, and the adventure of wilderness travel. They love their memories of beautiful places, and they love to dream of future journeys.

When identifying your ideal customers, you want to be as specific as possible. Define their typical age, gender, and income level. Are they married or not? If you sell wedding accessories, for example, your ideal customer is unmarried, though that is soon to change. Do your ideal customers have children? If you design and sew tunics for little girls, your customers will tend to have children, grandchildren, or nieces. What other things do your customers buy, love to do, and value? Are your customers part of a well-defined niche such as skiers, dog lovers, or gourmet cooks? What do they look at online? What do they need?

There are lots of ways to discover this information:

- Evaluate your current customers (the people who have purchased your work). Do not count family and close friends (they buy from you for different reasons), but look at the sales you have made to strangers. What things do your customers have in common?
- Selling in your studio and at fairs and events lets you connect face-to-face with buyers. Engage them in conversation. Find commonalities. Make notes later.
- On a marketplace website, you can view the profiles of people who buy things from you as well as the profiles of potential customers who simply like your shop and feature your items in treasuries and wish lists. You can discover their gender, and you may be able to get a feeling for their age. You can see what other items they have liked and get a feeling for what appeals to them.
- On your Facebook business page, you can collect all kinds of data about your fans. Just go to their Facebook profile pages and look for trends and common interests.
- Pinterest is a wonderful site for seeing what people love, and for getting a sense of their values and tastes. When anyone pins one of your pieces, pay attention to the people who like that pin or who repin it.
- Curated sites such as Threadless.com (*www.threadless.com*) invite you to submit a design and see what visitors have to say about it. Will your idea get a high score with the Threadless crowd? It's good information to test whether this is your target audience.

- Art shows, crafts shows, and online exhibitions—even your county fair—are great places to get a feeling for who likes your work, and perhaps win a few awards to enhance your professional resume.

Personalize Your Ideal Customer

Figuring out demographics, or the profiling of a group of people such as your customers, is a process of analyzing lots of data to identify common traits. Trained statisticians have this down to a science, but it can be challenging for small business owners to think in terms of populations, market segments, and psychographics. An easier, more intuitive, and often equally effective way to envision your target audience is to look at your history of sales and define several ideal customers. These are the customers you love and the people who would guarantee your success if you only had many more just like them.

Take all of your favorite customers and wrap them together into two or three imaginary identities, projecting as much as possible about their age and gender, likes, and values. Then give them names! Our wilderness artist, for example, after looking at the past couple years of painting and print sales, might define three typical customers:

- Billy Backpacker, an adventurous young hiker who loves bringing nature home.
- Sam Sportsman, a retired businessman who is an avid hunter/fisherman in the regions where our artist paints.
- Grandma Grace, a wealthy Sierra Club patron who treats her extended friends and family to frequent gifts.

The silly names help you to keep them in mind as you plan and carry out your online marketing. Your fictitious characters represent very real demographics, and whenever you think, "Am I writing this blog post for Sam Sportsman?" you easily remember everything that "Sam" represents, an entire group of customers you hope to reach.

The Attraction

The reason you are profiling your ideal customers is to be able to figure out the words and feelings they themselves might use, and to discover the other places they go on the Internet. With the very name you give your business, the way you describe your work, the look and feel of your product branding, you will enable your ideal customers to find you online. In addition, remember how very social people are on the Internet. Whenever you are successful at reaching one new ideal customer, you will also reach his friends.

ALERT

HubSpot (*www.hubspot.com*) has great articles on inbound marketing and free webinars for your learning pleasure. The HubSpot folks are perfect models of providing lots of free, useful content to attract future customers.

Branding Yourself and Your Work

Once you understand your ideal customers, you can begin to deliberately brand your business. "Branding" is not just getting a cute name and a logo; it is your signature style, the essence of who you are and what you offer.

You discover your brand by looking at your ideal customers and recognizing what it is that connects those people with your work. Take your ideal customers' loves and values, combine that with what is most special to you as an artist or artisan, then express the resulting feeling with words, colors, and images to create your "brand." When you get branding right, one quick view of your website or marketplace shop tells viewers exactly what is unique about your work. Your business name and the lettering style used to write it, your logo, all of your product photos, the way you write about your items, your packaging and labels, your newsletter . . . everything about your business will work together to create a single, expressive brand for your artwork.

For example:

- If you sell your paintings to wealthy art collectors, you will brand your online business as a luxury location for gallery work that exudes value, investment, and status.
- If you create decals and clothing for young skateboarders, your branding will be innovative, extreme, and funky (probably very much like your own personality).
- If your ideal customer values social responsibility, you will want your brand to include sustainability, recycling, and repurposing.

Kevin McCorkle puts his smiling face on going green with *Palletso*, rustic home décor made with recycled palettes. (*www.etsy.com/shop/Palletso*)

Good branding is a combination of your own values and the values and needs of your target customer. It's a two-way street, especially for artists and artisans. In the arts, your own personality and creativity are an integral part of the artwork you create. Your ideal customers appreciate that. It is more thoughtful, however, than just "being yourself." Your branding communicates an idealized version of yourself. Enhance your unique traits and talents. If you live in a spectacular place, make that part of your brand. Get out and do amazing things, then make that part of your brand. Tell your story. People buy the person as much as the thing, especially when buying handmade!

Put your face on it. You are part of your branding. You are the center of it, in fact. People may come to buy the artwork and handcrafts you create, but when they make the choice to purchase a handmade item, they are really buying you—and your talent, your passion, your skill, your unique way of looking at the world. So share yourself. Include your smiling face in your work. If you are shy about your appearance, invest in a photo session with a good photographer or swap some of your amazing work for a couple hours of their time and skill. Explain to them the look and feel of your brand, and ask for a series of friendly, smiling photos of yourself with your products, in your studio, in the surroundings where you are most inspired. Select the best of those photos and use them often. Your customers want to know who you are!

Here are a few branding guidelines to contemplate:

- Think of a great name for your business. If you are an established artist with a reputation, you can take the "traditional artist" approach and simply use your name. Or come up with a memorable name that communicates the values and essence of your artwork. Be creative. Check that no one else is using the name you are considering. Can you register it as a domain name and get a Twitter account in that name?
- Look at your competition. What artists, for example, have lots of sales on Etsy with items in the same category as yours? How do their product photos and descriptions communicate their brands? Read their seller's profiles and "about" pages. Follow links to their websites or Facebook pages. You may even wish to order something so you can see their packing, their thank you notes, and any other materials sent with a shipment. Use this information to create your own marketing materials. Make your brand distinctly different so you stand out!

- Design your shop banner, avatar, website banner, business card, and all other materials with consistent colors, carefully selected to communicate the essence of your brand. Use clean, easy-to-read fonts, not some sort of loopy, hard-to-read lettering. Incorporate a simple "logo" image that will instantly communicate the feeling of your work.
- Show that you care, in every aspect of your business, from your website to your Facebook page to the way you wrap and ship orders. It is often the smallest details that make the biggest impression. Carefully considering each part of your business shows that you care about your artwork and your customers.

Ashley of *Adam Rabbit* brands her business with packaging and labels stamped by hand for products at her Etsy shop. (*www.etsy.com/shop/AdamRabbit*)

- Branding is intuitive, but it does not need to be expensive. It's not essential to hire a professional designer or print expensive business cards and letterhead. That's great if you can, but as a creative spirit yourself, there are dozens of do-it-yourself ideas that fit perfectly with branding a handcrafted artisan business. All that's really necessary is to be consistent and carry your branding through all of your materials.
- Good branding is very important in developing the wholesale side of your business. When your items look good in a shop and your

products have a distinctive look, great labels, and a professional consistency, other retailers will be more likely to contact you about wholesale terms.

Develop a Marketing Plan

Your marketing plan is a document that states each year what you are going to do to attract ideal customers. How you will know if you are successful? Create your marketing plan once each year. Because the art and handcrafts industry builds traffic through the summer and fall, and culminates in the holiday gift buying season, January and February are great months to review your previous marketing plan, and make a plan for the future.

A simple marketing plan will include these elements:

1. What makes your business unique?
2. Who are you trying to reach? Which ideal customers?
3. What are the most important reasons they have to buy your handcrafted products?
4. How will you let people know that you can satisfy those needs?
5. What is it that you enjoy doing the most?
6. What are your measurable goals for this year? These would be things you have real numbers for, such as sales, your website stats, sign-ups for your newsletter, and so on. What are their current levels? Where do you want them to be after the end of this year?
7. What marketing actions will you do to deliver your message and achieve your goals?

Write a concise answer or answers for each element. Then post your marketing plan prominently in your office. Put step seven into action, and look back at steps one through four with everything you do. Keep monthly records for all the elements in step six.

Evaluate Your Progress

Visit the stats pages for your website, blog, and marketplace shop regularly . . . an hour a month at least, to note changes and trends. If your websites do not provide good stats, learn how to use the free services at Google Analytics (*www.google.com/analytics*).

Here's what you are looking for:

- Unique visitors. How many different viewers came to your website?
- Page views. How many times did different pages on your site, or different products in your marketplace shop, get looked at?
- Referral URLs. Where were visitors just before they entered your site? This lets you know where your traffic is coming from, which search engines have indexed your pages, and where other websites have linked to you.
- Angel links. These are other websites who have mentioned and linked to you "out of the blue." Suddenly you see significant traffic coming from their URLs. Go visit, introduce yourself, say thanks, and connect further with these websites, especially if they are bloggers or other small business sites who would be open to future collaboration, feature stories, or guest articles you could write.
- Keywords. If visitors have come to you from a search engine link, what words were they searching for when they saw and clicked your link? Track the main search words that are working or you.
- What time of day and week do most visits take place? Plan new blog posts to appear in time for these surges in traffic.
- Keep monthly totals of your sales at your various platforms. How many sales at your marketplace shop, from your new Facebook shop, from your website, and so on?
- Are you tracking any other numbers, such as how many Twitter followers you have, how many subscribers to your e-newsletter, and how many new Facebook "likes"? Observe and write down those numbers on a monthly basis.

Each year (or more frequently, if you wish), compile all your web stats and sales records and take a good, close look. Ask yourself:

- Did I do what I said I was going to do? How did that go?
- Did I correctly target my customer? Did I sell the things I would expect to sell if those people were actually coming to my site?

- Did a new customer type appear? Are my new Facebook "likes" a completely different group than what I expected?
- What products have I actually sold? Who bought them? Do I need to edit my ideal customer profiles in light of this year's real customers?
- Did something work especially well and bring in new viewers and lead to new sales?
- Did something not seem to work at all?

Your stats will drive your future marketing. When something works, do it again, more often and with more attention. When something does not work, do it differently, or stop altogether. Try, track, and repeat what works.

As a small business owner in the handcraft market, you have an advantage over large corporations and big business. You are flexible. You can recognize things that work well and make changes right away. You have personal access to your customers and can easily ask them questions. Why did you come to my shop? What inspired you to buy that item? Your analytics are important facts, but not as important as your personal relationships with customers. Invite feedback and listen to what they have to say.

The Happiness Quotient

The most successful businesses recognize that the happiness of their employees makes a huge difference in the success of the company. Innovative corporations like Zappos (*www.zappos.com*) and Google go way beyond normal expectations to keep the workplace happy and rewarding, and thrive because of it. As an artist or crafter with your own small business, you have the edge here. You are already creating the type of artwork you love. Now you have every opportunity to create an office, a customer service center, and marketing plan that you will also love.

Therefore, you include item number five in your marketing plan. What is it that you enjoy doing the most? If you really dislike spending time on Facebook but love every moment you spend on Pinterest, then make a change based on your own happiness quotient. Focus your attention on Pinterest, and spend just the minimum on Facebook. If you discover that you love writing short, sweet blog articles, then expand that part of your marketing. Post regularly, and seek out other blogs where you can write a guest article, or become a regular writer. Let your own happiness be a key part of your marketing plan.

While our culture makes us think that success will bring us happiness, the lab-validated truth is that it is our happiness that will bring us more success.

Sales, Coupons, and Giveaways

Coupons and discounts are time-tested ways to inspire sales in any retail venue, and selling arts and crafts online is no exception. They give customers an added incentive to buy something, and they give you a reason to contact your fans and followers to offer a special bargain.

Online customers were asked what would most positively influence their decision to buy something: 73 percent said free shipping, 62 percent noted sales and discounts, 56 percent said discount coupons were important, while 31 percent noted that a free gift offer would inspire them to make a purchase.

There are many different kinds of sales promotions:

- A price discount. $5 off spring flower prints through April.
- A percentage discount. 25 percent off all ornaments for Christmas in July savings.
- A grouping discount. Buy 3 get 1 free.
- A discount reward. Join our newsletter list and get a 15 percent off coupon to use at our online store.
- A gift. Free with your order, a copy of our PDF coloring sheets for kids.
- Free shipping. We'll ship all orders over $50 for free.

You can set up sales and coupons at marketplace websites, and with many shopping cart systems. Use your e-mail newsletter, Facebook, and Twitter to announce sales to your followers. Do these promotions one at a time, and carefully track the resulting sales to see what works best, so you can do it again.

Advertising on Other Sites

You will have abundant opportunities to advertise on other websites. Online magazines, arts and crafts websites, blogs about fashion and decorating, mommy blogs, sales representatives, marketing experts, and ad agencies will be delighted to help you set up all sorts of online advertising campaigns. Be very careful about extending yourself into these realms. Advertising online only works if it is very, very targeted. If you can figure out how to get your ad seen by your ideal customers at exactly the moment they are considering shopping for a gift or new item for themselves, then that particular ad might pay off. In general, however, online advertising is simply too broad to work well for the small arts and crafts merchant. But you have web stats to track traffic and a keen mind, so online advertising may be something you will test someday.

Paid Search Engine Results

Search engines offer promotional packages to display your link on search results pages. Google Ads (*www.google.com/ads*) is one of the most popular systems. With 85 percent or more of the search traffic, it makes sense to take a look at Google if a paid search campaign is part of your marketing plan. If your art or handcrafted items fall into a small and easily defined niche, you might get your money's worth. The Yahoo! Bing network (*https://secure.bingads.microsoft.com*) is the other major search engine program.

Paid search result programs usually work on a PPC (price per click) calculation. You set a budget and have an agreement that when someone searches for a particular term, such as "elephant art prints," your sponsored ad will show up at the top of that results page. If someone clicks and enters your website, you pay an agreed fee, anywhere from a few cents to a couple of dollars, depending on the words you specified.

FACT

The evaluation of Google Ads or any similar promotion is in your conversion rate. You want your ad and the search terms to be so well targeted that every click is a potential customer. If they're too vague, you'll end up paying for a lot of random curious visitors who aren't the least bit interested in buying your products. You need to send paid clicks to web pages that do an amazing job on inspiring sales so you actually convert them into customers. Most online merchants who use paid search engine ads set up special "landing pages" on their websites. You must track all the visits you are paying for, and figure out if you are making money or not with paid promotions.

Social Media Ads and Other Websites

Various ads and promotions are available on social media sites like Facebook and Twitter. Again, for such campaigns to be worth it to your business, you need to carefully target, test, and track results.

Banners are the standard advertising offer from other websites. Explore any opportunities that really promise to reach your target customers. If you do decide to try a couple of banner ads, test them for a few months and track carefully with unique landing pages. Your web stats will tell you how much traffic you get each month from the site where your banner ad is displayed. Only you can decide if the traffic is worth the banner ad price.

You will need to dig deep to discover how many of the visitors from any of these platforms actually became customers. A simple "How did you hear about us?" field on your shopping cart checkout page will help. You can e-mail a follow-up thank you to all your customers, and invite them to take a quick survey using free services at sites such as SurveyMonkey (*www .surveymonkey.com*). If you have phone contact with a customer, you can ask him directly.

Offer an E-Newsletter

One excellent online marketing tool is an e-mail newsletter! This is the ideal "permissions" marketing, because you only send e-mail newsletters to interested people who have specifically given permission for you to contact them by subscribing. Online newsletter systems keep track of the people who have signed up for your newsletter, adding new subscribers and deleting people who unsubscribe or e-mails that stop working. You can create sign-up forms for your web pages. The newsletter service will also provide all sorts of tracking statistics on each newsletter you send—how many folks open it, how many of them click through to web pages, and so on. Once you set things up, all you need to do is write a newsletter every now and then and keep track of your stats.

A business e-mail list is far too complex for you to manage yourself with your Outlook program or online system like Gmail or Yahoo! Mail. You absolutely need to have a subscription e-mail list service, and fortunately MailChimp (*www.mailchimp.com*) is great and free for up to 2,000 subscribers. Set up an account and learn the system. MailChimp's clever sense of humor will keep you entertained through your learning process. Set up a list, write a thank you note for the opt-in messages that subscribers receive, generate the code for a sign up form, and add it to your website and Facebook business page.

Other newsletter systems have a few additional features, more templates, advanced e-mail capabilities such as split testing, and live telephone support. They also have a monthly charge. Check out AWeber (*www.aweber.com*) and ConstantContact (*www.constantcontact.com*), the two main professional e-mail list services.

Your newsletter system will provide templates for designing an attractive e-mail newsletter, complete with photos and links that let readers click directly to your website pages. Select one of the newsletter templates that your system provides, and then tweak the colors and images until it blends with your business branding. It would be appropriate for artists and craft businesses to send a newsletter every month or two. The people on your newsletter list want to hear from you, to keep in touch with what you are doing, but they probably don't want to hear from you every week. Your monthly short e-mail newsletters can showcase recent new work, an exhibit or show you'll appear at, a special sale at your marketplace shop, or simply offer an inspirational note of good cheer.

Never send promotional e-mails to people who have not joined your list. It is considered spam and you will lose credibility with customers. If a colleague offers to "share" her e-mail list with you, ask her to send her own e-mail note to her subscribers about your products. Your friend can review and recommend your work, and include a link so her interested readers can click through to your website.

Videos

Videos are also a great Internet strategy to build your authority and attract new followers, especially for artists and crafters who know how to do amazing things. Simple, short videos (3–4 minutes) showing you working in your studio or demonstrating and teaching some unique technique can become very popular. A clever and creative video can easily get thousands of folks watching and sharing. Submit your videos to YouTube, Google Videos, and Vimeo, and be sure to tag them with keywords describing the content.

You can make good videos yourself if you are interested in learning how to use simple video editing software. Mac computers are especially handy for this. The easy iMovie program is included with the computer, and excellent teaching is available both at Apple stores and through the AppleCare support that comes with a new computer purchase. Small video cameras are sold everywhere—you can even use a smartphone to take video clips. Of course, be very critical of your own videos. Compare what you make to other online videos. If your visual or sound quality is poor, you would be wise to contact a professional videographer in your area. Search Google for "how to make a great how-to video" and discover lots more information.

Keep in Mind

Marketing on the Internet is all about being friendly, sharing items of interest, and giving to the online community. Attraction marketing simply means doing things online so that people come to you, rather than trying to seek those people out so you can make a sales pitch to them. All you need is confidence in the quality of your artwork, curiosity about your customers, and some commonsense intuition about what methods to try and test.

CHAPTER 16

Social Media Marketing

Creating a robust social media presence is an essential part of artists and crafters selling their artwork online. Websites such as Facebook, Twitter, Pinterest, and your own business blog are part of the new attraction marketing philosophy of the Internet, specifically called "engagement marketing." When used effectively, social media platforms are not just places where businesses merely advertise their products, they are where online sellers attract and expand a group of followers.

For an online arts and crafts seller, Facebook becomes a community of friends keeping track of one another and sharing ideas. Pinterest celebrates inspiration and helps expand innovative products far beyond the scope of a marketplace shop. Twitter becomes a mini-blog where artists and crafters can connect with followers and newcomers through short sweet sentences containing valuable tags and links. Other sites may be appropriate, such as LinkedIn, Google Plus, DeviantArt, Wanelo, Instagram, and more, depending on the target audience an artist or crafter wants to attract.

Using social media to build a following of faithful fans takes time, but there is no better time to invest in your future than right now. Take a close look at your customers and try to determine which social media platforms they are using; then choose a place to start and dive in.

Facebook

Facebook (*www.facebook.com*) may be the most popular social media platform. In fact, it is currently the world's largest social media website. Millions of people are on Facebook daily, and it is quite likely that your ideal customers are among this crowd. It is international, spans all ages, and is free. Facebook is mainly used to connect with real-life friends and family, but it is also popular with Facebook users to become a "fan" of favorite businesses and add them to the circle of friends.

It is an excellent idea to have a Facebook page for your business. You can post images, links, and brief comments, and use Facebook to share the ongoing story of your business and your creative process as an artist and artisan.

FACT

In 2011, a Nielsen study found that Americans spend almost a quarter of their online time on social media websites, a figure up 30 percent from the previous year and steadily rising. Sixty-seven percent of Internet users are on social media networks. Women are more likely to use social media than men, as are younger people, people with more education, and people with more income.

Set Up a Facebook Business Page

You must have a personal account in order to set up a business page, so if you are not already on Facebook, now's the time to learn this popular system. Sign up for a free personal profile, and then have a friend or family member who uses Facebook show you around. Spend a few weeks learning the system. Get a few Facebook "friends" and watch how people interact. What sort of things do they post and share? Observe how people like and comment on one another's posts, and feel free join into these conversations if you wish.

ALERT

Keep track of your Facebook username and password so you can easily log in later to add new comments, see what your friends are doing, and eventually set up your business page.

Investigate business pages by becoming a fan of a few interesting businesses. Etsy provides an easy way for shops to link their Facebook pages, so visit your favorite sellers on Etsy and click the button to "like" their Facebook page if they have one. Once you friend someone or like a business, you will begin seeing what they post on your news feed (the page that appears when you click the blue Facebook logo in the top left corner).

Remember that everything you say and do on Facebook is open to the public. Do not share anything you want to keep private. You may get hooked on Facebook for enjoyment, and your personal profile might become a central part of your life, the way you stay connected with far-off friends and family. Or you may find Facebook too time consuming and intrusive, and decide to never spend personal time there. It's up to you on a personal level.

But for your online business success, you will indeed want to build and maintain a Facebook business page. It is too good an opportunity to pass up! When you have spent a few weeks on your personal space and have an idea of how Facebook works, set up a business page for your artwork.

1. Log into Facebook and then go to *www.facebook.com/pages/create .php*. Click Local Business or Place, and follow the prompts to identify

your business and upload an avatar image. You can skip the Enable Ads part unless you plan to spend money advertising on Facebook.

2. Once you have created your business page, you can further decorate the page by clicking Add a Cover and choosing a photo with a long, wide area that communicates your work. A photo from your studio is ideal.

3. You now have two Facebook profiles, your personal profile and your new business profile. You move between them by clicking the tiny gear icon in the top right corner. To post to your business page, log into Facebook as an individual, then switch to your business profile. You can immediately begin posting and encouraging followers and friends to become fans by liking your new business page.

Posting on Your Facebook Page

Keep your Facebook business page professional, relevant to your studio, and updated often. You can easily post things every day, but this may be more time than you wish to spend. You should at least post things weekly. Decide how often you want to add to your Facebook business page, and then be persistent. Soon you will begin to see your fan base start to grow.

When you post something on your Facebook business page, you have three goals. First, you want the news you are sharing to be of interest to your fans. This way, when they see your post among all the others from their friends and family, they will at least smile and remember your business. Second, you hope that some of your fans will find occasional posts so interesting that they'll click to visit the web page you've linked in that post, which could be a page at your marketplace site or a feature on your own website. And third, you hope that at least a few of your fans will enjoy your post so much that they'll share it with all of their friends!

Most of what you share on your Facebook business page should be non-commercial. Follow the 80/20 rule: 80 percent of your postings should simply be interesting to your fans! You are not trying to sell something in these posts; you are trying to share the story of your creative business life. Twenty percent of your postings can be a promotion or sale-related, such as linking to a new product you've just put online or offering a discount coupon.

Things to post on your Facebook business page include:

- Where you are going, especially when amazing locations inspire your work
- Other innovative artists, artisans, and artwork you admire (collaboration!)
- The progress of a new piece you are working on
- A photo of your work displayed at the home of a recent customer, or worn by the customer in an fabulous location (encourage your fans to submit these photos too)
- A new product you have added to your marketplace shop (with a link to that page)
- A new article you have just written on your own blog (with a link to your blog)
- A beautiful photo from anywhere, a photo of your own, or one you have discovered elsewhere online
- Photos of yourself at work (Yes, you are a real person. Connect with your fans!)
- Success stories, like getting your 100th sale at Etsy or an award at a juried exhibition
- A question, like "Would you be more likely to buy one of my new summer sarongs in beige and sea blues, or in pink and peach?" to see what comments you get back
- Almost anything that is tastefully clever and relates to your fans

One-on-One Conversations

Many artists and crafters with Facebook business pages say that their favorite part of this platform is the ease of making a personal connection with fans and followers. The likes and comments on your posts provide great feedback from a self-selected group of "ideal customers." You can comment publicly on your wall, where all your followers can see the conversation, or you can send a private message to any of your fans.

Follow Banners and Buttons

You can create a "Follow Me on Facebook" badge to add to your website and blog. Badges are small chunks of HTML code you can place on your webpages or WordPress sidebar. When you are logged into Facebook, go to *www.facebook.com/badges*. There you will see a variety of badges for the pages you manage. You can edit a badge to look the way you want, and then click the Other button to get the HTML code. Have your webmaster or a computer-literate friend help you add this to your website. You can connect your Etsy or ArtFire marketplace shop with your Facebook account in those sites' profile management settings.

Shops on Facebook

It is now possible to add a store to your Facebook business page. It's a great way to quickly showcase your work, and perhaps catch a few sales from customers who may not want to click through to your marketplace shop. Adding an interactive store to Facebook is done by finding an appropriate app to add. There are Etsy store apps for Facebook pages, the Art-Fire Kiosk app, and many other apps for different shopping cart systems. Many experienced Facebook artists and crafters are testing various store applications.

People do not necessarily come to Facebook intending to buy things, but they do come for product information and to discover things that their friends like. New features such as the Facebook graph search (*www .facebook.com/about/graphsearch*) may become important as a social search function since it gathers information based on the "likes" of your friends. All a business needs to remember at this point is that the more likes your business page has, the more likely you will be to come up in the searches that fans and their friends may do.

FACT

Social networks play a growing role in influencing what people buy online. In a 2013 Digital Influence Report, 30.8 percent of consumers surveyed cited Facebook as an influential source in their purchasing decision. Twenty-seven percent said they were influenced by videos they saw on YouTube, 27 percent cited LinkedIn, and 20 percent noted that recommendations by friends at Google Plus were a factor.

Converting your Facebook visitors into sales is most often a process of encouraging people to come to your website, and reminding them that your products are available so they think of you when they need to shop. Gift giving is a big reason people choose to buy online. Your Facebook posts in the week before Valentine's Day, Mother's Day, and Father's Day are very important. You can post a photo of your packaging, suggesting how awesome it is to open one of your shipments, and emphasizing that you do the gift wrapping and shipping for the buyer. Try posting a special offer on Facebook, such as a discount coupon code, and see if your fans respond. Test, track, and analyze, and repeat what works.

Facebook Tips

Niccy, from the Midlands in the United Kingdom, calls herself Scrapunzel the sewing Faery. She offers a whimsical array of Faery Coats, Forest Fae jumpers, and very funky patchwork accessories at her own website and on a very active Facebook business page. "Hippy patchwork, elfin coats and shroom-covered skirts are all my specialty."

"I love making and designing clothing. I started at Etsy, which is sort of a natural choice to sell as a creative person. My online presence grew at my Etsy shop and my Facebook presence grew with it," says Niccy. "They both became a springboard in gaining a following. On Etsy it was a matter of using the teams, treasuries, and various promotional strategies that Etsy recommends. Through Facebook it was simply a case of generating steady and varied content. When I made the leap to a stand-alone site at Scrapunzel.com, it was much easier because of that initial following. In fact, it was invaluable, as building a site is scary and challenging enough!"

The Scrapunzel Facebook page has hundreds of fans, photos, regular postings, and an embedded shopping page. Niccy explains, "I set up a Facebook profile for Scrapunzel for the enjoyment of it and also to sell. I didn't see any reason why business shouldn't be fun. I post things almost every day. It's not a hard and fast rule though. My main priority is to be in the workshop creating, so I'm posting in short bursts. I get new 'likes' all the time. It's nice to get those thumbs-ups!"

The Scrapunzel Facebook page has frequent posts, comments, likes, and shares.

Niccy's Facebook posts are a mixture of products and personality, with an emphasis on fun. "How do I decide what to post on Facebook? If it makes people happy, if it contains a positive message, if it's colorful—it goes on. It's important to remember that Facebook is a social space first and a selling space second. Being as human as possible is very important. It shows my customers that I'm not a faceless business—and we have a lot of fun! Some people call it 'crowd sourcing' and 'PR,' and all kinds of marketing jargon. I just call it helping people and making them happy. I'm pretty simple at heart. If I take a break from creating my hippy-pixie clothing to skip through a forest, I tell people about it."

The Scrapunzel shop on Facebook connects with Niccy's store at her domain website *www.scrapunzel.com.*

The Scrapunzel shop on Facebook is a new feature. On the shop page, fans can view, share, and even buy products from the Scrapunzel website. "It's an extension of my website and my own shopping cart system, designed by a developer and one of the many third-party applications out there in the world of e-commerce. Customers can order items and their shopping cart shows up right on the Facebook site. Which is so clever, it sort of blows my mind a little. I am fortunate to have a technically minded partner to set up things like this!"

Niccy adds, "We are currently testing the Facebook shop concept. It is too early to tell whether it will be successful. Such things are not for every Fan Page, so I just take a policy of experimenting and asking lots of 'what ifs.'"

In addition to the website and Facebook page, Scrapunzel has an active Twitter profile and a regular e-mail newsletter managed through MailChimp for inspirational goodness, the latest news, and occasional kittens—and simply amazing wearable art. (*www.scrapunzel.com* and *www.facebook.com/ pages/Scrapunzel/106592056092749*)

Twitter

Twitter is the second largest social media site, with over 250 million users. Users post short sentences called "tweets" that often contain links to photos and websites. People usually tweet often throughout the day, and keep an eye on the tweets that are sent by people and businesses they have chosen to follow.

Twitter is a great way to connect with your customers, especially if your target audience is young and urban. The key, as with all social media platforms, is to use Twitter appropriately—not as a way to blast your followers with sales messages, but to connect and share interesting comments.

Getting Started on Twitter

Follow these steps to set up your new Twitter account:

1. Sign up for a free account for your business. If you are already using Twitter as an individual, be sure to log out first. Create a professional username, the same as your Etsy or ArtFire shop name, or your domain name. Fill out your profile, and upload your photo or the avatar you use on other websites.

ALERT

Keep track of your Twitter username and password, so you can easily log in later to post tweets and read the tweets posted by the people you follow.

2. Find some people to follow. Etsy provides an easy way for shops to link their Twitter accounts, so visit your favorite sellers on Etsy and click the

Twitter follow button if they have one. Once you follow someone, you will begin seeing what he posts on your Twitter feed. You can click the links embedded in tweets. If there is a photo attached to the tweet, click View Photo to see it.

3. Get some people to follow you. Connect your website and your marketplace shop page with your new Twitter account so your friends and fans know you are on Twitter.

4. Create your own tweets. Learn how to reply to someone (@), how to retweet (RT), how to use hashtags (#), and how to include a link and a picture in your tweets. Go to Twitter's support center (*https://support.twitter.com*) to learn the basics.

Twitter for Business

Twitter can be a quick and easy tool for promoting your new products and business successes, especially if your ideal customers are tech-savvy and the type of people who use and follow Twitter in their own daily lives.

- Send a few interesting tweets throughout the day. Only tweet things that your followers will find interesting. Different people check into Twitter at different times of the day, so scatter your tweets over morning, afternoon, and evening.

- Post comments, links, and information related to your artwork and to the interests of the people in your ideal customer profiles.

- Be consistent. If Twitter is an important way to communicate with your target customers, use it regularly. Don't blast dozens of tweets out all at once, and then log off for a week.

- Only use direct messaging (replying or tweeting with the @ tag) to honestly converse with someone. Never direct message someone with a sales pitch. A tweet such as "@kimsolga Thanks for the follow. Come buy my stuff!" is not appropriate.

- You do not have to follow everyone who follows you. Keep your own Twitter feed manageable by only following people if you really love reading their tweets. Your followers can always connect with you through @ direct messages.

- Make each tweet interesting. Make it worthy of someone's attention. Don't just say, "Just listed: Blue and gold quilt: *www.etsy.me/1a2b3c4d* . . ." Use you 140 characters your best advantage. "Go Bears handmade quilt inspired by pleasant #Berkeley #Cal football games on blue & golden autumn afternoons: etsy.me/1a2b3c4d"
- Shorter is better. Twitter gives you 140 characters. Studies show that tweets under 100 characters get a better engagement rate—people are more likely to retweet, favorite, and click shorter tweets.
- Use hashtags (#) in your tweets to make them searchable.
- Search Twitter to discover what is being said for any #word. A plein air painter, for example, might search for #pleinair and discover interesting conversations about the topic. If appropriate, click to comment, retweet, or follow any of the people. Get involved.
- Ask questions in tweets. This could be market research information (Should I glaze these vases in rainbow or neutral tones?) or simply something you want to know (Anyone have tips on travel to New Zealand?). Twitter is all about interaction.
- Whenever you add a new post to your blog, announce it to your Twitter followers. Compose three or four brief, interesting tweets, all different, linking to your blog post, and post them on Twitter at different parts of the day to catch the attention of your followers.

FACT

Where do customers go to figure out what to buy? In 2013, consumers said that blogs were the third most useful online resource (31.1 percent), behind store websites themselves (56 percent), and corporate brand websites (34 percent). Social media sites were also mentioned frequently as influential sources of information: Facebook (30.8 percent), Google Plus (20 percent), and Pinterest (12 percent).

- Use *www.hootsuite.com* or other free scheduling services to set up tweets that will be delivered later in the day or week.
- Now and then, feel free to share Treasuries you have been included in from Etsy, curated lists from ArtFire, events, sales at your shop, coupon codes, and other promotions. Of course you want to promote

your business, and your Twitter followers expect this. Just alternate your promotional tweets with lots and lots of other interesting stuff.

Pinterest

Pinterest is an especially important social network for the art and hand-crafts market; it's very popular with the people who also purchase hand-made arts and crafts online. Pinterest is completely visual. It creates bulletin board pages onto which people "pin" photos that link to their external website sources.

Pinterest exploded out of obscurity, with the website opening in 2010 and growing to become one of the top four most popular social media platforms by the end of 2012 (with Facebook, LinkedIn, and Twitter). By September 2012, there were nearly 12 million monthly visits to the Pinterest website. Pinterest's 85.5 million users, (most of whom are female, college-educated, middle-to-upper income, and between the ages of twenty-five and forty-four), spend an average of an hour each time they visit. Pinterest is compelling and fun. The colorful bulletin board format engages visitors immediately.

How Pinterest Works

Your Pinterest account is free. You can create as many themed boards as you want, giving each board a name and a topic such as "Style for the Home," "Yummy Recipes," or "Made Me Smile." Then you begin pinning images to fill your boards. To pin from the Internet, you locate and then copy the URL of a webpage with a great image or video, click Add Pin, and paste that URL into the Find Images box. Pinterest goes to that web page and presents you with the images it finds on the page. You select the one you want to pin. Choose which of your themed boards this goes into, type a short comment if you wish, then complete the pin. Each pin links back to its source page.

The pinned image shows up on the home board for yourself and all the people who follow you. It will start at the top, as the most recent pin, and then work its way down and ultimately off your home page as other people post newer pins. It will remain on your themed board unless you remove it. If you click the image in the pin, a new tab will open in your browser with the original source web page. Thus, if you pin one of your new products at Etsy, interested viewers on Pinterest can click and get right to your Etsy shop to buy the item.

ESSENTIAL

Etsy and ArtFire make it really easy to pin products. Each product page has a Pin It button. You add a plug-in to a WordPress website, such as Share Buttons by Lockerz / AddToAny, that will place a Pin It button on all of your pages. Find more buttons and widgets at *http://business.pinterest.com/widget-builder/#do_pin_it_button.*

Other people see your pins. Right away, everyone who follows you or that particular themed board sees the pin, but pins also have a long life span. Months later a pin will continue to be repinned and liked. People search Pinterest for topics, so random folks might stumble upon your pin at any time, especially if you have included popular search terms as hash tags. If your pin is interesting, anyone who sees it can "like" it, and they can also "repin" it onto one of their boards. Then, all of their followers get to see the image. And on it goes.

Getting Started on Pinterest

Follow these steps to set up your own account:

1. If you are a newcomer to Pinterest and simply wish to open an account for your business, go to *http://pinterest.com* and click Join Pinterest. There is no cost. Choose to sign up with your e-mail address using your business e-mail. Create a professional username, the same as your Etsy or ArtFire shop name, or your domain name. Upload your photo or the avatar you use on other websites, and create your account. If you are already on Pinterest as an individual, skip to step 4.
2. Pinterest will ask you to select five boards to follow, just to get you started. Categories to explore for artists and crafters would be Art, DIY & Crafts, Design, Home Decor, and Women's Fashion. Selecting a category will show a short list of boards that Pinterest users have created and listed in that category. Scroll through and select five interesting boards.

You will be able to follow many other boards, especially boards containing interesting and amazing images that can become repins for you. You can always unfollow any boards if they prove to be uninteresting.

Keep track of your Pinterest username and password so you can easily log in later to add new pins to the Pinterest boards you create. If Pinterest is just one of many online accounts, it might be worth it to create a word document devoted to your passwords.

3. Pinterest now shows you your homepage, displaying pins from the five boards you just selected. You'll also need to go to your e-mail and click the Confirm button to verify yourself. At this point, pull down from the About link in the top right corner to Help, and explore the basics of how Pinterest works.

4. Once you have played around for a couple of hours and understand the Pinterest system, go to the About menu again and click the For Businesses link. Click Join as a Business, and on the next page, click the Convert link next to "Already have an account?" Pinterest will have you log in again. You now complete your basic business information. The website you enter should be your domain site, the hub for all your online activities. If you do not have a website yet, you can use the URL for your marketplace shop.

If you do not yet have either a marketplace shop or website, just bail out of the business "Convert Account" form until you get something set up. Click the Pinterest logo at the top of the page and simply use Pinterest as an individual.

5. If you have listed your own website with your own domain name, the next important step is to verify it, which adds a clickable link to your profile. This requires you, your web designer, or a technically inclined friend to add an HTML file to the server space at your hosting company

or to add a META tag to your home page. At this time, you can't verify a marketplace shop, so if that's what you have, just type your shop URL in the About section of your profile. It won't be an active link, but people will see it and can copy the address.

6. To edit the profile information and add the links to your business Facebook and Twitter accounts, click Edit Profile. Make sure you are actively signed in to the accounts you want to connect.

7. That's it. Create boards and start pinning and repinning, following others, and enjoying when people follow you. Do not pin only your own products. As with all social media platforms, you are interacting with your followers as friends, not bombarding them with advertising. Pin things that inspire you, things created by other artists and crafters, and scenes from your studio. Keep your pins interesting and diverse. Only a small percentage of your pins should be your own products for sale.

Words of Wisdom

Artist Kat Selvaggio is a master of altered art. She uses vintage and new materials to create one-of-a-kind mixed-media jewelry, which she offers along with antiques and estate relics at her *In Vintage Heaven* shops on both Etsy and RubyLane. Her assemblage pendants are delicate sculptures, with bits and pieces from a dozen different sources layered into a colorful scene.

About a year ago, Kat discovered Pinterest and began creating a presence there for her business. "I thought it was an amazing site as it was so 'visual.' Since I have often used a physical bulletin board for inspiration, Pinterest took it to a whole new level of ease by being able to pin whatever inspires me. I thought it would also be a great marketing tool as it puts my own pieces out there for others to see and share with very little effort and time on my part," Kat says.

Each board on the *In Vintage Heaven* profile opens to reveal hundreds of fascinating images. (*www.pinterest.com/invintageheaven*)

Kat has a couple of Pinterest boards clearly identified for her own work, and many other boards for inspiration, networking, and tutorials. "Since I sell two different types of products, my own artisan jewelry and vintage jewelry, these were the first two boards that I set up." Kat's Artisan Jewelry board has over a hundred amazing images of her creations, making an impressive online portfolio.

Yet most of the pins and repins Kat adds to Pinterest are from other artists and websites. "I have always been a strong believer in networking and helping each other out when it comes to small business, and this is a great way to do it. I enjoy sharing the work of others and appreciate when they share mine also."

Pinterest is a social platform, and several of the boards on Kat's profile are community boards. "I have been invited into many group boards featuring specific jewelry or a style that fits my look, like Bohemian. I welcome this as it gives my page an eclectic collection of amazing things. Teaming up with people is a great way to widen your audience, build business contacts, and make friends along the way! Since the Internet is such a huge place, teamwork helps you get noticed easier with more exposure."

Kat does not track the use of the pins she adds to her Pinterest boards. "I do check the stats in my Etsy shop to see how many of my Pinterest pins have brought potential customers into my shop." But with hundreds of followers, it is certain that Kat's work is getting a wide exposure on the Pinterest platform. "I spend about 1–4 hours each week on Pinterest, depending upon if it is directly business related or if I am doing it for my own enjoyment. It is very easy to spend many hours there!"

Kat recommends paying consistent attention to Pinterest if you are using it as a promotional platform. "You do need to 'work' on your boards with pinning and repining in order to keep them active for others to see your pins. Whenever I list something new, I immediately pin it to the appropriate board. You never know where one of your pins might end up! They can be picked up for blogs, etc. It is quite organic in the way that your pins can move around. I just love it!"

(Visit *www.pinterest.com/invintageheaven*, and see Kat's shops at *www .rubylane.com/shop/invintageheaven* and *www.etsy.com/shop/InVintageHeaven*.)

In 2012, a study by Shopify.com analyzed data from 25,000 online stores, and found that Pinterest users who click through to Shopify-powered e-commerce websites are 10 percent more likely to make a purchase than people who come from other social networks.

Test, Track, and Convert

Simply watch your stats to tracking the effectiveness of Pinterest as a promotional tool. Observe how many visitors are coming from Pinterest. Are these visitors becoming customers? As with any external traffic, you'd need to dig deeper and actually ask the people who place orders how they found you. Pinterest Web Analytics, a new service launched in March 2013, will allow you to verify your domain website with Pinterest and have access to a wide array of information exploring how many items are pinned and re-pinned from your site and by whom. (See *https://help.pinterest.com/ entries/23296713-Pinterest-Web-Analytics*.)

Converting your Pinterest visitors into sales is the same as converting traffic from any other website. If Pinterest viewers click a pinned image and land on a page with clear sales information and a "call to action," they are more likely to take a step that will lead to becoming a customer. Perhaps they will buy your product then and there. Perhaps they will simply bookmark your site, or sign up for your free e-mail newsletter. You can increase this likelihood by making sure that there is a "call to action" on every page of your website, everywhere images are displayed that could become pins. This could be a Buy Now button, or a newsletter sign up, or simply a sentence saying, "Bookmark my site and return soon." When you pin one of your own product photos, make sure you pin it from a page that has clear action features, perhaps even a unique landing page you have created especially for this pin. Remember that only a few of the Pinterest users who see a pin will ever click through to visit your website, but if they do go that far, they are sincerely interested. Make sure they have the information they need to encourage a sale.

Because Pinterest is a platform for sharing amazing images, handcrafts and artworks are really popular. Artists and crafters can search for their names or their shop names on Pinterest, and will most likely discover images of their products that have already been pinned by others. By joining Pinterest themselves and taking part in the pinning pleasures, they can further increase the number of their product images available to be liked and re-pinned. Since the Pinterest user demographic fits the profile of an "ideal customer" for handmade crafts and arts, this is one social network that successful sellers cannot ignore.

Blogging

When professional marketers are asked, "What's the most effective piece of social media marketing?" the answer is always "blogging." Online businesses, including artists and crafters, become remarkably more successful when they have a frequently updated blog for interested fans to follow. Why?

1. A blog gives you a way to keep in regular touch with followers who want to hear from you.
2. A blog adds humanity to your business and lets you reveal your personality and the unique creativity that make your works more desirable.
3. A blog increases your authority as you share your expertise through tips, insights, and news.

4. A blog increases the chances that your website will show up in search engine results for your keywords and terms.
5. A blog with comments encourages your customers to engage with you.
6. A blog gives you a perfect opportunity to highlight new work and work in progress.
7. Writing a blog keeps your own skills sharpened as you put your interests, activities, and visions into words.
8. Your blog is an opportunity to network with other bloggers by sharing blog posts and guest articles.

ESSENTIAL

Incorporating a blog into a website can have a positive impact on its overall search engine rankings, simply by giving search engine robots additional content to index.

Even if your website is created with a different system, WordPress might be the perfect application to install within a subdirectory to use for your blog. Other popular blogging platforms on independent websites include Blogger (*www.blogger.com*), part of the many free services from Google, Typepad (*www.typepad.com*), with a monthly fee, and Wordpress.com with both free and paid space for blogs.

Whichever system you decide to use, begin by naming and designing your blog pages to fit your branded online identity. Use the same colors, graphics, avatar, and fonts that you use for your marketplace shop header and your website. Claim your blog on Technorati, a specialized search engine that specifically looks at blogs (*http://technorati.com/blog-claiming-faq*). Include your blog at Google Analytics (*www.google.com/analytics*) so you can track its use.

Start with some simple, interesting posts. Keep things short—400 words is a great article length. Remember to write for the Internet and divide your text into short, easily read paragraphs separated by meaningful subheads.

If you are wondering what you will write about in your blog or how to promote it on the Internet, no worries. Here are just a few ideas . . .

- New work completed. Show it off and link to your marketplace shop where you just added the new product. Don't sell things. Just talk about them. Blog for the love of it. Interested readers will click through to your shop pages to read the full product description, the price, and order stuff if they want.

- Works in progress. Are you working on a new painting, a new design for kids' playtime costumes, a new cable knit pattern? Share it. Readers are following you because they admire your work, so give them a peek into what's coming up. Each blog post should have a photo (you are a visual artist, after all, and people love "eye candy"). Photos can be as simple as a close-up detail of one of your new products. Don't show the whole item . . . keep the mystery alive and readers will hardly be able to wait for you to release the finished work.

- Techniques. Your readers are fascinated with your ability to create such marvelous stuff. Share how you do this. Talk about perfecting traditional techniques and inventing new processes (unless you want to keep them secret, that is). Offer helpful tips to readers who might be dabbling in the creative process themselves. Short do-it-yourself tutorials are especially popular and could end up getting you a lot of new readers!

- Evergreen content is information that does not go out of style. Write about subjects that people frequently want and will continue to search for in the coming years. This blog content does not become dated, and builds your authority as a dependable website with content that is forever useful.

- News! Have you been in the newspaper, donated a piece for a good fundraising cause, been featured by another blogger, or scheduled a booth for the summer art fair? Write about it. Brag about yourself. Include links to related websites. Other bloggers will see your link, and will be more likely to link back to you in the future. Remember to frequently include a photo of your own smiling face. You are your art!

- Blog about the Etsy Treasuries, other curated lists, or shows in which your work has been included. The CraftCult.com website offers a handy tool for including an Etsy Treasury on your own blog page (*www.craftcult.com/treasury_widget.php*).

- Participate on other blogs. Visit several new blogs each week. Think of something relevant to say and leave a comment on their most recent posts. You can generally include your own blog URL in your comment signature. The other blog owner will check you out and she could end up building a blogging relationship that includes sharing posts or guest articles.

- What inspires you? Blog about the things that enrich your life. Include a sweet little snapshot to illustrate: sunlight in the bushes outside your office window, the seashell you collected on your last vacation, the classic old movie you watched last night. A great example is Neil Pasricha's blog 1000awesomethings.com, entirely composed of short, sweet inspirations. Neil is a master at finding exactly the right photo to illustrate a post.

- Do not use other people's photography or pictures of other people's faces unless you have their permission. Learn how to find free and legal photos with the Creative Commons–licensed (CC) images at *www.flickr.com*. Start on Flickr's advanced search page *www.flickr .com/search/advanced*. Be sure to select all three Creative Commons conditions ("Only search within Creative Commons–licensed content," "Find content to use commercially," and "Find content to modify, adapt, or build upon"), then enter a search term and go hunting. Always give the appropriate credit or attribution that the photographer has requested.

- Network. Share the work of other artists and crafters. They may do the same for you.

- Research. Instead of telling your readers something, try asking them a question. "I am thinking of doing a series of cloth bunnies like this one from last spring. What colors and fabric patterns would you like to see me use?"

- Keep a notebook and pencil handy when you are on the go. Waiting in the dentist office or sitting on the beach are great opportunities to jot down a dozen ideas for future blog posts.

Even More Social Media!

Facebook, Twitter, and Pinterest are the three most important social networking websites for the arts and handcrafts market, but there are certainly many others. In each case, if you know that the people in your "ideal customer" profiles are using these sites, you should take a closer look. The following are some sites your customers may use.

Other Sites

Google Plus is Google's social networking platform, with over 65 million users. If you've ever registered for a free Google service, from Analytics to Webmaster tools, you can use Google Plus (*https://plus.google.com*). Google Plus users gather and follow a circle of friends, and have access to many advanced networking tools, such as video chats, photo albums, and trending topic feeds. People on Google Plus most often share links and photos. A business owner would participate in Google Plus as an individual, which is ideal for artists and crafters who are themselves their "business."

DeviantArt (*www.deviantart.com*) is an online community for artists and art lovers. It's most often used for digital art and artwork from video games, popular culture, TV, movies, and literature.

Wanelo (Want-Need-Love) (*www.wanelo.com*) is gigantic social store curated by users. Wanelo users share products that they want, need, or love (hence the name Wa-Ne-Lo). It's like Pinterest with a shopping feature built in, and targets females aged twenty to thirty.

LinkedIn (*www.linkedin.com*) is a social networking site geared for business; basically an online resume and network of business associates. It's a good resource if selling business-to-business is part of your ideal customer definition.

Tumblr (*www.tumblr.com*) is a visually oriented blogging platform where you can easily upload pictures and videos to share with followers.

Flickr (*www.flickr.com*) is a social photo sharing website. Many Flickr users have chosen to offer their work under a Creative Commons license, which is a great location to find photos for your blog, and to offer photos of your work under CC license for expanded exposure. (*www.flickr.com/creativecommons*)

Instagram (*www.instagram.com*) is a photo sharing application integrated with Facebook and Twitter, with features that make it easy to edit and enhance photos and then share them through tags. An independent website at *http://i-am-cc.org* also works with Instragram users to share photos through a Creative Commons license.

Forums

Forums are not a specific website, but rather a social feature used by a huge variety of websites on different topics. A forum allows people to interact with one another, and can be a great way to promote your work if you have plenty of time to read and respond. Join online discussion forums that would be relevant to your ideal customers, forums where they themselves are participating. For example, if you sell handcrafted knitting stitch markers, you might find it valuable to participate in knitting forums. Read forum questions and topics, and make comments when you have something thoughtful and relevant to add to the conversation. Include your URL in your signature, thus creating backlinks to your website. Curious readers will follow your link to discover your work. This enhances your online reputation, increases your site's visibility, and may attract new customers.

Your 40-Minute Social Scene

Social media is an essential part of Internet marketing, but alas, managing your different profiles tends to take a lot of time. If keeping up with your networks is eating into your production and the customer service side of your business, then it's advisable to set a schedule and stick to it.

Assuming that you have already invested the time to learn how each of these systems work, you can indeed get all your social media responsibilities fulfilled in 40 minutes each work morning. You simply have to start with a plan and follow a path, depending on which networks you use. The following is an example schedule from a crafter who uses Twitter, Facebook, Pinterest, Etsy, and e-mail from her own website:

Five days a week

1. *10 minutes*. Start with your e-mail. Begin by opening, glancing at, then deleting or filing any e-mails that do not require a reply. Answer any others immediately and briefly. Do not get distracted with clicking links in e-mails and surfing the Internet. You can do that later at your leisure. Right now you are at work. Leave your e-mail open to glance at through the day and respond to new e-mails as they come in.

2. *6 minutes*. Go to Twitter. Log in. Respond to any @ direct messages that have been directed your way. Glance through the tweets from the people you follow. Retweet anything appropriate. Write three or four tweets for the day. Post one right away. Go to HootSuite.com and schedule the others for later in the day. Log out.

3. *8 minutes*. Log in to Facebook and switch immediately to your business profile. Look through your recent posts to see if people have commented, and like their comments or reply back if they have. Post something new with a link or a photo. Do not switch to your personal profile. You are at work. Log out.

4. *6 minutes*. Log in to Pinterest. Look at your homepage board and immediately repin anything that is appropriate from any of the people you follow. Quickly check the back-link on an image before you repin, just to be sure it leads to a reliable website. Click like on a couple more pins, and comment on a few others. At least once a week pin one new image yourself, sometimes a product or photo from a blog post of your own, more often something interesting that you have discovered on the Internet. Log out.

5. *10 minutes*. Go to your marketplace shop on Etsy. Check your convos. Answer any immediately. Look at the recent activity page to see what the people you are following have recently posted or liked. Click to view any items that catch your eye. Favorite a few of these. Favorite one new shop. Comment on every Treasury you have been featured in. Then move on with your workday, but stay logged in through the day to watch for new orders and respond to convos right away.

Once a week, spend your 40 minutes writing a new blog post, and skip the other things on that day.

On the seventh day, rest! Take the day off. Do not even look at your computer. Go do something amazing with your family and friends.

When you decide to use social media to promote your online business, always remember that this is a new style of marketing. You are not on social networks to sell your products, but to share yourself and to share the creative process that leads to your products. If all you do is post new things you have for sale and discount coupons urging people to buy stuff, your fans will soon stop looking at anything you send. Focus instead on sharing things your readers will find interesting, things that inspire your work, books that look at the world in a special way, music you listen to while you create, and walks on the beach that lead to a new seashell-colored glaze. Be upbeat and positive and friendly. Your fans will check out your shop on their own at the perfect time for them to buy your work.

CHAPTER 17

Customer Service

Your customers should emerge from their experience with your business feeling as if their needs have not only been fulfilled, but that your service exceeded their expectations in every respect. Your ability to receive each order with joy and treat each customer as a new friend will ensure that they become fans, return to your shop, and recommend your products.

Word gets around. Even in the seemingly impersonal arena of the Internet, or perhaps especially on the Internet where it is so very easy to leave feedback and share your story, word of mouth is the main way you will get new sales. Make sure that the stories your customers share will be positive. Great customer service will slowly but surely float your business to the top of the thousands of other similar artists and crafters, just as poor customer service will sink you like a stone.

The good news is that artists and crafters who sell online are primarily sole proprietors, especially at the start of their business. You are personally providing this excellent customer service. You don't have to hire the right employees, train them, and keep a constant watch to make sure they care about your customers because you are doing it all yourself. It is far easier to greet each new customer with joy when you are the business owner. Customer service comes second nature to artists and crafters who love what they create in the first place, and who love to share their works with others.

Quick Response Time

Good communication is essential to Internet sales. The Internet is an impersonal place to shop, and the buyer has no other way to connect with you, no shop door to enter, no way to know if you are real or not—except for the messages you provide.

Make a Connection

As a business owner, your number one priority is making sure your customers are happy. The following suggestions will help you keep everyone smiling:

- Answer e-mails and convos the same day. The Internet has made this possible and at the same time has made this the expectation. Even if you don't know an answer right away, shoot back a quick note telling the customer you got her message and are working on it. Let her know what to expect.
- Be exceedingly polite and friendly in your e-mails. Customers can't see you, hear your tone of voice, or have any of the other clues that humans

use to connect with one another, so your e-mails should go out of the way to be positive. Check through your notes before you click the send button. Rewrite any parts that have even the least hint of impatience or attitude, especially when you are dealing with problems.

- Keep buyers updated. Send a note when you get their orders, and let them know the shipping dates. Send a confirmation note when you ship items, and give them a tracking number. And in a week or two, say thank you again! Ask what they think about their purchase and invite further conversation. Include a discount coupon to encourage return orders. With regular, friendly communication, customers will be far more likely to take the time to leave positive feedback, send you a happy testimonial, and recommend you to their online shopping friends.

- Keep your promises. If you regularly have orders packed and shipped in 2 days, then promise 3 days. People will be even happier when they receive their order a bit faster than expected. Be realistic. If you can't meet the 3-day goal, simply change your processing time to 5 days or 7 days. Customers respect that you are a working artist as well as a small business owner, and as long as you fulfill their expectations, they will be satisfied.

QUESTION

How it is possible to respond to e-mails when I can't be online every day?
If you will be out of the office and out of e-mail range for a day or more, set up an auto-responder or vacation response. Almost every e-mail system has this capability. Simply write a note explaining when you'll return, then set a start and end date. Your e-mail system automatically mails this responder to all incoming messages during that time period, and people know what to expect.

Handling Problems

Issues will arise with customers. A package will arrive damaged, an item won't meet expectations, or a gift will not get there in time for the event. It is inevitable. The way you handle their problem will define your customer service.

ESSENTIAL

Studies show that a satisfied customer will tell two to three people about their good experience. An unsatisfied consumer will gripe about it to eight people or even more. An unsatisfied customer whose problem was successfully resolved, however, is the most likely person to become a loyal fan of the business. Customer problems are great opportunities to gather new supporters.

The Sins of Customer Service

Online buyers are a chatty group, and freely share their best and worst experiences. If they receive bad service, you can bet that the word will get out. Here's what deeply annoys buyers. Make sure you are never guilty of such poor customer service.

- Slow delivery time. "Their shipping policy said 3–5 days, but my order didn't arrive for 2 weeks. And the seller was from my state. No e-mail or anything about the delay . . . so disappointing."
- No communication with the seller. "It really annoys me when my order just shows up, with no note included or e-mail thanking me."
- Packages that smell of cigarette smoke, cats, or food. "I know many crafters have home-based businesses, but at least keep the studio clean."
- Overpriced shipping. "I hate seeing that I paid so much more for shipping than the postage actually cost. I know there's a cost for mailing envelopes and tape, but not that much cost."
- Flimsy packaging. "I ordered a pair of expensive earrings, and they arrived in a lightweight envelope, no padding or anything."
- Shipping in inappropriate product boxes. "I am all for recycling, and I never mind when an order arrives in a good, reused cardboard box, but shipping in used pizza boxes, tampon boxes, or diaper boxes is not a good image."

- Items that are a different color than the photograph showed. "It wasn't even close."
- Sellers who have too much bad customer feedback. "I know sellers can't block bad reviews on Yelp or at their marketplace shop. I tend to ignore a few sour grapes comments, but if there's lots of negative feedback, I start to believe the criticism."

Here are a few insights into dealing with customer issues that will end up scoring big points for your online business. First, when there is a problem with an order, recognize your customer's distress and make it personal. Send them an e-mail that says something like: "I understand. I hate it when I open a box and the item is just not the color I expected. I remember when I painted that silk scarf that the greens were particularly vibrant." Then ask the customer what they need. Let them suggest a solution. Most customers will be more reasonable than you can imagine, especially when your conversation reminds them that you are not a huge business, but a solo artist creating handcrafted goods. When the customers become part of the solution, they are far more likely to be satisfied, even enthusiastic, about the outcome.

Go out of your way to make it right. "I'll ship you a replacement scarf in the muted mossy colors. It's on my desk right now and I'll get it into Priority Mail today. Go ahead and repack that first scarf and send it back. Our boxes will cross in the mail." Trusting your customer will almost always work out perfectly.

Use each problem as a way to improve your own marketing and avoid similar issues in the future. In the example of the vibrant green silk scarf, the artist can adjust the colors of product photos to more realistically represent the item. Look at photos on different computers and different monitors—just because you have a state-of-the-art screen that displays your photos perfectly does not mean that your customers see the images in the same way. Add a handcrafted disclaimer to the product descriptions, "The imperfections and color variations inherent in handmade work are part of the beauty of one-of-a-kind, wearable artwork." Customers will not only understand that the product they buy is not mass-produced and uniform in appearance, they will celebrate this with you!

FACT

Of over 5,000 consumers in a consumer survey early in 2013, 82 percent said that their number one measure of good customer service was "getting my issue resolved quickly." Other top customer service elements mentioned included: "Dealing with a friendly customer service representative," "Having follow-up after the inquiry to ensure I am satisfied," and "Having a personalized experience."

Returns and Guarantees

Specify your return policy on your website or marketplace shop. What is your satisfaction guarantee? A typical policy might be, "All orders are guaranteed for 30 days after purchase date. During that time, the item can be returned for a full refund of the item cost or an exchange, no questions asked." What is your policy on product failure? Will you repair or replace items that develop defects? A typical policy for this might be: "If any defects in construction appear within the first year, send the item back, following our return shipping process, and I'll repair it for you." And speaking of return shipping, what do you require there? "A returned item must be unworn, undamaged, with all original tags intact. The customer is responsible for the cost of return shipping, unless I made a mistake. All 'on sale' items are final, and cannot be returned." Look at the policies of other shops and decide what is appropriate for the products you create. State your policies plainly.

Learn how to ship your products safely. An item damaged during shipping must be replaced. The buyer is inconvenienced. Even if you can put in an insurance claim with the shipping carrier, it still takes a chunk of your productive time. Go out of your way to wrap and pack orders so they can withstand the wear and tear of shipping services.

All of Sarah's handbound journals, notebooks, and guestbooks from her *Renewed Upon a Dream* shop on Etsy are shipped with a satisfaction guarantee. (*www.etsy.com/shop/reneweduponadream*)

Boxes, Labels, and Packaging

One of the easiest ways to impress customers is to pack each shipment as if it were a gift to your best friend. It is a perfect opportunity to remind them why shopping for handmade items directly from the artist is a rewarding experience, and to ensure that they will return to buy more gifts and treats for themselves. Taking a few extra steps with your packaging can be fun, creative, and incredibly effective.

Presentation Counts

Here's a list of ways to make sure you're package looks its best:

- Your packaging materials reflect your brand. Choose the colors, materials, and patterns of your boxes and envelopes to blend with your website, photos, business graphics, and products. See all sorts of examples at the Etsy Packaging group on Flickr.com. (*www.flickr .com/groups/etsypackaging*)

- Wrap products beautifully before you pack them into sturdy shipping containers. Many handcrafters find that brown paper and colorful baker's twine or decorative tape create a look that is both economical and goes with their brands. Other sellers with more elegant products use glossy gift paper, tissue, and silk ribbon. Whether an order is specifically sent as a gift, or is simply your "gift" to your customer, opening a shipment from your shop should be a special occasion.

The natural colors and brown paper theme of the Authentic Arts website is continued in the materials Jenny uses to pack and ship orders. "Bunny approved" by the iconic Pisky, her mascot rabbit. (*www.jennyhoople.com*)

- Using repurposed materials in your product wrapping is a great way to make a statement. Sellers have used roadmaps, nautical charts, and sheet music to wrap orders while also enhancing their image.
- Hand written notes and stickers add a personal touch to any order.

- Simple folding techniques can give you amazingly clever gift boxes for jewelry and small items. An origami evening with an old movie can result in dozens of handmade boxes for future orders.
- Rubber stamps are often used by handcrafters to economically brand packaging materials. You can draw your own design and have it made into a rubber stamp. You can also carve your own stamp blocks with E-Z Cut printing blocks. You can order a custom stamp from a number of online artists. Just search Etsy for "custom stamp block."
- Along with making rubber stamps of your own hand-drawn designs, you can have your artwork printed on stickers and labels in a wide variety of shapes and sizes. PsPrint.com (*www.psprint.com*) and Vistaprint (*www.vistaprint.com*) are two of the many online printers that provide inexpensive custom stickers, as well other kinds of business stationery.
- If your particular artistic skills do not lend themselves to doing your own graphic design, hire the services of an illustrator or designer to create a couple of images that you can use in your branding. Always ask if a swap is appropriate.
- The outer packaging for a shipment, while mainly selected for strength and the safety of the wrapped object inside, can also be embellished with your business name, stickers, stamps, or other handmade touches. Make every part of your packaging a celebration. You may discover that several of your new customers are mail carriers and delivery drivers who have been impressed with a creative box they encountered.
- Tuck-ins are tiny gifts that unexpectedly show up as part of packaging materials. Excellent handmade examples are a painted clothespin that clips packing slips together, a blank greeting card of one of your paintings enfolding a handwritten thank you note, or a bonus fridge magnet with a cute design and your website address. These freebies impress your customers and make them eager to order from you again.

Beth from *Mad Scientists Designs* encourages gift purchases by including a product photo showing how beautifully her items are wrapped. (*www.etsy.com/shop/MadScientistsDesigns*)

Shipping Services

As a seller, you will discover the shipping service that works best for your location, your products, and your ideal customers. In the United States, businesses generally choose between the U.S. Postal Service, UPS, or FedEx as their preferred method of shipping. U.S. Priority Mail may be the most convenient and economical choice, though for heavier or expensive products UPS or FedEx ground delivery may prove a better value. Explore all the shipping options convenient to your business, and decide which combination of costs and services works best for you. Remember to calculate not only regular shipping, but expedited shipping (if you want to offer fast delivery service to attract rush orders) and international rates. Here are a few handy links:

- U.S. Postal Service information is found at *www.usps.com*
- U.S. Priority Mail, with free envelopes, boxes, and flat rate options, can be found at *www.usps.com/ship/priority-mail.htm*
- The UPS (United Parcel Service) website is at *www.ups.com*
- FedEx (Federal Express) is at *www.fedex.com*
- Canada Post information is at *www.canadapost.ca/cpo/mc/business/system/language*
- UK Royal Mail information is at *www.royalmail.com*
- Australia Post is at *http://auspost.com.au*

The way you set your shipping prices depends on the shopping cart system you are using. On Etsy, shipping is generally set per item, with one cost attached if this product is the only thing a customer orders, and another cost if this is the second or third product in an order. Other cart systems use the cost of the order as a basis to calculate shipping, or the actual weight of each item. Whatever method you employ, you will be making your best guess at what the shipping will actually cost in each situation, and seeking to come up with a fair "average" price. When your shipping rates are correctly figured, some shipments will cost you less than what the customer paid, other shipments will cost you more, and on average you will break even.

Shipping insurance is completely for your protection as a shipper. It does cost more, and is a factor in the shipping rates you set. As a business owner, you are continually juggling between your costs to fulfill orders and the customer's tendency to not even place an order if your shipping rates are too high. You may decide that it is more cost effective to set your internal policy to buy insurance only on packages valued above a certain amount, and not buy insurance for lesser values, in order to keep your shipping prices down. You may lose a couple of packages through the year, and it is always your responsibility to replace that item for the customer, but the cost of a few replacement items may be cheaper than purchasing insurance for every little thing you ship all year long.

One online seller, for example, has set $100 as her insurance threshold. For any packages worth $100 or more, she buys the appropriate insurance. Any packages valued less than $100 are sent U.S. Priority Mail without additional insurance. Over the course of a typical year, she has to re-ship a few orders that were damaged or lost, generally less than 1 percent of the total order volume. This system has worked successfully for several years, and the merchant is convinced that her lower shipping prices contribute positively to overall sales.

International and expedited shipping require not only a higher shipping price, but also more work for you. Rush shipping implies that you are available to process orders every day and have the ability to meet Next Day or Two Day expectations. Only you can decide if this level of service is a sustainable practice for you in your business. If it is not, do not lead customers to expect it. International shipments require customs forms and a wide variety of delivery expectations. Certain services, such as package insurance, are not even available to some nations. Certain materials cannot be shipped to other nations. Gold, silver, and precious stones, for example, are subject to strict regulations in Australia, and they cannot be sent via certain services. Be sure that the cost you charge for international shipping covers everything that is involved.

Once you have decided on the shipping method you want to use, figured out the average cost of sending your packages, and entered this information into your shopping cart systems, post your rates and policies clearly on your website and at your marketplace shop profile.

Plan ahead for busy times. December is always the busiest month for online sellers, especially for artists and crafters whose products make great gifts. Know the "last date for delivery" for orders sent to different places. Have plenty of shipping boxes and packing materials on hand before the rush begins. Stock up on your bestselling products in autumn. Make arrangements for extra childcare or for a friend to come help if things get really hectic. Holidays are excellent opportunities for profit as long as you have things under control.

Words of Wisdom

For the best ideas on customer service, go directly to your customers. Discover why they are shopping with you and selecting your products. Let them tell you what sort of services they expect.

Kim is not an artist or crafter selling online, but she is a regular customer that buys handcrafts online. With a few purchases for herself and over 75 percent bought as gifts for others, she places around 40 orders for handmade items each year. She very well could fit the profile of one of your ideal customers.

"I love ceramics, letter press cards, and creative mailing materials, but generally I shop for gifts and look for something specific to a special person. For my dad's birthday I found a vintage celluloid football player from his era (he played football in school). I am also drawn to far-away cities and countries I've visited. Just for example, I recently searched for something from Costa Rica, and for small white ceramics for a table setting, and for shell necklaces from Hawaii for our garden figurine," says Kim.

Kim describes herself as being "happily in the clutches of Etsy's marketing." She says, "I was introduced to Etsy by a niece who had a shop early on and by my son who wanted a nerdy but hip T-shirt from a specific artist. Because of this, I was guided in and never had to flounder around. I am on Etsy's daily serve list and glance at what they send me so I can learn of new people."

Kim orders from a wide variety of shops. "I only tend to return to shops about 10 percent of the time, but I have six or seven that I have gone to more than once. I buy my journals from a bookmaker in Brooklyn. I follow two or three ceramicists, a painter in Portland (where I was born), a mixed-media artist in the southwest, and a couple who have a letter press shop using an antique press in Florida. Most of the time, though, I buy from new artists and crafters."

Good customer service is always appreciated. "I love a personally e-mailed 'Thank you,' even if it is brief. Many artists have a way of using inexpensive, everyday material to package creatively, which makes receiving the order fun. Often a written thank you is tucked in. Mostly what I appreciate is a timely ship. Reasonably fast shipping implies so much—that not only my choice to spend my hard-earned money in their shop is appreciated, but so is my time. I have had e-mails from sellers in Europe who have been very concerned about mailing times and stayed in close touch. I found that so considerate. It is always delightful to fall in love with artists' work and discover they themselves are equally special," she says.

Favorite artists are always a treat to visit on Etsy. As Kim Explains, "I very much respond to Cathy DeLeRee's found-object, mixed-media art, which is both sacred and playful, the divine and the all-too-human (*www.etsy.com/shop/CathyDeLeRee*). I am drawn also to her palette. She puts time into wonderful, openhearted notes welcoming me back that she encloses with her items."

Kim also orders custom items. "Rae Dunn (*www.etsy.com/shop/raedunn*) puts words on her ceramic napkin rings and as a poet I had my own ideas. She was welcome to that and worked with me. I checked with Barbara Dunshee (*www.etsy.com/shop/barbaradunshee*) before ordering multiples and she too was approachable and made me a special order."

Online shopping is definitely a part of life for this ideal customer. "I think many artists and crafters feel that online selling lacks the personal touch, but for someone like me whose time is premium, I am grateful I can shop in my jammies and not always tramp all over town."

So what advice does Kim have for online handcraft sellers? "Offer a clean, eye-catching website with top-notch, well-lit, simple images of your work. As a past administrator of a small cultural center, I found that creativity grounded in integrity brings benefits, although exactly how these arrive can't always be predicted. If artists and crafters put themselves—their true selves—into their art, I think it's very probable that miracles will come their way."

CHAPTER 18

Learning as You Go

Successful online business owners are sponges for information. They never stop learning about the different aspects of the business they have created, especially in an environment that changes as frequently as the Internet. Artists and crafters have double the challenge. Not only will you continue to learn more about the world of Internet marketing, you also have to keep up with the innovations in your creative field as you improve your own amazing artwork. Learning as you go is part of any profession, and certainly is an essential element of starting your own business. Understanding this is actually quite liberating. There's no way you are going to know everything ahead of time, so why not jump in and get started?

The Seven Steps to Creative Problem Solving

It is inevitable that you will run into things you don't know how to do as you begin to sell your work online. Your world will expand in unexpected and amazing ways. You'll find yourself in need of information to solve problems you didn't even know existed. Curiosity is the key to figuring things out with the least amount of stress. When the accounting software won't connect with your bank account, or your favorite supplier goes out of business, or your orders continually get shipped too late, just take a deep breath, put on your Sherlock Holmes hat, and solve each puzzle as it appears.

1. **Define the problem.** Exactly what is going on? What is missing that you need to have? What specific part of the system or machine is not working?

2. **Describe the cause.** Is this problem due to poor equipment, to software that you do not understand, to factors beyond your control? Knowing the cause leads you to the solution.

3. **Get more information.** The Internet is your best tool. If you can ask your question correctly and specifically, a search will most likely return a wide variety of tech support pages and forums where other people have dealt with the exact same problem. Try asking your question in different ways to get to the most valuable information. Read through search results, taking care to evaluate the reliability of any information you find. Always remember how quickly things change with computer and Internet issues. A solution from 2007 may not be the least bit valid in 2013.

4. **Identify multiple possible solutions.** If your printer stops working during the holiday rush, there may be several ways to deal with the problem. You could fix the printer yourself. You could hire a service person to come in and fix it. You could buy a new printer. You could use someone else's computer and printer for the time being.

5. **Decide which option is best in this moment.** If you choose a temporary fix, schedule when you will deal with the problem for a more permanent solution.

6. **Carry out the strategy.** Work slowly and keep track of what you try, step-by-step. It is especially helpful when using telephone tech support to very carefully explain what you are experiencing, each thing you do, and what results you see.

7. **Evaluate the effectiveness of the solution.** Is everything fixed? Or is there still a problem here?

QUESTION

Can you learn to start an online business?
Yes. There are classes, books, workshops, and programs to teach the specific skills needed to be successful. But the bulk of entrepreneurial learning does not come from a classroom or a manual. It happens in real time through hands-on experience as you solve the problems that arise when running a small business.

Learning as You Grow Your Business

When artists and artisans first begin selling their handcrafts online, it's usually as a sole proprietorship working either part-time or full-time. As business owner, you wear all the hats, from producing the artwork to managing, marketing, bookkeeping, and fulfilling every order. Because you are talented, smart, and a great online marketer, your business expands, slowly at first, and then in leaps and bounds. All these tasks become more and more demanding, until it is clear that one person simply cannot continue to do everything. Learning as you go and planning ahead for business growth is essential in keeping a healthy business.

Work Smarter

When you are doing everything yourself, your tendency is to multitask and run through each day doing a little of this, some of that, mixing jobs together. You will usually emerge with everything accomplished at the end of a day, but it will take longer and be less satisfying than if you are able to focus. Learn how to concentrate on the task at hand. Get rid of distractions as much as possible. Turn off the TV. Log out of social media websites. Create step-by-step processes that you can follow and repeat.

ESSENTIAL

Psychological research shows that multitasking can reduce productivity up to 40 percent. Although human brains can hold more than one task at a time and switch back and forth between them, this ability comes at a cost to our efficiency. Multitasking leads to distraction, inefficiency, and stress.

Use Your Computer

Your office computer is not only for managing your Internet profiles and answering e-mails. It is a powerful tool for making your work more efficient. Invest the time to learn how to use an accounting program that will make bookkeeping and end-of-the-year taxes a simple click of the button. Use time management systems to keep track of appointments and deadlines. Learn to pay bills online rather than by hand. Keep track of your inventory with an online system. The more you learn to automate business tasks, the more time you will have to create and market the artwork you love.

Establish Systems

Plan ahead for the day when you won't be the only person doing each job. Separate the different parts of your business into specific tasks. Now that you have created step-by-step processes to make your own work more efficient, write these down. When it comes time to subcontract that job to another professional or to hire an employee, you will already have a complete job description and a training program.

Outsource

Begin to identify business tasks that are simply not your strong suit, and learn how to hire someone else to do these particular jobs. The most typical tasks that a small business will send to an outside provider are bookkeeping and accounting, taxes, payroll (if you expand to hiring employees), technical website tasks, graphic design, copyediting, photography, and video production. Your decision to hire other professionals to do these tasks can be pretty simple. Is your business more successful and making more sales when you pay someone else to do these tasks and free up your own time for more profitable activities? As with every other business decision . . . try, track, and evaluate.

QUESTION

When is a worker a subcontractor and not an employee?
In general, a subcontractor completes a specified task at his own location, on his own schedule, and following his own processes. If a person works in your location during hours that you specify and is following a process that you oversee, then he is your employee, not a subcontractor. Many small businesses outsource tasks to subcontractors. There are different rules and regulations—from taxes to permits to insurance—that will apply to your business when you hire employees.

There are a few parts of your online business that you are best advised to keep in your own hands. Obviously, creating your art or craft is something you do yourself. If a marketplace shop is an important part of your sales plan, realize you have confirmed that the items you sell are indeed handmade, not mass-produced. This does not mean that you have to print all of your own giclée prints, or can't work with friends and title your shop a cooperative producing amazing knitwear. As an artist or artisan, you are responsible for original design and quality control for every item you sell as a handmade product.

You should keep control of your online marketing—writing your blog, managing your social media profiles, answering e-mail, and sending out a regular e-mail newsletter. There are many marketing companies on the Internet who will offer to take over your social media tasks for a fee. But since you as the artist are so personally identified with your business, no one but yourself can truthfully "be you" online. This is one part of a successful online arts or crafts business that you should do yourself.

You are also the most efficient person to write your own product descriptions, since you know each product so intimately. However, it might be an excellent idea to hire a good writer to edit what you write, correcting grammar and checking for SEO.

Move Customers to Your Own Website

While most online sellers begin with a marketplace shop on Etsy, Art-Fire, or other arts and crafts selling platforms, serious sellers soon develop their own websites with blog and shopping cart capabilities. They encourage their customers to come to their domain websites. The reason is simple: no distractions. Customers see your work and only your work. They are far less likely to go surfing off to see what other artisans offer. On your own website, you control the branding, the presentation, and the experience of your viewer. You can offer more. Even if you decide to keep your marketplace shop as part of your integrated online presence, learn how to use coupons, special offers, your e-mail newsletter, and your blog to encourage customers to buy directly from your domain website.

Your Go-To Learning Resources

Use the following resources to help solve problems and expand your knowledge as you build your successful arts and crafts online business. Expand this list with helpful materials and websites you discover on your own.

- **SellingArtsandCraftsOnline.com.** Now that you've read the book, follow the blog! SellingArtsandCraftsOnline.com is your source for expanded information, new tips and tricks, and networking. You can connect with other artists and crafters following the path to online success, and have an opportunity to be featured in the success stories.
- **The U.S. Small Business Administration "Starting a Business" pages**, *www.sba.gov*. Though this site targets businesses in the United States, the information at this website is useful to businesses everywhere. Search for "small business startup support your-country" or your-state, your-province, your-city to discover more specific information.
- **Find a mentor!** The number one most helpful support system as you get started is to find someone already successful in your field that is willing to offer advice and counseling as you grow. In the United States, the SCORE Association (Service Corps of Retired Executives) (*www.score.org*) is a nonprofit association dedicated to entrepreneur education, and may be helpful in locating a mentor. The marketplace

websites, Etsy, and others are great sources of teams and individuals willing to help with critiques and advice. Remember to give in return, give your advice to others who are starting out, and give back to those who mentor you.

- **Create a mastermind group.** Locate four or five other artists or crafters in your town or region who are likewise in the process of starting to sell online. Get together once a month for lunch or happy hour to share stories, troubleshoot each other's problems, and support and encourage each other.
- **The Everything® Guides** offer wonderful books on a wide variety of business topics, from accounting to basic business startup to project management. If this book has been useful to you, check out the other titles at *http://shop.everything.com/everything-business-personal-finance.*
- **Tech support people are your friends!** The reason you host your website with a hosting company that offers free telephone or live chat tech support is so you can ask questions. The same is true for any of the equipment and services you purchase for your business. The availability and the reputation of a company's phone support should be a significant factor in your decision to go with that product. Always treat tech support people politely and respectfully, even when you are frustrated with the problem you are discussing. If you do not seem to be getting anywhere with a particular tech support operator, thank them and end the conversation. Take a break. Call back after a few hours to try again with a different support person. Live online chat is often a good option. Typing your questions requires you to work a bit more slowly and carefully, and being able to save a copy of the written conversation is valuable for dealing with that issue again at a later date.

Free Online Information

Online marketing has a rich community of learning resources. Many websites offer an abundance of free materials as part of their own attraction marketing philosophy. You can soak up as much free advice and information as you can hold, and decide for yourself whether any of their purchased materials or services are worth the investment.

- **Handmadeology** (*www.handmadeology.com*) is a fantastic resource with lots of blog articles, e-books, and services on the science behind selling handmade goods online.
- **The Etsy Seller's Handbook** (*www.etsy.com/blog/en/2012/the-seller-handbook*) is, of course, your first and best source of information on all things Etsy.
- **Take Control of Your Internet Marketing** (*www.takecontrolofyourinternetmarketing.com/art*) offers a series of inexpensive online video lessons on social media marketing and building a WordPress website, with lots of free information on their blog *www.takecontrolofyourinternetmarketing.com/blog*.
- **The Abundant Artist** blog at *www.theabundantartist.com/blog* has plenty of free content to explore, and offers an online course as well as paid services.
- **HubSpot** provides free webinars and materials at *academy.hubspot.com* to attract customers for their professional marketing services and software.
- **Copyblogger** (*www.copyblogger.com*) offers a free online marketing course to attract customers to their professional services.
- *Empty Easel* is an online art magazine with practical advice, tips, and tutorials for creating and selling art. Find lots of business advice for artists at *http://emptyeasel.com/art-business-advice*.

There are a wide variety of websites and organizations dedicated to small business startups. *The Everything® Start Your Own Business Book* lists all these resources and much more to help you get off to a solid start (*shop.everything.com/everything-start-your-own-business-book-4th-cd*).

CHAPTER 19

Your Startup Checklist

So what's next? You've read this book cover to cover. You've spent some time at the main marketplace websites, and peeked into eBay and the products-on-demand platforms. You've contemplated where an office space might fit in your house or studio, and imagined how to create hours in your day to devote to working a new business. You have experience selling at craft fairs and in local shops, and are ready to make the big move to selling online. What's next?

Begin with Your Artwork!

This is the foundation for your online selling success. Collect your very best for-sale pieces into one spot. Simply look at what you have right now. Create a simple inventory list with everything you have to offer at this moment.

- Give each item a name that makes sense to you. You will improve these names later when you title them online using powerful keywords.
- Write each item's essential specifications. Size. Color. Materials.
- Assign a price category to each item: inexpensive, mid-range, expensive. Don't put in an exact price yet.

How many pieces do you have? If you only have a few, you could consider auction websites as a good starting point, where one-of-a-kind objects can be successfully displayed and sold. To open a marketplace shop, such as space on Etsy or ArtFire, you should have a variety of different items you can offer for sale. Depending on your particular field, this could be anywhere from ten to fifty or more different pieces.

- Make more items to sell. How many price levels do you have? Do you have smaller, less expensive pieces as well as larger works of art? A successful marketplace shop needs to have "foot in the door" pieces so interested viewers can make a small purchase and test your service and the quality of your work. Likewise, artists and crafters with a wide array of inexpensive items can create sets and groupings to promote higher average sales.
- Make some inexpensive items. Package small items into sets to create higher-priced products.
- Are all of your pieces finished and ready for sale? What do they need before you can pack them into a box and send them off to a customer? Do your fiber art and clothing pieces need a small label stitched into a seam to become professional products? Do you need simple earring cards and small plastic jewelry bags for your handcrafted earrings? So you need a stock of clear plastic sleeves and cardboard or foam board backing sheets to package your fine art prints?
- Get what you need to complete your products. Research DIY solutions and inexpensive online sources. Create or order what you need. Get your products ready for sale.

It is possible to "bootstrap" your business, starting up without the need to raise a pile of venture capital, and reinvesting your profits as you go. Many successful online artists and crafters began this way—most of them, in fact. But there are a few essential tools you absolutely must have. In order to start your online business, you do need to empower yourself with:

- A decent computer
- A good Internet connection
- A good digital camera

Determine if the equipment you already have is sufficient. If not, research what you need to get. Explore options such as used and refurbished equipment and hand-me-down equipment, as well as brand-new retail purchases. List your top choices for each item.

Find the money you will need to make the necessary purchases—ideally from your existing savings or with a savings plan you will start right now. If you get a startup loan from family, friends, your own credit card, or your bank, be very careful to borrow responsibly with the lowest possible interest, and plan to begin paying off your debt immediately with regular, manageable payments. Get the equipment you need.

Know Your Competition and Customers

Most crafters and artists can begin by going to Etsy.com and searching for items that are similar to what they themselves create. Locate ten different sellers who sell items like yours. Expand this list by going to Craftcount.com (*www.craftcount.com*) and looking at the top sellers in your category until you locate one or two additional shops selling items like yours. Now look closely at the twelve sellers you have discovered. Make a chart with the following information:

- The name of each shop.
- The URLs of the Etsy shops.
- When did each shop open on Etsy?
- How many sales does each shop have?

- Do the math: How many items has each shop sold per month on average?
- How many total items does each shop offer?
- How many followers does each shop have?
- How much feedback does each shop have?
- Does each shop have an About page?
- Does each shop have a Facebook and Twitter link?
- Sort each shop by lowest price. What are the least expensive items?
- Sort each shop by highest price. What are the most expensive items?

Analyze the information you have gathered. Which shops have the most sales? Which shops have the fewest sales? What do the most successful four shops have in common? Look at their photography, their product names, the way they write their product descriptions, their prices. How have the leading shops branded themselves? What makes these shops different from the shops with the lowest number of sales? Were you able to easily discover shops that create items similar to yours? Having lots of competition is not a negative for you. Instead it means there's a well-developed niche that you can join, an existing flourishing market. This is far easier than trying to create a brand-new market with products no one knows about.

Expand your research beyond Etsy. Locate and analyze similar online sellers who sell from their own websites and on other market platforms by searching Google.com for artwork or handcrafts like the items you create yourself.

Identify Your Customer

Create a "perfect customer profile" by using everything you know or can guess about the people who have already purchased your work. If only one single person has ever bought something from you, describe that person. If you have sold at art fairs, to friends of your friends and family, and at a local shop, compile your awareness into one or more perfect customers. Since many arts and crafts buyers are women, we'll assume female for these questions, but switch from "she" to "he" if you your customers are mostly men.

- What is her age?
- What sort of work does she do? What is her income level?

- What is her family life like? Single? Married? Children? Grandchildren?
- What are the significant relationships in her life? Family? Her partner? Circle of friends? Work colleagues?
- How does she dress? Clothing can tell you a lot about her culture and interests.
- What special interests does she have? Hobbies? Sports? Political or social passions?
- What does she do online? Use e-mail? Social media sites? Shop online stores?

Write your perfect customer profile. Do you have more than one perfect customer? If you sell equally well to both men and women, create two perfect customer profiles. If you have two distinct age groups among your customers, create two perfect customer profiles.

If you simply have not sold enough to know much about who will buy your work, set up a booth or table at local farmers' markets, craft fairs, holiday gift shows, and art walks where you can meet buyers face-to-face. Join a local arts cooperative and sell items at the co-op shop or gallery where you can work regular shifts and talk to shoppers. Enter your work into shows and exhibitions. Get out there and sell stuff to real people.

Take a Simple Survey

Ask your most important question to twenty-five of the most appropriate people. Who? People who are already interested in the things that you make—your friends, their friends, your neighbors, anyone who is your customer. The question? "If I were to begin selling my artwork on the Internet, where do you think I should set up a shop?" You will discover how much your typical customers already know about Internet sales for arts and crafts and where they automatically see your products fitting.

Conduct your survey. Write the answers. Remember to use simple surveys often with your customers as you plan new products, choose between different promotional offers, or essentially decide anything about your business. People enjoy giving you their opinions, and you get better information than anything you could imagine all by yourself.

Set Yourself Up for Success

Start branding yourself. Come up with a business name that you can . . .

- Use on a marketplace website such as Etsy.
- Register as your own domain name.

Only then can you begin to use your new business name on all your materials.

If you are planning to start with an Etsy.com shop or another marketplace website, search to see if the business name you are considering is available. Remember, there is a twenty-letter limit, and all words are run together in a shop name. As you type into Etsy's search box, one of the options will be "find shop names containing ___." If there is no other shop using the name you want, you will most likely be able to register a new shop with it. But before you do, search a domain registrar company such as GoDaddy (*www .godaddy.com*) to see if you can also get this as a .com domain name. Keep trying different business names on these websites until you can get a business name you can use for both.

ALERT

If you are *not* planning on opening a marketplace shop, you only need to think of a business name that can be registered as a .com domain name.

Register at Etsy or the marketplace site you wish to use. Register your domain name with GoDaddy or the domain registrar company you wish to use. You do not need hosting space for now, only simple domain registration. Once you have done these two steps, begin using your business name on all of your marketing materials.

Last but Not Least

Which two social media websites does your ideal customer most commonly use? This could be Facebook and Pinterest, though that might differ, depending on your audience. Open your business profile at the two social media sites you have identified.

QUESTION

How do I know which social media websites my customers use?
Ask them. If you have contact with previous customers, use e-mail or the phone to get in touch with them. If you are selling things in person at a craft fair or farmers' market setting, ask as you conclude each sale. Explain that you are expanding your work online and are taking a survey to find out which social networks are important. Your customers will tell you, and probably offer interest and encouragement that will inspire you to keep going.

Decide what legal matters you need to complete right away. Register for a resale license with your state sales tax office, or whatever governmental system is appropriate for your location. Buy a business license. Do any other official steps that you decide are needed.

You have your items ready for sale now (see Step 1). You have a digital camera and a good computer (see Step 2). You know what the photos from successful sellers look like (see Step 3).

Take at least a dozen photos of each item.

Download the photos to your computer. View and select the best five photos of each item. Rename the image files or organize these photos in a way that makes sense. Use a photo editing program or online service to crop and optimize your photos.

Finally, begin selling online.

Resources

Many more resources exist in every one of these categories. Use a search engine such as Google (*www.google.com*) to search for others.

Artists and Crafters Featured in This Book

Adam Rabbit jewelry
www.etsy.com/shop/AdamRabbit

Anderson Soap Company
www.andersonsoapcompany.com/products and
www.etsy.com/shop/AndersonSoapCompany

Blue Sky Pottery
www.blueskypotterycolorado.com

Brandon Bird
www.brandonbird.com

Carol Jenkins
www.caroljenkinsart.com

Clay de Lys designs in polymer clay
www.etsy.com/shop/ClaydeLys1

Conscious Art Studios
www.artfire.com/ext/shop/studio/ConsciousArtStudios
and *www.consciousartstudios.com*

David Joaquin paintings
www.twohawksstudio.com and *www.etsy.com/shop/*
PaintedMoonGallery

Designs in Tile ceramic tile
www.designsintile.com

Dodeline Design cards
http://blog.dodelinedesign.com and *www.etsy.com/*
shop/dodelinedesign

Holdman Studios
www.holdmanstudios.com and *www.stores.ebay.com/*
Holdman-Studios

Humperdincks art prints
www.etsy.com/shop/Humperdincks

In Vintage Heaven altered art jewelry
www.rubylane.com/shop/invintageheaven and
www.etsy.com/shop/InVintageHeaven

Jackdaw jewelry
www.etsy.com/shop/Jackdaw

Jenny Hoople Authentic Arts
www.jennyhoople.com and *www.etsy.com/shop/*
AuthenticStone

Kim Solga watercolors
www.solga.com and *www.etsy.com/shop/BlueOtterArt*

Knotty Needle knit fiber and wire
www.etsy.com/shop/TheKnottyNeedle and
created pookalooka.com

Lauri Sturdivant
www.lauristurdivant.com

Mad Scientists Designs jewelry
www.etsy.com/shop/MadScientistsDesigns

Mandy Budan
www.budanart.com

Palletso rustic home décor
www.etsy.com/shop/Palletso

Papertique paper goods
www.etsy.com/shop/papertique

Prairie Primitives folk art
www.etsy.com/shop/PrairiePrimitives

Rhody Art whimsical collage
www.etsy.com/shop/rhodyart

Ruddle Cottage gifts
www.ruddlecottage.net and *www.etsy.com/shop/*
ruddlecottage

Scrapunzel pixie clothing
www.rscrapunzel.com

**Spool + Sparrow handprinted natural fiber clothing
and décor**
www.spoolandsparrow.com and *www.etsy.com/shop/*
spoolandsparrowshop

General Business Resources

Australian Business License and Information Service
https://ablis.business.gov.au/pages/home.aspx

Canada Revenue Agency
www.cra-arc.gc.ca

The U.S. Small Business Administration
www.sba.gov

The Word Bank's Doing Business
www.doingbusiness.org

Intellectual Property

Creative Commons online image licensing
www.creativecommons.org/licenses/by-sa/3.0

Intellectual Property Rights from the U.S. Small Business Administration
www.sba.gov/content/intellectual-property-law

The U.S. Copyright Office
www.copyright.gov

The U.S. Patent and Trademark Office
www.uspto.gov

Marketplace Platforms

ArtFire
www.artfire.com

CraftIsArt
www.craftisart.com

DaWanda
www.dawanda.com

Etsy
www.etsy.com

Folksy
www.folksy.com

ICraftGifts
www.icraft.ca

Madeitmyself
www.madeitmyself.com

ShopHandmade
www.shophandmade.com

Silkfair
www.silkfair.com

Yessy
www.yessy.com

Zibbet
www.zibbet.com

Auction Platforms

Art on eBay
www.ebay.com/chp/art

Crafts on eBay
www.ebay.com/chp/crafts

DailyPaintworks
www.dailypaintworks.com

Tophatter
www.tophatter.com

Products-on-Demand Platforms

CafePress
www.cafepress.com

RedBubble
www.redbubble.com

Society6
www.society6.com

Zazzle
www.zazzle.com

Prints-on-Demand Platforms

ArtistRising
www.artistrising.com

CanvasOnDemand
www.canvasondemand.com

DeviantArt
www.deviantart.com

FineArtAmerica
www.fineartamerica.com

GreatBigCanvas
www.greatbigcanvas.com

Imagekind
www.imagekind.com

Books-on-Demand Platforms

Blurb
www.blurb.com

CreateSpace
www.createspace.com

Lulu
www.lulu.com

Build Your Own E-commerce Website Platforms

Amazon Webstore
http://webstore.amazon.com

Big Cartel
www.directory.bigcartel.com

Shopify
www.shopify.com

Silkfair
www.silkfair.com

WordPress
www.wordpress.org

WordPress themes directory
www.wordpress.org/extend/themes

Domain Name Registrars

GoDaddy
www.godaddy.com

Network Solutions
www.netsol.com

Register.com
www.register.com

Hosting Providers with WordPress Support

Bluehost
www.bluehost.com

HostGator
www.hostgator.com

HostMonster
www.hostmonster.com

E-commerce Resources

Bead Manager Pro handmade bead management system
www.beading-software.com

Bizelo inventory management
www.eretail.bizelo.com

Craftybase inventory management
www.craftybase.com

Google Analytics
www.google.com/analytics

Google Webmaster Tools
www.google.com/webmasters

inFlow inventory management
www.inflowinventory.com

Intuit QuickBooks accounting
http://quickbooksonline.intuit.com

Jewelry Design Manager jewelry management system
www.jewelrydesignermanager.com

My Art Collection artwork management system
www.my-artcollection.com

Outright accounting
www.outright.com/etsy

PayPal payment gateway
www.paypal.com

Run|Inventory inventory management
www.runinv.com

SoapMaker handmade soap management system
www.soapmaker.ca

Stitch Labs inventory management
www.stitchlabs.com

Wave accounting
www.waveapps.com

Photo and Graphics Resources

EtsyBannerGenerator.com
www.etsybannergenerator.com

FotoFlexer
www.fotoflexer.com

FotoFuze
www.fotofuze.com

GIMP
www.gimp.org

Google Plus photo editing
https://plus.google.com

iPiccy
www.ipiccy.com

Paint.net
www.getpaint.net

Picasa
www.picasa.google.com

PicMonkey
www.picmonkey.com

Pixlr
www.pixlr.com

Social Media Marketing Networks and Resources

AWeber
www.aweber.com

Blogger
www.blogger.com

ConstantContact
www.constantcontact.com

Facebook
www.facebook.com

Flickr
www.flickr.com

Google Plus
https://plus.google.com

Instagram
www.instagram.com

LinkedIn
www.linkedin.com

MailChimp
www.mailchimp.com

Pinterest
www.pinterest.com

SurveyMonkey
www.surveymonkey.com

Technorati
www.technorati.com/blog-claiming-faq

Threadless
www.threadless.com

Tumblr
www.tumblr.com

Twitter
www.twitter.com

TypePad
www.typepad.com

Vimeo
https://vimeo.com

Wanelo
www.wanelo.com

YouTube
www.youtube.com

Shipping Resources

Australia Post
http://auspost.com.au

Canada Post
www.canadapost.ca/cpo/mc/business/productsservices/shipping

FedEx (Federal Express)
www.fedex.com

UK Royal Mail
www.royalmail.com

UPS (United Parcel Service)
www.ups.com

U.S. Postal Service
www.usps.com

U.S. Priority Mail
www.usps.com/ship/priority-mail.htm

Online Learning Resources

Abundant Artist blog
www.theabundantartist.com/blog

Copyblogger
www.copyblogger.com

Empty Easel
www.emptyeasel.com/art-business-advice

Etsy Seller's Handbook
www.etsy.com/blog/en/2012/the-seller-handbook

Everything® Guides
www.everything.com

Handmadeology
www.handmadeology.com

Hubspot
www.hubspot.com

Lynda.com online training tutorials
www.lynda.com

Selling Arts and Crafts Online, the blog community for this book
www.sellingartsandcraftsonline.com

Take Control of your Internet Marketing
www.takecontrolofyourinternetmarketing.com/art

Index

We Have

EVERYTHING.

on Anything!

With more than 19 million copies sold, the Everything® series has become one of America's favorite resources for solving problems, learning new skills, and organizing lives. Our brand is not only recognizable—it's also welcomed.

The series is a hand-in-hand partner for people who are ready to tackle new subjects—like you!

For more information on the Everything® series, please visit *www.adamsmedia.com*

The Everything® list spans a wide range of subjects, with more than 500 titles covering 25 different categories:

Business	History	Reference
Careers	Home Improvement	Religion
Children's Storybooks	Everything Kids	Self-Help
Computers	Languages	Sports & Fitness
Cooking	Music	Travel
Crafts and Hobbies	New Age	Wedding
Education/Schools	Parenting	Writing
Games and Puzzles	Personal Finance	
Health	Pets	